Learning Technology

CONTENTS

LIST OF FIGURES AND TABLES

PREFACE

You are reading my writing, in a printed book, which you have probably bought online, which you searched for using a computer (AI) on the internet to find. That is what this book is all about, the history of learning technology.

Learning technology, arguably the technology that underlies the invention and creation of all other technologies and human culture, has been around as long as our species, from cave paintings to the Metaverse, yet oddly there is no book that exhaustively covers its development and history. It is about all sorts of shifts: the shift from one learning technology paradigm to another, gear shifts in scalability, the shift from teacher to learner. It is also about the role of technology in the modern world.

Beyond history, this book is about something deeper, that learning technology is something unique and fundamental to our species. It may be the most important form of technology we have invented. We are *Homo sapiens*, Latin for 'knowing man', or more correctly, 'the people that learn to know'. For 3 million years we have been creating technology that has shaped our cognition and enabled social and cultural transmission. What underlies our progress and the invention of all other technologies, is learning technology – from the earliest days of stone tools and cave paintings, through manuscripts, books and printing, to computers, smartphones, the internet, AI, neurotechnology and the Metaverse – all these have melded to create minds, institutions and the cumulative legacy that is civilization.

I was lucky enough to have caught the technology bug, albeit by accident, at Dartmouth University in New Hampshire. I had played around with punch cards at school, and during a trip to a huge mainframe in Edinburgh, wrote some simple programs which we input into the Colossus. Sure enough, it spat out the solution. It was mesmerizing.

Dartmouth College, in the United States, was the place where the modern era of AI started in 1956, the year of my birth. AI was the subject of my first book *Artificial Intelligence for Learning*, so the stars were aligning. Although doing a degree in philosophy, all students got access to the IBM mainframe on the campus. One thing I've always liked about US Higher Education is that it gives students a broader set of perspectives and opportunities. After playing a few games of Battleships, they allowed us to write short programs

(Basic was invented at Dartmouth). If you've ever written any code and seen it executed, you will know that it gives you a God-like feeling. It is an act of creation like no other – from some simple lines of symbols, you can make amazing things happen.

When I returned to Edinburgh, I bought a Commodore 64. The computer industry was built on the back of a consumer craze by amateurs and my first thought was to create something useful. I was travelling to the Soviet Union with my future wife Gil that summer, so I wrote a piece of teaching software that taught me first the Cyrillic alphabet, then some basic vocabulary. It worked a treat, and 40 years later, when I revisited Moscow to talk about artificial intelligence, with my son Callum, I could still read the Cyrillic alphabet and remnants of my Russian remained.

The rest of my adult life was in learning technology. First, with two others, building a learning technology company, Epic, in Brighton, which we floated on the Stock Market in 1996 and I sold in 2005. Many of the people who worked at Epic then went on to form other successful learning technology companies and Brighton is still a major hub. Free from the tyranny of employment, I became a board member of Learning Pool, which has gone on to great things on a global scale. As a Director of Learndirect, I worked on the delivery of basic skills using technology across the whole of the UK. When it was sold, I was instrumental in using the proceeds to set up a £54 million funded charity, the University for Industry, to fund projects using technology in vocational learning. As a Director of City & Guilds I continued my effort to support vocational learning, something I've supported all my life. Even as the Deputy Director of the Brighton Arts organization responsible for three theatres and an annual festival, I was always promoting the use of technology. I also invested in other learning technology companies, including CogBooks, an adaptive learning company, which was sold to Cambridge University in 2021. More recently I have been CEO of WildFire, the world's first company to use AI to create online learning content. That was the subject of my first book, *Artificial Intelligence for Learning*, published in 2020.

I have worked with almost all the technologies mentioned in this book. Having been commercially active in using computer-based learning since the early 1980s, I have designed, developed and delivered learning on videotape, the very first IBM, Apple, PET, BBC Micro and other home computers. Designing for the crop of storage devices that came along included computer-controlled video and audio tape devices, Laserdiscs, CDi and CD-ROM. As computers became connected, I designed for distribution across large area networks (LANs). I've used many authoring tools to design and build various types of learning program, from text only to text and graphics with interaction to scenario-based learning, as well as many different types of simulation, gamification, games and VR.

Having designed, developed and delivered learning technology solutions for over 40 years, for schools, colleges, universities and public and private sector organizations, I recently wrote *Learning Experience Design* (2021), a book that covers project design methods, text, graphics, audio, podcasts, video, animation, scenarios, simulations, VR, AR and AI. This was written during a period when learning technology became a global phenomenon, as educational institutions had to close because of the Covid-19 pandemic.

As for delivered platforms, I've worked on web portals, LMSs, LCMSs, LXPs, LRSs and MOOC platforms. Different devices have included every imaginable computer, tablet and smartphone. I also started and ran a large computer-based learning testing lab (Epicentre) that tested for quality, usability, accessibility and technical compatibility. More recently, I've been involved in the delivery of AI and data-driven solutions to create chatbots, create and curate online learning, do sentiment analysis and semantically interpret open input. I've also been heavily involved with VR and Metaverse projects.

Above all, this has all been informed by evidence-based learning theory. I have written pieces on over 200 learning theorists, produced a series of podcasts on 'Great Minds on Learning', covering 2,500 years of learning theory, as well as hundreds of articles on research and learning theory.

This is my third book and one where I hope to show that learning technology is far more important than many give it credit for. It has far greater reach back into history and is the driving force behind progress and almost all of our human achievements. There is no other technology or area of human endeavour that does not rely on rudimentary forms of learning technology, be it the simple act of writing – a technology in itself – using pencil and paper, again the technology of learning. It has given us evolutionary and cultural advantages that have allowed us to conquer the globe, understand who we are, where we came from and, as we leave this planet, where we are going.

What does the book cover?

History, as they say, is just one damn thing after another, but this is not a blow-by-blow account of what technologies appeared and when. It is not strictly chronological, as many of the technologies overlap in time, and while it serves as a history of learning technology, it also discusses the pedagogic and at times social implications of a particular piece of learning technology. Technology is not always successful, so it is presented warts and all.

We start by uncovering some generic phenomena underlying technological development and learning technologies, such as cultural impact, exponential growth and scaling capability. They also draw from consumer technologies and meld hardware and software. Technology tends to augment teaching and learning, enabling new pedagogies and extending cognition. Although often initially viewed as a threat, once adopted it is seen as normal. It also has a moral dimension in having good but also bad applications and consequences, and these apply consistently across time.

The first chapters cover the earliest forms of learning technology and their development over time, which may surprise those who assume that it is really just modern computer technology. Learning technology has been around for as long as humans have existed, and this book aims to show how it has shaped us as a species. Teaching and learning, informally and formally, is the primary means of cultural transmission. We now know that the creation of tools is an intense learning experience, taking hundreds of hours to master and clearly involving language, so the book goes back to evolution and prehistory to throw light on the earliest possible uses of technology in learning. This led, eventually, to the dominance of one species – *Homo sapiens*, whose cognitive revolution led to larger social groups coming together in social spaces to create and learn from magnificent cave paintings. These can still be seen 50,000 years later and are increasingly interpreted as learning experiences. We rarely recognize this period as being one where learning technology shaped our progress, but it profoundly extended our physical and cognitive capabilities. Through cultural evolution came technologies that scaled group transmission through learning, making us the only teaching *and* learning species.

Just like geological ages, there are identifiable ages in the development and evolution of learning technologies, with significant new technologies exploding onto the scene. As with many evolving phenomena, it had its Cambrian explosions and some notable extinctions.

Writing, as a learning technology, had an incalculable impact on the creation of culture, which could now be created, captured and distributed across time and space. It led quickly to the production of written cultural artifacts, scaling through crafted copying, stored in libraries and carried to far locations. Indeed, many of these early texts are still with us today, having survived for over 5,000 years. Writing is not often seen as a learning technology, but it is arguably the most important form of scalable learning technology our species has invented. It extends the life of our ideas for others to read and act upon. Importantly, it allows us to learn without the presence of another human as teacher, as it transcends speech. Writing was the 'Big Bang' of learning technology history, but it was limited by the hand-crafted nature of handwritten language on non-replicable technologies such as scrolls and manuscripts.

Printing scales writing and images through an automated process of replication, so it reaches out to many more people and learners. For more than 500 years, printing has amplified cultural transmission, producing individual printed texts that spread across continents. This spread of ideas led to the Reformation and Scientific and Industrial Revolutions. The products of print – books – literally created the world we know today, their scale through mechanical replication has widened the creation, capture and communication of thought.

The broadcast media of radio, film and television, as scalable consumer technologies, have provided informal and formal learning in the home and classrooms for decades. They brought another form of scale, defined by Sarnoff's law, where anyone with a suitable receiving device could receive learning experiences. Their obvious limitation is their one-way transmission but, as radio and television became global media, their reach was, and still is, immense. Although usually seen as consumer technologies, they have been used for over a century as learning technologies.

Teaching technologies are little commented upon, but the apparatus of teaching and learning, including writing instruments, papyrus, parchment and paper through to a myriad of tools used to teach and learn, have been around for thousands of years. They scale teaching and allow generative learning. This includes the technology of punishment, which until recently was ubiquitous in formal education.

Teaching machines arose in the late 19th and first half of the 20th century and were an interesting bridge between the machine and digital age. As the psychology of learning started to grow academically, early behaviourist and cognitive theorists built teaching machines. They were built on the back of pedagogic theory but proved too unsophisticated to deal with the complexities of learning. A precursor to the digital age, they nevertheless gave an idea of how the scaling of learning could be tackled.

Computers arrived in the 1970s, and alongside these consumer products were storage devices such as Laserdiscs, CDi and CD-ROMS. Computers, scaled through Moore's Law, put the power of teaching and learning in the device itself, with the screen, input device, multimedia capabilities and printer enabling the learner to be in control of their learning. The pendulum had now swung towards remote, self-paced learning. As computers, tablets and smartphones swept the world, they became personal, powerful devices for teaching and learning.

But it was the internet and the ability to search that had a profound effect on what could be done by learners, as well as more formal online learning. This allowed many forms of online learning, using all types of media, to be delivered to billions around the world, and included consumer services such as video repositories and social media. As a learning technology, the internet may prove to be even more important than writing. It adds an exponential dimension to computers, as defined by Metcalfe's Law, where the number of connections between nodes gives huge expansive power on connections. Reed's Law adds even more exponential power by factoring in social connections, providing another order of magnitude on scale.

With the internet came platforms, lots of them: VLEs (virtual learning environments), LMSs (learning management systems) and now LXPs (learning experience platforms), LRSs (learning record stores) and other species of social and performance support platforms. These are still hugely relevant in the learning landscape, delivering learning on an organizational scale. These enterprise-wide learning platforms provided a single source to store, manage and deliver online learning and manage offline events. They provided efficient management, consistency, security and scale. Today, they have matured into personalized, adaptive and performance support platforms, supporting learning as a process, rather than a series of events.

Learning *content* is also a form of learning technology, and is the crossover point between the teacher and the learner. Although we tend to still think of content as recent digital content or online learning, it began with simple geometric marks through cave paintings to writing, printing, broadcast media and the internet. Now learners (and teachers) have access to diverse types of content on every conceivable subject that could be delivered anytime, anyplace to anyone on the internet.

Artificial intelligence is in its infancy as a learning technology but already promises to grow into something beyond our imaginations. It brings something quite different as it scales personalization, as well as many other facets of teaching and learning, such as the creation and provision of learner support, feedback, adaptive learning and assessment. It is the first technology that actually learns, and which, in certain tasks, outperforms humans. Search was its first impact, a huge pedagogic change, but there will be many others. It is undoubtedly the key learning technology of the future. When combined with neurotech, it may well lead to a new era of brain mind interfaces (BMI) that have real impact on cognitive phenomena, helping with disabilities, mental health and of course learning.

One leap into the future that looks certain to happen is the Metaverse, the creation of a parallel world where everything has a digital twin, in a multiuser, 3D world. It will certainly be a place for entertainment and games, but, like all mass consumer phenomena, learning will also take place there. It is not entirely a leap into the unknown as we already know a lot about immersive learning, and some lessons can be carried forward from VR. However, this is a new level of participation activity that will create new pedagogies.

The book also looks at a few interesting and perhaps surprising topics that do not fit neatly into any of the above. These include the role the telephone has played in learning, the success of assistive technology, the technology of punishment in schools and cheat technology.

Of course, the story never ends. Learning technology goes from strength to strength. It turned out to be a saviour during the Covid-19 pandemic when schools, colleges, universities and workplaces closed. We have the exciting prospect of AI with data that promises to deliver solutions to make us smarter. On the horizon are virtual reality, the Metaverse and neurotech. It is important to see this as an ongoing story.

LIST OF ABBREVIATIONS

ADL	advanced distributed learning
API	application programming interface
AR	augmented reality
ARPA	Advanced Research Projects Agency
CPD	continuing professional development
DAP	digital adoption platform
EPSS	electronic performance support system
GDPR	General Data Protection Regulation
IoT	Internet of Things
L&D	learning and development
LAMM	learning analytics maturity model
LCMS	learning content management system
LMS	learning management system
LRS	learning record store
LTI	learning tools interoperability
LXD	learning experience design
LXP	learning experience platform
MOOC	massive open online course
Moodle	modular object-oriented dynamic learning environment
MR	mixed reality
NFT	non fungible tokens
NIH	not invented here
NLP	natural language processing
OER	open educational resources
PLA	personal learning assistant
RFI	request for information
RFP	request for proposal
ROI	return on investment
SaaS	software as a service
SCORM	sharable courseware object reference model
SME	subject matter expert
UI	user interface
UX	user experience

VLE	virtual learning environment
VoIP	voice over internet protocol
VR	virtual reality
W3C	World Wide Web Consortium
xAPI	experience application programming interface
XR	extended reality
XRSI	extended reality safety initiative

01

Learning technology

Learning technology is the most fundamental form of technology, the point of departure for all other designed technologies and cultural endeavours. It is the foundational technology that created all other technologies, as it underpins all cultural capital.

We need a deeper understanding of technology in terms of its history, the story of accelerating technological change. On the bedrock of several million years of cognitive development, from bipedalism at around 5 million years ago, through a long era of stone tool use, we had the first meaningful marks at 500,000 years, the cognitive revolution and cave painting at around 50,000 years, writing around 5,000 years, printing 500 years, computers 50 years and AI at 5 years. This accelerating progress, with shorter and shorter periods of innovation and adoption, may well be the result of learning technologies' capability to speed up and spread teaching and learning.

This book is about more than history though, it is about this single idea – that learning technology has been the most important form of technology our species has created. The idea that learning technology has been a driver of cultural transmission and the success of our species is new and unexplored. For over 3 million years we have been creating tools and technology. We are *Homo technus* but behind all of this, we are the learning species and the most important technology, the one that underpins the invention and use of all others, is learning technology. From the stone technology that defined the cognitive capabilities of our hominid ancestors through cave paintings, writing, pencils, pens, alphabet, manuscripts, books, printing, computers, internet, AI and possibly neurotechology and the Metaverse, this is a history of technology with a difference, one that looks at the technology that lies at the root of all our success.

We are distinguished, as a species, through our ability to create and use tools and technology. Other species, such as birds and primates, do use tools

FIGURE 1.1 History of learning technology

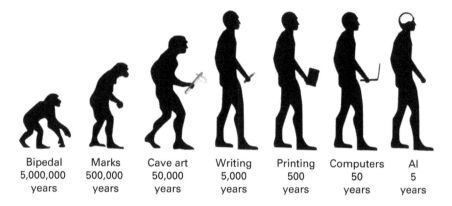

| Bipedal
5,000,000
years | Marks
500,000
years | Cave art
50,000
years | Writing
5,000
years | Printing
500
years | Computers
50
years | AI
5
years |

in a rare and limited fashion, but the first of our genus *Homo habilis* (handy man) through to *Homo sapiens* (knowing man) are by far the most successful of these competing species. We had better tools and technology, and our ability to harness technology to help us learn is what allowed us to become the most successful species. This is the core idea behind this book.

This learning technology needs to be defined as fundamental to the progress of our species. It is the technology that precedes and enables the creation of all other technologies, as, without learning, we have no cultural transmission and progress. It is important, therefore, to consider the science of technology – techn-*ology* – and lay out the ways in which technologies in this area evolved.

Techn-*ology*

The study of technology is stuck somewhere between science and engineering. We need a renewed focus on techn-*ology* as a field of study, like psychology, biology or sociology, and a deeper understanding of its history and role in history. Our aim, therefore, is to look towards the science of technology, specifically learning technology, as identifying useful laws of technology. Not like laws of physics, but rules that emerge from the way we innovate, develop, use and perceive learning technology.

Technology has certain dynamics that have to be considered before one can understand the role it plays. It constantly disrupts long-established practices, which is why it naturally and predictably invokes strong opinions, even fierce resistance. The dialectic between technology and human affairs has always caused friction. Learning technology, in particular, is contentious and creates more friction than usual, as it lies at the heart of human development.

Learning technology is clearly a subset of technology. It is fitting, therefore, to start with a general definition of 'technology'. This is not as easy as it sounds. Going back to the earliest technologies, stone tools, we need to say that technology is:

- found or made
- separate from the body
- changes the state of things, other organisms or ourselves
- is purposefully used with intentional cognitive goals.

Many books on technology start in the 18th century with the Industrial Revolution. Mumford's *Technics and Civilization* (1934) was novel at the time, as it extended that time back to the monastic clocks of the 10th century, when monks needed to mark time with devotional prayers. His was the first systematic overview of technology as a force in the development of civilization. Mumford goes further in seeing the relationship between the inner cognitive world and the physical world of technology. It is in this tradition of the dialectic of mind and technology that this book falls. Technology over the last few million years has become more combinatorial, less proximate, more powerful and more autonomous. We evolved from *Homo habilis* into *Homo sapiens*, not in a linear fashion but through a complex process of migration, crossbreeding, genetic change and cultural transmission, starting with tool augmentations to our hands and bodies and eventually into the augmentation and extension of our minds.

Technology tends to be seen in purely mechanical and material terms. Most texts about technology, such as Usher's *The History of Mechanical Invention* (1929) discuss technology as physical, tangible, mechanical devices, yet many of our most important advances have been intangible technologies, such as writing, alphabet, audio, images, video, software and different forms of media. So we must also include symbolic tools and technology, such as writing and software. The cognitive dimension is also fundamental to our definition. Technology is a social artefact, the result of cognitive effort and can be tangible or intangible, and in learning technology it is often both.

Learning technology

That brings us to the question of what we mean by learning technology. The word technology comes from the Greek *tekhne* (art, craft) and *logia* (writings), something we can reflect upon as something that is used for learning. This brings us back to our definition above that it is found or made, separate from the body, changes the state of things, other organisms or ourselves and is purposefully used *to teach and/or learn* with intentional cognitive goals.

Note that learning technology need not be consciously used to teach and/or learn, one can be aware of that function or not, only that it is used for that function.

It can be technology that already exists, technology that is used unintentionally for learning, consumer technology co-opted and used for learning, technology that is designed specifically for learning, not just hardware but also software, even technology that learns for itself, such as AI. The scope of learning technology is wider than most imagine.

The key to understanding this interplay between ideas and technology has an underlying story around the generative power of teaching and learning. It was the role of technology in shaping cognition during the millions of years we used tools that necessitated teaching and learning. This was largely oral but eventually, around 5,000 years ago, writing emerged in societies with an agricultural surplus, the alphabet came later, then printing, broadcast media, computers, the internet and AI. These mediating technologies, when used for learning, are a necessary condition for all other significant technologies and what we know as cultural capital and civilization. They are the technologies that helped expand and improve the mind and therefore the march of progress. All technology is designed, and that design requires learning. Learning technology is therefore generative, the flywheel that allows ideas to be generated, communicated, passed on, acquired, archived, reused, discarded and improved upon. Each of these steps allowed civilization to scale and eventually envelop the entire globe. The cultural and economic consequences of technology are immense and the catalytic learning technologies that underlie this process are worthy of study.

A usable definition of 'learning technology' must therefore include both hardware and software. Modern hardware invariably has, as an integral part of its function, input and output, software. Pens, pencils, erasers and paper are all hardware but have writing as their software. Manuscripts, codexes, printed books and papers are all hardware but have writing and images as software. Computers and their networks and even the cloud is hardware, but the internet is also software, and the world wide web has every imaginable media type as its software, with code that controls the logic of delivery. In learning technology, hardware is entwined with and inseparable from software.

Technology and learning

Technology is the embodiment of our cultural achievements. It manifests and enhances our powers, physical and psychological. With our first hand-held axes, we used natural materials turned into tools to hunt, survive, expand and thrive. We felled trees to create the energy for extracting and shaping metals into even more powerful tools. Tools begat more powerful tools. What is less known is the role that *learning* technologies have played in human progress.

There have been several stages in the invention and use of *learning* technologies: prehistoric cognitive development, writing, alphabet, printing, broadcast media, computing and internet, AI and data and now neurotechnology and the Metaverse. At key moments in our history, fundamental learning technologies were invented that unlocked massive cultural growth.

Writing was first invented in the advanced agricultural civilizations of Mesopotamia, Egypt and later China and Mesoamerica, and supported advanced economies in those regions. The phonetic alphabet lies at the root of the advanced Greek, then Roman civilisations with their science, philosophy, poetry and drama. When there was little that was new in the way of learning technology, there was a hiatus – the scholasticism of the Dark Ages. Printing in Europe then gave rise to the Reformation and Scientific Revolution, Enlightenment and Industrial Revolution. Computers moved us into knowledge economies, and the internet gives rise to the global online economy.

These learning technologies share some common rules of technology that determine their adoption, use and impact. These rules overlap with the general rules of technology but in some cases are specific to, or more relevant to, learning technology.

There are 10 rules or premises for our inquiry. The first five major rules explain the ways in which learning technology has been and will be an increasingly important force in cultural progress; the second five are features of learning technology that specifically define its cognitive potency. As we progress with the story of learning technology, we shall see how these general rules have shaped not just learning but our entire cultural history.

1 Learning technology has cultural impact.

2 Learning technology growth is exponential.

3 Learning technology scales.

4 Learning technology is combinatorial.

5 Learning technology gets demoted.

6 Learning technology is seen as real life.

7 Learning technology extends cognition.

8 Learning technology swings teaching to learning.

9 Learning technology enables new pedagogies.

10 Learning technology can be both good and bad.

Learning technology has cultural impact

There is a rich literature that reads history as being catapulted forward by innovations in technology, in economic cycles. No one has applied that logic to *learning* technologies. Our toolmaking had to be taught and learnt, writing and reading require detailed teaching and learning. This undoubtedly led to leaps in cultural and economic progress. The alphabet gave eastern Mediterranean culture a cardinal role in early science, philosophy and literature, particularly in Greece, a cultural source that remains strong in Western culture.

A lengthy aberration during the Dark Ages followed, when culture and progress were suspended because writing technology was stuck in manuscript production. These were written in Latin, a language of exclusion held in the hands of the few, namely the Church and monarchs. Nevertheless, manuscripts enabled cultural transmission across and through cultures, with even the works of classical Greece reaching us via Arabic culture and writing.

Western Christendom then flourished, and by the 12th century many cathedral schools had become universities. Places of study were not new and had existed in Ancient Greece and Muslim madrasas, but the universities of, for example, Bologna (1088), Paris (1150), Oxford (1167), Cambridge (1209), Padua (1222), Salamanca (1227), Prague (1347), Vienna (1367) and St Andrews (1410), while originally places for training the clergy, laid the foundations for the more secular institutions that now exist globally.

Teaching and learning then sprang into life with the advent of printing, its cultural impact being enormous. Printing put learning into the hands of anyone that could read, in their own language, and caused the Reformation and Scientific Revolution that led to the Enlightenment. All of this resulted in an explosion of learning and learning institutions.

The Industrial Revolution began in Britain in the 18th century and by the mid-19th century it was clear that a literate labour force was becoming increasingly necessary. The rise of mass manufacturing had also led to a management class that needed to be trained. This led to the introduction of more widespread schooling and, to meet this demand, the mass production of pencils, pens, slates, paper, textbooks, notebooks and blackboards. These literally educated the masses, widening and increasing the cultural capital of the world.

Then came computers that sped up technological progress. They energized and accelerated the building of new knowledge economies. Hot on their tail came the internet, itself a research and learning network, which globalized learning resources through search, Wikipedia, YouTube and other services, as well as retail, finance and economics.

One can see how the underlying technologies of writing, printing, broadcast, computers and the internet have not just been technological revolutions but learning technology revolutions. It is hard to see how any of these wider technology and cultural revolutions could have taken place without learning technology being available. It is learning hardware and software that enabled human minds to build such political, economic and technological systems.

Finally, we are now in the era of artificial intelligence, or AI, the age of algorithms and data that promises to free up what Daniel Dennett calls 'pedagogical bottlenecks'. For the first time we have learning technology that doesn't just help us teach and learn – it can learn itself. Only now do we see that teaching and learning is not the sole domain of our species but a feature of our newly created technology – AI.

Learning technology growth is exponential

Writing, printing, broadcast, computers, the internet and now AI, are all learning technologies that liberated exponential growth in knowledge and learning. Our ability to document, write, calculate, explain, plan, execute, teach and learn about what we normally think of as technology (mechanical, electrical, chemical and physical) has always relied on learning technologies that underlie their ideation. The great leaps forward in the history of our species have been leaps of the imagination, that envisioned technologies that would allow us to teach, learn and document our imaginative output, time after time, to further cultural transmission and development.

These leaps gave rise to science and advances in medicine, commerce, great art and every peak of human achievement.

Learning technology is not simply additive, it is a cultural and economic multiplier and one of the root causes of cultural paradigm shifts that is often categorized in terms of materials, namely stone, bronze, iron, water, steel, steam or silicon chips. Alternatively it is seen as mechanical devices: mills, ships, steam engines, looms, railways, automobiles, domestic devices, airplanes, rockets, satellites, computers, tablets and smartphones. But what lies beneath their development is teaching and *learning*, enabled by learning technologies. We mistakenly describe the more obvious visible and physical manifestations of technology when they are actually the effects or products of deeper and unrecognized learning technologies. Learning technologies progressively accelerate learning, compounding output, and with each successive creation of learning technology we get a shift in civilization.

Learning technology is still mostly ignored in favour of the obvious physical and mechanical categorization of technology. This fails to recognize that the history of technology has a deeper, hidden story of cognitive effort and progress that made this more obvious technology possible. Generative learning technologies lie beneath the physical manifestation of technology. These cognitive technologies allow the brain to create, document, manipulate and share ideas. 'At a few times in history, people have hit upon technologies that multiply, indeed exponentiate the growth of knowledge', said Stephen Pinker in *Enlightenment Now* (2018). These learning technologies are inflection points in the history of our species.

This has been defined in economics as relatively modern periods of technological change, for example in Schumpter's *Theories of Economic Development* (1911), with cycles of economic development driven by sudden changes in innovative technology. Carla Perez in *Technological Revolutions and Financial Capital* (2003) expands on the Schumpterian idea to identify more fine-grained cycles of over-effusive investment and slumps, then periods of fruitful investment, resulting in significant improvements in productivity and economic progress.

To place learning technologies in context, we need to go back to our origins as a species. Learning technologies go back to the origins of our stone tool-making species, which in a virtuous loop of cognitive development, allowed us to make several leaps.

Learning technologies

More recently, it can be said that we overestimate technology in the short term and underestimate it in the long term.

Learning technology scales

Scale matters, but we often fail to address the real meaning of the word and the various species of scalability. Teachers are not scalable. Classrooms and lecture rooms are not scalable. When delivery is tied to both, it limits scalability. Tied to the tyranny of location and time, learning remains non-scalable.

Technology, by contrast, is intrinsically scalable. The ability to create and store writing gives it longevity and portability, the alphabet accelerates the efficacy of writing, printing duplicates writing and images, broadcasting reaches millions simultaneously, computers duplicate digitally, the internet duplicates globally and AI delivers personalization and created content. They all scale up successively in orders of magnitude.

There are four laws that quantify raw scaling in technology: Sarnoff's Law, Moore's law, Metcalfe's Law and Reed's Law.

David Sarnoff had a long career in radio and television and was head of the Radio Corporation of America (RCA). His law defined the scalability of broadcast technology that sees the value of a broadcast network as proportional to the number of viewers. The advantage of broadcast technologies, such as radio and television, is their simultaneous transmission of learning to large public audiences.

In 1965, Gordon Moore saw that the number of transistors in an integrated circuit was doubling every year. He revised this in 1975 to doubling every two years. This meant that the processing power grew exponentially and that all the devices we now use doubled their processing power every two years while remaining affordable.

Metcalfe quantified the growth of value in networks. As the number of potential connections between nodes always outstrips the number of nodes, so connecting networks always create a value greater than the simple sum of the two networks, more accurately defined as the value of a network being proportional to the square of the number of connected users of the system n^2. This defines the scalability of computer networks and the internet.

Reed saw that the value of large 'social' networks scale exponentially rather than proportionally. Social use across networks is therefore behind the real growth of use on the internet. He defined this as a network with n

members having 2^n possible groups. There are cognitive limits to group formation, but this is still exponentially huge. In one sense it defines the learning power of a network – the potential connections, teaching and learning between brains on the network.

This explains the exponential scaling of learning technologies from one-to-many teaching, through the multiplier of printing, then the wide reach of broadcast media, the growth in power and functionality of computers and the massive exponential effect of the internet. In terms of the potential value for learning, it is linear for printing and broadcast networks, across a network with nodes it is squared and with social groups it is exponential. We shall see how this unfolded across the 20th into the 21st century.

Quite simply, as learning technology evolved, its scale and reach increased. With the invention of writing, we freed knowledge from the tyranny of space and time and were able to externalize our thoughts. Knowledge was captured, archived and distributed to many others in many different places, at many different times. Printing accelerated this same process, as identical copies could be mass produced and distributed nationally and internationally. This was scaled up again with broadcast media and went global and social with the internet.

Learning technology also scales in the sense that it is cumulative. Writing benefited from more efficient alphabet technology and then from more portable formats such as scrolls, followed by books. Printing takes these technologies and duplicates exact copies in batches for distribution. Once digitized on computers, they also feed through digital capture, distribution and access.

Learning technology all comes together on the internet, with broadband, cloud services and streaming lessening the need for local storage. Most learning technology platforms are now cloud-based, and streaming has led to a renaissance of video and podcast learning. Access is available at anytime and anyplace on any device with an internet connection. The internet is a single, global source for storage and access, meaning that peripheral devices such as tablets, smartphones, audio devices, VR, AR and the Internet of Things can multiply its use. Most learning technology services are responsive in being smartphone ready. Ubiquitous smartphones allow access from almost anywhere on the planet.

Another dimension of scalability is personalization through AI and data-driven learning, where relevance can be scaled using personal and aggregated data. We have seen this with search, smart interfaces, knowledge bases, translation, transcription and globally delivered learning, such as Duolingo.

A new form of scalability in learning technology is machine and AI learning which allows software to learn and improve with use. This uses data, not just to train AI systems, but also to dynamically improve the systems as they are used. This is the scalability of Google search and translation. It is also true of learning systems such as adaptive platforms and learning experience platforms.

The digital reformation has led to an age of digital abundance, the only real, scalable solution for ideas and content, as digital replication is possible at almost zero cost across the entire planet. From Gutenberg to Zuckerberg, scalability is the key to accessible, ubiquitous, low-cost learning.

Learning technology is combinatorial

Combinations of technology are seen by Brian Arthur (2009) as the unrecognized driver of technological innovation. This is also true of learning technology. From writing instruments, inks and papyrus, parchments or paper, combinations of technologies have always been necessary. It is these, along with advances in technologies for reading, that make learning technologies fly.

Printing was not a single technology. It was the combination of presses, moveable metallic letters, ink, paper and binding that gave us printing, with copied texts being the replicable distributable entities.

Broadcast media is a complex combination of image and sound creation and capture, along with electromagnetic wave technology and the receiver technology of radios and televisions. There were many breakthroughs and applications in physics involved in the creation of this consumer and learning technology, with its immense reach.

The computer, with its combination of input device, processing unit, keyboard and printer, brought together a huge number of combinatorial possibilities.

A more intimate form of combination is between hardware and software. Learning technology almost always involves the combination of the tangible and physical (hardware) and intangible and psychological (software). Learning is, in essence, psychological, and learning technologies lead to relatively stable changes to long-term memory.

Combination also means cumulation. We see on the internet the cumulative delivery of all media types – text, images, audio, video, AR, VR – and different forms of communications in different configurations. There is no technology that has been as combinational, cumulative and communicatively complex as the internet, with its network protocols for identification, transmission and presentation to a global audience for learning. It delivers a huge variety of options, including text via Wikipedia and other knowledge bases, video from YouTube and others, social media, podcast services for audio and many other free learning resources. Learning technologies have always been combinations of physical technologies, used to expand their breadth and depth, using all possible media. For example, immersive VR is a combined multimedia device, with stereoscopic vision, sensors, haptic gloves, bodysuits and treadmills brought together in the multiuser environment that is the Metaverse.

Learning technology gets demoted

When defining the evolution of technology, it is almost compulsory to state Douglas Adams' (2013) wonderful description, and to be fair, his wording has not been bettered:

1 Everything that's already in the world when you're born is just normal;

2 Anything that gets invented between then and before you turn thirty is incredibly exciting and creative and with any luck you can make a career out of it;

3 Anything that gets invented after you're thirty is against the natural order of things and the beginning of the end of civilisation as we know it, until it's been around for about 10 years when it gradually turns out to be alright really.

Technology is often a solution to a problem that has been forgotten. This is true of technology in general, but particularly true of learning technology. We are born into a world of writing, pens, pencils, paper, printing, books, chalkboards and so on, seeing them not as technologies but just there in the background of everyday life. Learning through computers, smartphones and the internet falls into the category of being exciting and certainly something one can make a career out of. Artificial intelligence, data, neurotechnology and the Metaverse are, of course, the end of civilization as we know it! With learning technologies, we move like a wave, with old technology no longer seen as technology, contemporary stuff as exciting and leading edge, and future tech as an abomination. It was ever thus.

We therefore have to recognize that what we see as technology tends to fade and get declassified as technology or de-technologized. The technology of the day quickly becomes the technology of yesteryear and eventually not really technology at all. This book attempts to save learning technology from that fate.

Learning technology is seen as real life

Byron Reeves and Clifford Nass (1996) are two Stanford academics, who laid down some foundational research studies on media in learning. Their compelling case, backed up with empirical studies, showed that people confuse media with real life, a beneficial confusion as it is what makes movies, television, radio, video and online learning work. These 35 psychological studies all point towards the simple proposition that people react towards media socially even though, on reflection, they may believe it is not reasonable to do so. People think that computers are people.

There is no reason, therefore, why online learning experiences should be any less 'human' in feel than what we experience in the classroom. As long as media technology is consistent in its social and physical rules, we readily accept it. However, as Reeves and Nass found, when media technology fails to conform to these human expectations, we tend to reject the experience.

The spell is easily broken. We have a visceral response to awkward pauses and unnatural timing, so slight pauses, waits and unexpected events cause cognitive dissonance. Asynchrony, such as poor lip-synch or delays, and poor quality of sound result in negative evaluations of the speaker and are problems that are cognitively disturbing and hamper learning.

Many modern theorists have begun to research different aspects of learning theory in relation to learning technology. From the actual physical use of technology in Papert and Harel's 'constructionism' (1991) to Norman (1998) and Nielsen's (1999) work on design and usability and Mayer and Clark's (2003) 500+ studies on what works in online learning, research has flourished in a slew of works on the cognitive interaction between technology and the mind.

Learning technology extends cognition

Technologies often protected and extended our bodies (think of clothing, weapons and tools), while other technologies extend the mind (spectacles, pens, books, computers and digital voice assistants, for instance). The emergence of language began millions of years ago, writing came about thousands of years ago, printing arrived hundreds of years ago, broadcast media a hundred or so years ago and now, in just a few decades, computers, the internet and AI have appeared. We are now, especially with the advent of AI, seeing innovation in 'cognitive' technologies such as brain computer interfaces (BCIs).

We represent, replicate and scale our thoughts through cognitive technologies, such as speech, writing, alphabets, mathematics, audio, images, video, VR and other media. These external media allow our minds to directly create, express, manipulate and distribute our inner thoughts. From another perspective, they also allow our minds to listen, read, understand and learn. Pens, pencils, keyboards and touchscreens can be seen as extensions of consciousness, part of one's mind and body.

But where does the mind stop and the rest of the world begin? Chalmers and Clark answer this fascinating question in *The Extended Mind* (1998). They see the components of learning technology as literally an extension of our consciousness, the very things we use to learn. These philosophers put forward the idea of extended consciousness or cognition as an alternative theory of consciousness.

Once written, a text is a piece of captured consciousness that can be read by others. To create this archived realm is to escape the tyranny of time and place. Written words can be read at any time in any place, as they are objects in themselves, separated from their creator. This is how learning happens and escapes from the consciousness of the human teacher. As a learner or teacher, learning technology extends and bridges minds in several possible dimensions. First and fundamentally, it changes long-term memory, which is the primary aim of learning. With that change we can recall and think about the past as retrieved history and create future possibilities. Our imagination is fuelled by this recall of knowledge and skills.

We can also escape the tyranny of location, to learn about and imagine places beyond our current location. Paper maps, then Google Maps and Street View and sat nav devices have become commonplace. Technology that extends the mind extends capabilities, foresight and creativity, allowing other forms of human capabilities and culture to develop.

Learning technology swings teaching to learning

The history of learning technology is the history of technology becoming more accessible, scalable, frictionless, even invisible. A consequence of the scaling of learning technology is that it has gradually reduced the dependency on human teaching in learning. This process is now accelerating.

If we start with the hypothesis that cave paintings were social spaces where clans came together for learning, then we can see how one-to-one instruction, on say tool making and hunting, becomes a one-to-many teaching and learning experience. This drift towards one-to-many has been enabled by technology that reflected the mind of the teacher to a group of learners, and exponentially increased the ratio between teachers and available knowledge, as well as teachers and learners.

This is not to say that technology has or will replace teachers, only that the ratio has changed. With economic progress more countries have the ability to deliver more education and training, but learning technology has allowed us to transcend the family, clan, classroom or lecture hall as units of educational transmission. Instead it is now increasingly online, borderless and global.

We spend only a fraction of our time in classrooms and in formal learning; most learning therefore no longer takes place in the presence of a teacher but in other contexts, often made possible by learning technology. We now search, read, write, watch videos, listen to podcasts, access the vast knowledge base on the internet, use smartphones and voice assistants, with increasing levels of sophistication. All of this is in the increasing absence of teachers, even other humans. We should not let formal 'schooling' blind us to this fact, as this is not where the majority of learning takes place.

Each successive innovation in learning technology changes the way we learn. Technology changes pedagogy, with the locus of learning shifting away from live, synchronous teaching to asynchronous learning. It is an uncomfortable truth for many but from the invention of writing onwards, the pendulum has always been swinging away from formal teaching to technology-based learning.

Learning technology enables new pedagogies

McLuhan (1994) saw that technology shapes not only what we learn but how we learn. So learning technologies, both old and new, have all had a profound effect on the process of learning. Learning technology also brings with it an implied pedagogy. McLuhan's idea that technology shapes how we see and think about the world has accelerated, and billions now search for knowledge and solutions through search engines such as Google and learn at a distance using technology. The printed encyclopedia was killed stone dead by Wikipedia; video has expanded as a learning medium and social media has exploded in popularity. Other forms of technology, such as

AI, BCI, the Metaverse and as yet unknown innovations will come in time. All of this has already had a profound influence on how we teach and learn and will continue to enhance the learning landscape.

New learning technologies create and enable new pedagogic techniques. The humble pencil and eraser allow one to fail, erase and retry as one learns. This is a simple example of technology enabling pedagogy. The chalkboard also allows the teacher to erase and rewrite when dealing with worked examples and is still popular in universities. With computer technology, the ability to cut, paste and edit all help one to write, while tools can be used to spell and grammar check, check for plagiarism and provide feedback on one's writing. We also have powerful search, research and citations at our fingertips, when only recently this meant browsing the shelves of libraries.

Allowing learners to do cognitively effortful, generative learning by writing on an internet-enabled computer and then distributing and publishing their work enables them to do things on their own in their own time and place. This is just one example of how a piece of technology can enable a range of pedagogic advances.

The internet creates more pedagogic opportunities since it frees delivery from time and place and enables the delivery of different media and complex interaction through scenario-based learning, simulation and gamification, to name but a few. Flight and medical simulators, for example, are clear examples of technologies creating sophisticated pedagogic options for pilot and physician training. The free live video communications that flourished during the Covid-19 pandemic are another example of pedagogy being enabled by technology.

AI and data-driven systems allow pedagogic techniques like personalization through adaptive learning, delivering to the right person, the right experience at the right time. There is also the algorithmic delivery of deliberate practice, spaced practice and motivational pedagogies such as behavioural, nudge learning. An enormous set of pedagogic options can be blended into an optimal blend suited to specific groups of learners and types of learning. This is not just about learning delivered solely through technology. Offline learning can also be designed, delivered and managed through technology.

Learning technology can be both good and bad

The pen is said to be mightier than the sword but most technology, including learning technology, has an ethical dimension. With learning technology, these ethical issues are fairly minor compared to say weapons of war, the use of fossil fuels and even driving cars. We continue to drive cars despite the fact that nearly 1.5 million people die every year in car crashes, with the number injured even higher. This is a casualty number larger than that of an annual world war. Plastic syringes may save lives, but plastic is killing our oceans.

Learning technologies have no lethal consequences, but there are still downsides. In printing, paper production means felling trees and is one of the most polluting manufacturing processes ever invented. Billions of plastic bricks have been produced by the famous Danish toymaker, yet single-use plastic is a menace. The internet and AI have created ethical issues in social behaviour, crime and politics. Astonishingly, even the humble learning management system has had a genocidal consequence. In 1939, Tom Watson, CEO of IBM, flew to meet Hitler and sold him a punch-card called the Hollerith system. As we shall see later, it stored data on skills, race and sexual orientation, and was subsequently used to select people for slave labour and the death trains to concentration camps.

At a more prosaic level, although some learning technology in schools, universities and the workplace is admirable, it also is not without ethical problems. Learning technology can be used for good, for example, as assistive technology for those with physical or psychological problems and during the Covid-19 pandemic when there was no alternative. However, some argue that its use increases social inequalities by ignoring the digital divide, being selective and elitist and using time and money that would be better spent elsewhere. This seems to be an eternal problem with technology and learning technology, its Janus-face as a force for both good and bad.

Dialectic of learning and technology

Learning theory has always been the product of the larger cultural milieu it finds itself in, and that is both productive and limiting. So what has 2,500 years of learning theory and practice taught us? Firstly it has been remarkably compliant to religious, philosophical and political movements and shifts. It not only bends with these winds, but it also hangs on to them, long after their real effect on society has waned. In a sense, the learning landscape reflects the past more than the present or future. Old theories and practices get locked in, often through institutional inertia. Education and training can be slow to learn.

The lecture today is not that different from those delivered at Plato's Academy 2,500 years ago. Even when new theories and practices are adopted, such as learning styles, they can be faddish and ill-researched. Technology is always ahead of sociology and even in education, the technology and associated pedagogies used by learners tends to leap ahead of their teachers and institutions. Almost all learners with access to internet technology are, to some degree, online learners.

We learn over a lifetime, yet the focus is largely on schooling. Schooling remains a stable offering, with standardized curricula, tests and teaching the norm. Most learning theorists have focused on formal learning along with taxonomies of learning and defined instructional models. Yet little of our learning across a lifetime is formal. Apart from one major bout of formal schooling between the age of five and one's teens or early twenties, the rest is largely informal. Pre-school is almost wholly informal, and, in the workplace, research consistently shows that the great majority of learning is informal.

A common refrain from educators is that this is not about technology but learning. So was it learning then technology, or technology then learning? This idea is flawed, as the relationship between the two is a complex dialectic. The technologies that shaped the learning landscape were writing, alphabets, writing instruments, books, broadcast media, computers and the internet, yet none of this technology came from the 'learning' community. The technology came first, its use in learning second. What did come from the learning community was the technology of the lecture hall and schoolroom, such as lecterns and blackboards. However, a lot of learning technology has been shaped by learning professionals who make it usable and productive. It has been a *dialectic* with constant cross-pollination.

The real world of learning is messy, a combination of formal and informal learning. We are a nurturing species and child development is an intense learning experience but not one that is especially formal – parenting is not teaching. We then nurture through a legally enforced period of schooling, and many now continue with formal learning beyond school. Of course, it does not stop there, as beyond formal schooling is work and life. Workplace learning is mostly incidental and unintentional. In life itself, we often learn for pleasure. It is not so much lifelong learning but a life of constant formal and informal learning.

Learning technology does not only exist in the structured world of educational institutions and organizational training. The real world creates lots of consumer technology that is useful outside of these environments. Just because it is not seen in the classroom or lecture hall does not mean it is not used in learning. After formal education most adult learners become fairly autonomous. In some cases learning technology emerges, without reference to learning, yet has a profound pedagogic effect on the way people learn. Google is a good example. It changed the way we access knowledge, find academic papers, do research and solve problems when learning or at work. This irreversibly changed the way we learn. Wikipedia, a crowdsourced knowledge base, was also a major leap forward in terms of the way knowledge could now be dynamically created, edited, discussed, distributed and accessed. YouTube has become a learning platform, accessed by huge numbers of formal and informal learners, where 'how to' learning is globally accessible. Many MOOCs, Khan Academy, Duolingo and other services came not from within education but from outsiders who shaped the learning landscape through innovation.

There are many examples of technology that are sensitive to learning theory and learner needs. All manner of useful content creation and delivery, communication, collaboration, assessment, learner management, learning management, simulation, spaced practice and adaptive, personalized systems have been developed with learning in mind, often by educators. Moodle and open educational resources (OER) are good examples. Moodle, built by Martin Dougiamas, created an open source system used by educators around the world.

Culture, in the short term, tends to trump technology, until that technology is assimilated into culture, where it often drives that cultural norm. Institutional inertia needs to be overcome for technology to succeed. Learners often use learning technology that is not provided by or even approved by their organization. All sides produce friction when they stick to their prejudices. The learning technology side when they overreach and overpromise, the learning side when they refuse to consider change and overreact.

We have seen the disastrous consequences when both tech and teachers get obsessed with 'devices', leading to the wrong focus on short-lived 'mosquito projects' when what is needed are 'turtle projects' – slower but long-lived – leading to sustainable change. It sometimes leads to the procurement of tech that is expensive and poorly implemented, with a lack of support for teachers. Writing was by no means popular when learning theory was discussed by Socrates and Plato. Printing was seen by many as the Devil's work. Broadcast media were seen as a cultural evil. In the computer age, the internet, social media, smartphones, Wikipedia and AI have all come under heavy fire. Every learning technology revolution has been dismissed as irrelevant and harmful, but eventually turns out to be useful and often essential in learning.

Compromises are often struck. Blended learning is a good example, something almost everyone on the technology sides agrees with, but it remains difficult to implement because of the technology versus teaching wars referred to above. Blended learning proposes the use of both offline and online, classroom and internet, and is designed to optimize learning opportunities and experiences. Learning is a process not an event, and freeing it from the tyranny of time and place will continue to be beneficial for learners.

In practice, it is a complex dialectic. Over millennia, technology has played an increasing role in teaching, and more importantly, learning. The teachers versus technology argument is specious because it fails to recognize that learning has always been an accommodation between the two. Technology evangelists can overplay their hands with excessive, even egregious claims and marketing, while educators can also overplay their hands, putting up resistance to defend the traditional against any form of change. Both sides have their purists but most eventually see this as a synthesis.

Even when they work together, applying new technology to old thinking doesn't always result in progress. The simple transfer of books to screen, theatre to cinema, lectures to online and so on, is not optimal. A new synthesis, often blended learning, sometimes a radical shift, is almost always better.

Far from being a 'black box', something separate from us, learning technology has profoundly shaped our evolution, progress and culture – it will shape our future even more, as we increasingly depend on being smarter to survive. This complex dance between ourselves and technology is far more multifaceted than the simplistic trope, 'it's about people not technology'.

Technology matters

There is a much bigger historical and philosophical story around technology here that is worth laying out before we take our deep dive into learning technology. Plato's articulation of the philosophy of technology in his *Timaeus*, as the work of an 'artisan', sees the universe as a created entity, a technology. Aristotle is less metaphysical and makes the subtler observation in his *Physics*, that technology not only mimics nature but continues 'what nature cannot bring to a finish', a good description of both learning and technology. Both set in train an idea that the universe is *made* by a *maker*, the universe as a technological creation.

What followed was a 2,000-year history of Western culture that still believed that the universe was a creation. William Paley, in his formulation of the argument for the existence of God from design, used a technological analogy, the watch, to prove the existence of a designed universe and therefore a designer, called God. In *Natural Theology or, Evidences of the Existence and Attributes of the Deity* (1829), Paley used the argument from analogy to compare the workings of a watch with the movements of the planets in the solar system and concluded that it showed signs of design and that there must, therefore, be a designer. God as technologist and watchmaker has been the dominant philosophical belief for two millennia. Richard Dawkins cleverly titled his book *The Blind Watchmaker* as a counterpoint. Modern Paleys, and there are many, have resurrected his watch argument, notably in the Pennsylvania school district trial in 2004, where the expert witness on both sides used the watchmaker argument to present their case for and against 'intelligent design'.

Technology clearly helped generate this metaphysical split, this binary separation of the subject from object, that allowed us to create these new realms, both real and apparent. Technological progress has always invoked both utopian and dystopian visions and as learning technologies are close to the developing minds of children, they are seen as particularly suspect.

The farming cultures in the fertile crescent of the Middle East, using the spade, plough and scythe, had time to reflect on the back of their technology-aided labour. If technology fuels ideas, learning technology fuels the dissemination of ideas. Interestingly our first written records, on that wonderfully permanent piece of technology, the clay tablet, are largely the accounts of agricultural produce and commerce. At heart, we are accountants, with our great religious books of accounts, the first global best sellers, holding us to account for our sins.

Learning technology has not, historically, been seen as dystopian, yet when it starts to put power in the hands of the learner or free us from the tyranny of the teacher, with computers and the internet, the dystopian visions become a flood. When we invent technology that learns by itself, AI, the dystopian visions almost give way to hysteria.

The learning technology that was writing may have suggested, then created, God, but in the end, it slew him. The very technologies, writing and books which captured these beliefs and fuelled the evangelical spread led to the invention of the printing press, which in turn promoted the learning culture that rejected religious hegemony. Printing, with its rapid duplication of religious texts, was seen as spreading the word, but soon all sorts of alternative worldviews emerged.

Copernicus, drawing upon printed, technology-generated data and mathematics, displaced us from being at the centre of the universe; we ended up not even being at the centre of our own little twirl of planets. Printing continued, fuelling science until Darwin destroyed that last conceit, that we were unique as a species and created by the hand of God. Now the product of the blind watchmaker, double-helix and genetically encoded algorithms, not a maker but reduced to mere accidents of genetics, the sons and daughters of genetic mutations and variability.

We were suddenly adrift, anchors lost; but we had learnt to be a cunning species. We make things up, but we also make things and make things happen. Our new solace was not from being created forms but by creating technology ourselves. We scaled agricultural production through technology in the agricultural revolution and then abandoned the fields for the factories. We then created technology that scaled factory production in the Industrial Revolution and went on to scale mass production in the consumer revolution. We have even learnt, with AI and data, to make machines that can know and think on our behalf. Technology literally shapes our conception of ourselves.

René Descartes, as a dualist, thought of mind and body as separate. Although failing to explain how one causally interacts with the other, he did see the physiology of the body as a machine and in this context we began to see 17th-century robots, such as Jacques Vaucanson's 1738 flautist, that astonishes even now. But it was Gottfried Wilhelm Leibniz who was the true progenitor of AI, with his theory that language mirrors thought, and a universal language may be written that manipulates symbols representing concepts and ideas using logic to simulate reasoning. This is to see the mind in terms of a computational model. He was precise on this idea as, in 1666, he quoted Hobbes as having proposed the same theory: 'Thomas Hobbes, everywhere a profound examiner of principles, rightly stated that everything done by our mind is a computation'. Note also that Descartes and Leibniz made significant contributions to algebra, geometry and calculus, influencing AI in other, more purely mathematical ways.

AI has suddenly made the dialectic between man and machine a lot more complex. Martin Heidegger said, 'Only a God can save us'. What did he mean by this? That technology has become something greater than us, something we now find difficult to even see, as its intangible hand has become ever more invisible. It now teaches us, and we learn from it. We must reflect on this technology, not as something separate from us, but as being of us. We must face up to our own future as makers of technologies that in turn make us.

The postscript is that artificial intelligence and neurotechnologies may, in the end, be the way forward, with learning technology that makes us better learners, augmenting our intelligence. AI may be better explained as augmented intelligence. In the same way that the brain has limits on its ability to play chess or GO, it may also have limits on the application of reason and logic. AI that teaches us to learn may be the God that saves us from ourselves.

Conclusion

These are the major questions this book addresses, with a focus on learning technologies. We track learning technologies over the entire period of their existence, looking at how they enhance and amplify learning. Sometimes they push other technologies out, making them obsolete, such as scrolls, manuscripts, videotapes and the printed encyclopedia. Sometimes technologies from the past are resurrected and given a new life, such as out-of-print books now digitized and made available on the web. Sometimes older media is used in radically new ways, such as video and stereoscopic vision in VR.

Online learning technology enhances, increases and amplifies knowledge and learning globally. The history of learning technology shows that, in general, it democratizes, decentralizes and disintermediates the learning game. Personal computers and the internet have been the real source of pedagogic change over the last 25 or so years and are something that has changed the behaviours of learners, independently of teachers, teaching and education.

What is notable about many of these breakthrough learning technologies is that they came from outside of the orthodox system. All have changed how, where and when we learn, with radical shifts in the way we search, communicate, collaborate, create, share, play and learn. Technology is now a pedagogic engine, changing and shaping the very way we learn, and it is accelerating, resulting in more pedagogic change in the last 25 years than in the last 2,500 years. This book is the story of that acceleration and its impact on our species.

References

Arthur, W B (2009) *The Nature of Technology: What it is and how it evolves*, Simon and Schuster, New York

Adams, D (1999) How to Stop Worrying and Learn to Love the Internet, Douglas Adams.com, https://douglasadams.com/dna/19990901-00-a.html (archived at https://perma.cc/EE4R-78PT)

Archer-Hind, R D (ed) (1888) *The Timaeus of Plato*, Macmillan, London

Black, E (2012) *IBM and the Holocaust: The strategic alliance between Nazi Germany and America's most powerful corporation* (Expanded Edition), Dialog Press, USA

Clark, A and Chalmers, D (1998) The extended mind, *Analysis*, 58(1), 7–19

Dawkins, R (1996) *The Blind Watchmaker: Why the evidence of evolution reveals a universe without design,* WW Norton & Company, New York City

Dennett, D C (2017) *From Bacteria to Bach and Back: The evolution of minds*, WW Norton & Company, New York City

Leibniz, G W (1989) Dissertation on the Art of Combinations (1666) In: Loemker, LE (eds) *Philosophical Papers and Letters*, The New Synthese Historical Library, 2, 73–84, Springer, Dordrecht https://doi.org/10.1007/978-94-010-1426-7_2 (archived at https://perma.cc/2FXV-6MHC)

Mayer R E and Clark R (2003) *E-learning and the Science of Instruction*, Pfeiffer and Company, Hoboken, NJ

McLuhan, M (1994) *Understanding Media: The Extension of Man*, MIT Press, Cambridge MA

Metcalfe's Law https://en.wikipedia.org/wiki/Metcalfe%27s_law (archived at https://perma.cc/LWR9-HGKK)

Moore's Law https://en.wikipedia.org/wiki/Moore%27s_law (archived at https://perma.cc/Q7UL-JBS4)

Mumford, L (1934) *Technics and Civilizations*, University of Chicago Press, Chicago

Nielsen, J (1999) *Designing Web Usability: The practice of simplicity*, New Riders Publishing, Thousand Oaks, CA

Norman, D (1998) *The Invisible Computer*, MIT Press, Cambridge, MA

Paley, W (1829) *Natural Theology: Or evidence of the existence and attributes of the deity, collected from the appearances of nature*, Lincoln and Edmands, Boston

Harel, I and Papert, S (1991) Constructionism: Research reports and essays 1985–1990, Ablex Publishing Group, Norwood, NJ

Perez, C (2003) *Technological Revolutions and Financial Capital: The dynamics of bubbles and golden ages*, Edward Elgar Publishing, Cheltenham

Pinker, S (2018) *Enlightenment Now: The case for reason, science, humanism and progress*, Penguin, London

Reeves, B and Nass, C (1996) *The Media Equation: How people treat computers, television, and new media like real people and places*, Cambridge University Press, Cambridge

Reed's Law https://en.wikipedia.org/wiki/Reed%27s_law (archived at https://perma.cc/65B3-LSP4)

Sarnoff's law https://en.wikipedia.org/wiki/David_Sarnoff (archived at https://perma.cc/4PKV-XMSA)

Schumpeter, J A (trans. R Opie) (1983) [1934], *The Theory of Economic Development: An inquiry into profits, capital, credit, interest, and the business cycle*, Transaction Books, New Brunswick, NJ

Usher, A P (2013) [1929] *A History of Mechanical Inventions*, Courier Corporation, North Chelmsford, MA

02

Prehistoric learning technology

We are the technological ape. *Homo sapiens* evolved not in a linear fashion from apes but as the most successful of a number of early species that used tools and technology. Bipedalism literally set us on our evolutionary way 10 million years ago. It allowed us to run and sweat, it also freed up our hands and the increase in muscles and nerves in our palms and fingers allowed us to carry and, more importantly, make and use tools. In shaping our tools, our tools shaped us. We could imagine things in 3D, make them and throw them precisely and with force. Tools could be used to impress and so played a role in sexual selection.

These scrapers, blades and axes literally gave us an edge. They allowed us to hunt, fish, kill, dismember, skin, crush and cook. Hand and hefted axes gave us increased power and precision, while spears, bows and arrows enabled us to become lethal predators while at the same time preventing us from becoming prey.

Lamps and ochre allowed us to express our imagination on the walls of caves. Clothing, also a form of technology, allowed us to move into new habitats. Tools and technology distinguish us from other species and without this period of several millions of years of learning, our brains would not have their disposition to teach and learn. That is why this examination of the infancy of our evolution as a species is so important.

Homo technus

We could be better described as *Homo technus*, using tools and technology to conquer the entire planet. Our supreme achievements right up to walking on the Moon and reaching other planets was built on our earlier ability to create learning technologies such as writing, manuscripts, printing, books, computers, the internet and now artificial intelligence, a technology that learns itself and may transcend us.

With artificial intelligence we are breaking new ground, with smart technology that surpasses some of our own cognitive achievements. First, at automating our factories, then in beating us at our own games such as chequers, chess, GO, poker and computer games. Now sophisticated skills in finance, healthcare, transport and education are in sight. It is not yet clear how far this will take us and at what speed, but its transformative effect is clear, as explained in Clark (2020). As *Homo technus* we have tamed technology, but ultimately it may tame us. Time, as they say, will tell.

This book makes the case for us being *Homo technus*, but also focuses on one facet of our relationship with technology – teaching and learning. We are the species that learnt to teach and learn. This, I believe, is our real advantage, and our use of technology to teach and learn is our greatest achievement. This is the hidden story of how we used technology to turn us into the *learning ape*, tooled up to expand our mental capabilities, physical reach and geographical dominance. Cognitively, we had language, the ability to learn and memory capabilities that turned us into planning, scheming apes. We learnt to reach out into the future and see what we could achieve, then work towards that goal. We learnt to communicate those goals to others and become social animals.

A neolithic axe is a thing of beauty, but also a thing of clear purpose and use. I found one near my home on the South Downs and to hold it in your hand takes you back to the person who held and used it millennia ago. It feels familiar, comfortable to hold, useful and possibly lethal. I have also stood in a field of axes in the Rift Valley in Ethiopia, where Early Man was so prolific there is literally a sea of axes strewn across a large area, made of basalt as well as obsidian. Our earliest ancestors were prolific in their manufacture and use of this technology and these hand tools were as common as smartphones now. They have the same appeal in terms of functionality but also status.

But my most exhilarating prehistoric experience was entering the Caves of Altamira in Northern Spain, walking back through the cave with a torch and seeing images that were created, hidden deep in the back of the cave. There before our eyes were images that gave us a window into the minds of these men, women and children. Their handprints on the walls and superb renditions of the animals that were their prey but also predators. The rehearsed stories of the animal hunt.

They were drawing from their imagination, a capability that eventually developed into writing language from imagined words and sentences. On a visit to Ur in Syria, then on to Damascus, I saw the famous tablet, the first alphabet that emerged from that ancient city. That aside, we tend to ignore the fact that writing, alphabets and printing are our greatest cultural and technological achievements but not seen as such, since technology is usually framed as new technology. Technologies, as they become obsolete, are no longer seen as technologies.

Books are no longer seen as technology but something preceding technology, even under threat from technology. Writing, when done on paper, is not seen as using the technology of pens, pencils, clay tablets, papyrus, parchments and paper, but as something that is in danger from those who now read on-screen or touch type. Yet *all* of this fuelled the future – the foresight, drawing, organization, design and innovation – for other more obviously 'technical' technologies.

More recently, I visited the Nicholas Tesla Museum of Technology in Zagreb, a cavernous building that had a huge room of spades, then a vast collection of ploughs. The spade and the plough are the two forgotten heroes of technological progress through farming. It was this technology that allowed us to move from being a nomadic to a pastoral species, allowing us to settle and form larger groups and communities. Technology that led to scaling up food production gave us the leisure time to invent and apply our writing skills 500 years ago and imagine new futures. The museum continued through the era of mass-produced household goods, such as irons, washing machines, cookers and so on. It reminded me that everyday physical technology tends to render itself invisible. The fact that it was an authentic Museum of Technology seemed odd, but that is exactly what it was.

From the hand-held axe to smartphones, they all serve that basic human need to survive and to communicate. It is the symbolic technology of cave art that allowed the art of drama and theatre to scale through film, radio, television and now the internet and Metaverse. We are social animals, and the internet has facilitated an undreamt-of level of communication, expanding local ties to global ties.

The history of our imagining, designing, using and abusing technology is the real history of our species. History leans toward the recent, when things were recorded and prehistory (a telling term) suggests something sparse, hidden, largely lost. If we are to learn from history it has to be through a longer, deeper view that encompasses how we really got here. We created the tools that ensured, not only our survival, but also our smartness and dominance. In the beginning was not the word but the tool.

From stone axe to smartphone

Darwin thought there were three things that led to the success of our species: tools, fire and communications. It is through technology, in particular learning technology, that we have overcome the indelible stamp of our lowly origin. Where we stand apart most significantly is in cultural accumulation and transmission. Many animals learn. Only humans teach. Adam Rutherford (2018) claims this is the result of us being social creatures that can disseminate ideas through time and space. Culture evolves very much faster than genes, with the ratchet effect building upon previous technological innovations.

Holding a prehistoric stone axe is to put yourself in the mind of someone who held that same axe tens, even hundreds of thousands of years ago. It seems familiar, even more comfortable than your smartphone. One can learn a lot from the experience of holding and using such tools but also learning how to make them. To watch an axe being made or make one yourself, creating the shape from a core with a hammerstone, then using an antler or soft hammer for edging, is to see or experience a masterclass in manufacture. We can enter the minds of our ancestors and identify the cognitive skills needed to make these marvelous tools.

Darwin sparked great interest in the study of our ancestral species, and in 1865 John Lubbock named and separated the Stone Age into the earlier Paleolithic and later Neolithic. The Paleolithic (Old Stone Age) was characterized by simple struck and knapped stone axes, the Mesolithic (Middle Stone Age) was a more hunter and gatherer society defined by flaked tools and the Neolithic (New Stone Age) was defined by polished stone axes. Technology in the form of hand axes was already defining the epochs of human evolution. Even more recent prehistory continues to be defined by the shorter Chalcolithic, Bronze and Iron Ages. A pattern emerges here of technological revolutions, defining bouts of cultural progress, taking place over shorter and shorter periods: at first millions of years, then hundreds of thousands, tens of thousands, then hundreds, and now decades.

These stone tools carry the indelible marks and shapes of internal, intentional activity. Their complexity and variability reflect our cognitive growth as a species, from simply struck rocks, to more carefully shaped tools, and eventually to superbly crafted blades. This evolution of mind and technology, in tandem, also implies a growth in the ability to teach and learn. Research on the relationship between this technology and our progress as a species has identified cognitive, social, teaching and learning features intimately connected with the use of such stone tools. Experimental archaeology has shown that the skills needed to imagine, plan, resource, make and finesse such tools require that they be taught, and that such learning is not easy. These stone tools helped shape our cognition but also the leap into social and cultural transmission that allowed our species to soar.

Hand axes, as the primary evidence for learning in prehistory, show intent and are a window into the cognitive abilities of our ancestors, as well as their capability to learn and teach. We have been making, and teaching others to make, these tools for over 3 million years. It started with Oldowan technology, with pebbles that were struck against other rocks to produce edges. Then, around 1.8 million years ago, a new technology appeared, the Acheulian 'teardrop' hand axe, used as hand tools but also hafted into wood and antler. About half a million years ago the technology changed again, to the Levallois, with bladed stone tools that had more varied uses.

Stone tools can be seen as artifacts or objects, but they are made for a predicted purpose. It is no accident that they are similar in size to modern smartphones. Designed from 1.8 million years onwards to be portable, we see that their average size fits the range for portable tools that gave significant advantages for bipedal hominids.

Teaching

Imitation must surely have been the way much early learning took place, but is there evidence for teaching? Chimps have been occasionally observed being taught in the wild. Boesch (1991) gives an example of the repositioning of a nut on a larger stone and repositioning a stone in the hand of the younger chimp, to affect a better hammer-like strike. But tool 'making' through being taught by adult animals is extremely rare in the wild.

With hominid stone tools, observed studies show that demonstration alone is not enough and that being taught through language is necessary for both instructing best techniques as well as corrective feedback.

Stone tools are fiendishly difficult to manufacture and before attempting to do so, one needs knowledge of the suitability of the material, to identify differences in terms of hardness and texture, along with its potential for the correct type of fracture. A knowledge of local geology, the nature of suitable materials and the right size of cores need to be selected. It is clear that our ancestors traveled far to select the right materials for tool creation. One must then hold, in one's mind, the desired 3D shape, with the right dimensions, symmetries and thickness throughout the process of manufacture.

Then come the knapping skills which require fine motor skills, using tools to make tools. Later axes required hard hammers for flake production then soft hammers for edging. As one strikes, it is easy to make mistakes, as one must predict the fracture. It needs constant adaptation and problem solving, and not just the application of a set of fixed rules. Beyond these skills lie higher-order mathematical skills, such as transformations to scale. Gowlett (1993) has shown that axes of exactly the same shape were made to different sizes, showing an ability to scale. Even today, few master the skills of these highly skilled, prehistoric nappers.

Stone tools are the best proxy we have for tracing the development of teaching and learning, as we can replicate the effort in the lab. Experiments with graduate students show that Levallois tools take up to 500 hours to learn how to make, the joke being that only graduate students have that much spare time! More than this, almost all scholars in this field, having gone through the complex process of knapping, claim that it needs to be taught and that language is necessary for that teaching. John Shea (2018) calls this the 'no, you're doing it wrong effect'. More than this, the necessity for teaching and learning on such a scale sets up the constant habit of learning and the spread of knowledge and skills down through generations. The creation of tools gives selective advantage, the teaching and learning of toolmaking gives us communication, social expectations around the accumulation of social capital and further intergenerational advantages down through time.

Another feature of stone technology is that it is more than just an item of utility. It is also a symbol, with a meaning and purpose beyond its use. Huge hand axes, such as the Furze Platt Giant in London's Natural History Museum, and many other finely worked examples, suggest that axes were also for 'show'. We find stone tools that are stained, far too large to be useful and so perfect they are assumed to have been unused. It is highly probable that they gave their owners status and perhaps had value in bartering. This symmetry, Kohn (1999) argues, may reflect fitness and therefore sexual selection, something some evolutionary psychologists think is needed to explain the sheer reach and longevity of axe production. Axe production certainly went way beyond utility into cultural and social significance. It may have been that having the skill to make an axe was in itself the hallmark of fitness and social status.

At Cissbury Ring in Sussex and Grime's Graves in Norfolk, Neolithic flint mining, down deep shafts and along horizontal passages, took place on an industrial scale. High value axes from Langdale in Cumbria and the Alps were manufactured at scale and followed trade routes across the whole of the European continent. The process of finding precise geologic sources, creating blocks for polishing elsewhere and quality manufacture was commonplace. This axe technology was reflected in the megalithic monuments built by these first settled people. Axes appear inside their burial mounds, standing stones and dolmens.

The evolution of hominids is indicated as much by the abundance of durable stone tools they left behind, as rare and delicate fossil bones. Links between the fossil evidence and the stone tool evidence show a cognitive progression. As the toolsets become smaller, more sophisticated and more differentiated in use (a little like computer technology in the modern world that went from huge mainframes to smartphones), early humans developed a technical intelligence in the working of stone that is hard to replicate, even today. Stone axe manufacture was profligate and shows that we developed, not only the ability to use the technology of tools, but also the ability to teach and learn the rapid manufacture, using a wide range of cognitive and motor skills. Technology always has a cultural significance, and the evidence suggests that the role of stone tools in social and cultural life was significant.

The stone axe is only obliquely a learning tool, but it is clear evidence that technology played a significant role in our cognitive development and laid the groundwork for our future as what I refer to as *Homo technus* (technology man) – masters of tools and technology. Hand-held tools from the stone axe to smartphones are omnipresent in our long evolution as hominids and provide evidence of the development of sophisticated learning and teaching. We see this in the brushes used in cave paintings, while reed pens, clay tablets, books, pencils, chalk, blackboards, cameras, calculators and mobiles have been used to enhance and accelerate our ability to teach and learn. The very first marks made by our ancestors 500,000 years ago put learning literally into the hands, and by implication the minds, of the learner.

Fire

Fire is a manufactured and manipulated technology. We need to distinguish between fire as it naturally occurs as a result of lightning strikes and so on, and the creation of fire, which must be either from the 'strike and light' percussion of rock striking rock or through friction using wooden tools. Fire use is also different from fire creation. Fire is a technology, created using tools and so becomes a tool in itself. For 250,000 years, the period of our own species *Homo sapiens*, the use of fire has become commonplace.

Some, such as Wrangham (2009), claim it goes back further to *Homo erectus,* where there is evidence that the use of fire for cooking led to an increase in cognitive abilities. In *Homo erectus* we see increased brain size, changes in the shape of teeth and a reduction in the size of the gut, as fire is increasingly used for processing food, firing of tubers and cooking meat. Drying meat for consumption in lean times is also made possible, and fire kills dangerous parasites.

Fire can also be used to hunt, corral and trap animals for hunting. The move towards a high protein, fatty diet, with increased calorie intake was achieved through hunting, with fire being used to create finer flakes of stone and fire-hardened wooden tools. It is also useful for protection from predators, especially in caves, where predators lurk. Fire made cave art possible, as a source of illumination not only for their creation but viewing. As a source of warmth at night and for geographic expansion into colder climates, fire has played a significant role in our success as a species.

Fire is a technology that requires a combination of tools, intention, skill, teaching and learning. It is also a learning technology. For the entire history of its use by our species, until very recently, fire was in a hearth. Indeed when fire had to be maintained, it may have encouraged the creation of a fixed base or hearth, increasing the size of a social group, along with fire being used to clear trees and brush from around the campsite (Gowlett, 2016).

> Fire is, in a sense, the first and most long-lived form of the classroom, where language and social communication became important along with the transmission of stories and cultural knowledge, from old to young, from those with knowledge and skills to those that needed them. It became a focal point for teaching and learning.

By extending human interaction into the hours of darkness, around the hearth, after the day is done, fire becomes an extended time for cultural transmission and learning. There is evidence that we have longer waking days as our circadian rhythms changed with the use of fire. It may also have led to an increase in group size, more care for and by older members of groups, with group size being an important accelerant of cultural transmission through teaching and learning.

Learning technology simulators

Deliberate, geometric marks first appeared around 500,000 years ago, but around 50,000 years ago something quite astonishing happened. Symbolism appears in objects and on surfaces, especially in caves. This was the Cognitive Revolution.

Cave imagery

Discovered in 1994, the Chauvet cave had been hidden by the scree of a rock fall some 20,000 years ago. Deep in the pitch dark of the cave lay exquisite paintings of animals, some such as a pride of lions, are those of animals on the hunt. These people lived in a dangerous carnivorous world where they were clearly both predator and prey.

So sophisticated were these paintings that for decades after their discovery, people simply did not believe that they could have been produced by our prehistoric ancestors. Such expressions of the natural world stimulated interest in the cognitive development of our species, as this first renaissance of expression clearly showed we had developed the ability to produce tools to create representations designed to teach and learn. The creators of such images were not so much savages, as savants, people of real aptitude and capable of teaching and learning.

The idea that this is 'art' in the sense of deliberately produced aesthetically pleasing images was a Victorian perspective, an aesthetic theory that saw these works as 'art for art's sake'. That this so-called art is in deep, dark, inaccessible caves encourages us to dismiss the romantic notion of Paleolithic humans as 19th-century Romantics. Shamanic theories, such as those put forward by Lewis-Williams (2002), that read in these images magic, mythological, totemic, initiation and religious meaning, have also been demoted. More recent work on cave imagery points firmly towards practical and utilitarian goals. The images show, overwhelmingly, predators and prey. Strikingly realistic and naturalistic and shown in poses that aid recognition, many of the images are strewn with wounded animals and spears and seem clearly instructional. These were people who hunted and were in turn hunted. Knowledge on being successful in the former and avoiding the latter was literally a matter of life and death.

Cave imagery as learning

This more realistic hypothesis relies on the simple fact that, for millions of years, teaching and learning was a necessary social activity. Cave imagery is dominated by animals that early humans relied on for their food, clothing and survival, as well as dangerous killers to avoid. These images seem intentionally instructional and what better place than the cold dark interior of a cave, that early chalkboard or simulator, where you literally, in the flickering darkness, experience the simulated fear of being the predator and also prey.

I once swam into a deep, dark Mayan cave in Belize. I still remember the immediate heightening of the senses and as I moved further into the darkness, as the natural entrance light disappeared, the fear was intense, as was the claustrophobia. Entering the Cave of Altamira was a similar experience, as it twists and bends for over 250 metres, with the images located well away from the entrance. A cave can be viewed as an ancient cinema, and as the light dims, provides the perfect psychological condition for learning – heightened attention.

There is a reason for so many of these images being set deep into the darkness of the caves, often in awkward places, where there is no natural light. That reason is not shamanism. This is exactly what you would design for revealed instruction. They are deliberately placed to be seen suddenly, inside passages, on the roof and in places so difficult to access they are still being discovered.

Seeing these images in Altamira, for the first time, I saw glimpses of stunningly realistic images by torchlight, one by one. This is important, as we know from the carbon marks left on the walls that these images were created and viewed by burning wicks and torches. The sudden reveals bring these creatures suddenly and vividly into view, exactly what you want if you need to teach people to spot fleeting glimpses of animals that need to be killed or avoided as they may kill you. There is an emotional dimension to this learning, as it is necessary to overcome the fight or flight instinct. A quick flash of a head, rump or legs will provide the powers of control needed to hunt and survive, just as a flight simulator teaches a pilot to keep a cool head when dealing with terrifying situations.

In France, deep inside the Chauvet Cave, dangerous predators such as hyenas, lions, panthers, bears and rhinos can be seen with startling realism. The large larder mammals such as bison, mammoths, deer, aurochs, ibex and horses are also there, many driven to extinction by hunting. Context is all, and these images mirror the real world that these people inhabited. These animals can kill and are difficult to spot and examine close up, so this may have been the first time young humans saw their predators and prey. It is a risk that has to be understood by everyone in a wild environment, especially the young, as one may live with predators but rarely, if ever, see them. When taken into the darkness of the cave they would have felt fear and apprehension. The experienced hunter could then have given them lessons on how to hold their fear, spot prey, identify colours that may be different in different seasons and avoid predators. We know the young were brought into these caves in numbers, from the common ochre-blown silhouettes of their hands.

The beautifully painted animals are never benign, always prey or predators. Around 15 per cent of the Altamira animals are depicted as wounded, and as wounded animals are dangerous, this adds to the instructional motivation for these cave images. Human images are rare and are usually sketchy and schematic. Many of the animals are shown on the move. and with views of all four legs, they have an astonishing range of poses. One herd of bison, shown in different poses cover the roof. Their point was surely to show the herd from a bird's eye view, something that needed to be understood when hunting a fleeing herd of bison. It is this variety of prey and predator imagery that is indicative of instructional intent.

The level of simulated realism or naturalism is further evidence of their pedagogic quality. This naturalism also supports the role of these images as learning tools. Simulations are about both physical and psychological fidelity. You need to have enough graphical realism to make the experience seem real and memorable, as well as enough psychological reality to make you do the right thing at the right time. The wonder of these paintings is their graphical realism; they are literally masterpieces. You are in no doubt about what species you are looking at from their poses, colours and behaviours.

More than this, however, is the emphasis on chiaroscuro, using colour, contour and outline. Deep in the cave the rock has been used as a sculptural form, with faces painted on natural forms that look like the heads of the animals they represent. Three-dimensional bison hang down from the ceiling on rock outcrops. In Chauvet, walls were scraped clean and outlines etched to achieve a stunning three-dimensional effect, and the rounded contours of the rock cleverly used to give an even more dramatic effect. Contrast and contour are used to great effect. There is also the teaching of the materials used to create these paintings – charcoal blacks, ochre reds and yellows, haematite reds and the brownish black of manganese oxide. Their deliberate choice of colours has been shown to match different seasonal coats of the animals depicted.

Marc Azéma and Florent Rivère (2012) have uncovered remarkable new interpretations of the hunting stories represented by attempts at movement in cave paintings and inscribed objects. They claim that most cave images and inscribed art show movement that can be brought to light through partial reveals and flickering torches. A good example is the Chauvet Cave painting which seems to show a huge 10-metre hunting scene, with lions stalking bison and other animals. Multiple, superimposed heads, limbs and tails suggest running and they later lunge at their prey.

Large numbers of carbon dating samples have also shown that images were amended and improved over thousands of years, showing that, whatever their true purpose, they were found to be useful by many generations. These people were hunters and gatherers, pre-farming, who moved around in small groups. The problem with small groups is that they need to come together to breed in order to avoid genetic problems, and to share knowledge about their main concerns, hunting and survival. One theory is that they came together in such places to share and learn from each other. The Cognitive Revolution marked the appearance of larger groups of up to 150 individuals, with co-operation across larger groups and increased innovation.

These astounding caves seem to be the very first, carefully designed, learning technology simulators, full of exciting and useful learning experiences. The evidence suggests that they were carefully rendered teaching and learning aids, early classrooms that encouraged social learning, which undoubtedly poured out when viewing these images. Social cohesion could well have been fostered through the need for collective learning.

Baldwin effect

A powerful idea that has been recently resurrected is to understand how technology, with its accompanying teaching and learning skills, can affect evolution itself. You may never have heard of James Baldwin, yet he may be one of the most significant learning theorists that ever lived. He proposed the Baldwin effect, in the late 19th century, which has been recently revived in evolutionary biology. It places learning at the very centre of evolutionary theory, as Baldwin saw learning giving individuals significant survival and reproductive advantage. Learnt behaviours become instinctual through genetic transmission.

The idea is that learnt behaviour, such as tool production and use, and not just environment and genes, influences the direction and rate of the evolution of psychological and physical traits. The Baldwin effect places 'learning' on a larger theoretical canvas, lying at the heart of evolutionary theory, no longer just a cognitive ability, albeit a complex one with many different systems of memory involved, but a feature that defines the very success of our species. Note that this is not Lamarckism, as it does not claim that acquired characteristics are passed on genetically, only that the offspring of an adaptive trait (physical or psychological) may be genetically better at learning. This creates the opportunity, as it creates the conditions and successful population survival, for standard selection to take place.

It has some impressive supporters. Hinton and Nowlan revived the idea in 1987, as did Richard Richards (1987). But it is Daniel Dennett (1991) who has done most to popularize the idea. He posits the Baldwin idea that learnt behaviour, especially sustainable innovative behaviour, if captured in substantial genetic frequency, can act as what he calls a 'sky crane' in evolution. Weber and Depew (2003) have since published an excellent explanatory and supportive book of the Baldwin effect.

More than just language, adaptation to new environments through tool-making, responding to climatic and food pressures and other changes that require quicker adaptation through selected teaching and learning, may have played a role in the rapid success of *Homo sapiens*. Dennett (1991) proposes the actual creation of selective pressure on others by sustained learnt behaviour. This is where it gets interesting for technology.

Significant advantages could have occurred through the relatively rapid learnt ability to create technology, namely the production of tools. Technology scales the ability of its producers, owners and users to avoid predation, become better predators through hunting and fishing, be protected against climate (needles, cloth, clothes), use fire and preserve food. There is the relatively new idea that technology is the real runaway success, especially that which allowed us to create social groups in which teaching and learning could thrive.

This flavour of the Baldwin effect, the runaway success of learning to make things, may be most important causal factor it bestowed on our species. Note that *Homo Sapiens* was not the only species to thrive on the success of tools and technology – all other humanoid species did so, only not with the same levels of success. The history of toolmaking shadows the history of different hominid species and gives us a window into the development of consciousness. The trail of stone tools is often as significant as the fossil bone evidence and our advantage, for example, over our nearest, recent rivals, the Neanderthals, seems to have been based on superior minds, tools and technology.

The Baldwin effect gives 'learning' high status but learning technology, the product of learning, is also significant. One can go further and claim that learning, especially the development of cognitive systems such as episodic and then semantic memory, gave the production and use of technology a privileged status. In an interesting twist of fate, Hinton and Nowlan (1987) claim to have demonstrated through computer technology (simulations) that learning could shape evolution. The Baldwin effect may, through its own efficacy, have created the technological conditions for its own proof! The brain, through consciousness, may have created a fast-developing structure that in turn accelerates learning and thus evolution.

Evolution and learning

Learning theory has a lot to learn from evolutionary biology, as the predictive power of evolutionary theory can explain why some things are easy to learn, such as our first language, walking, talking, listening and so on, while other skills such as reading, writing, mathematics and counterintuitive science, are more difficult to teach and learn.

Geary (2005) has shown how attention to evolution pays dividends in teaching and learning. He explains why some things, like speaking and listening, are easy to learn, while others, like reading and writing (the subject of the next chapter) are hard. He distinguishes primary from secondary learning and sees this as determining the limitations of how and what we learn.

Primary learning is our folk psychology – our capacity to acquire our first language, understand others' minds and intentions and recognize faces. These come naturally to us and do not have to be learnt. Similarly with folk biology, we understand about food and animals that may be good or bad for us. This primary learning, our evolutionary heritage, constantly interferes and thwarts attempts to teach and learn new knowledge and skills. Secondary learning means overcoming primary learning to learn complex and counterintuitive knowledge and skills, which is the purpose of most education.

Geary brings evolution and biology back into learning, explaining why learning can be so easy in some instances, but hard in others. Without understanding evolution and prehistoric learning technologies, we cannot understand teaching and learning.

Conclusion

The advances we have examined are related to the scalability of learning technology. In the Paleolithic era, teaching and learning was limited by the cognitive capacities of our ancestral species. Nevertheless we saw technical advances linked to our ability to both teach and learn through language, leading to more sophisticated toolmaking, along with the invention of fire. Millions of years of toolmaking shaped our cognitive development and abilities. Group size was also significant, as larger, settled groups emerged in the Neolithic era. At this point, we get massive scalability as writing provides a form of cultural transmission that is freed from oral constraints – this is examined in the next chapter.

References

Azéma, M and Rivère, F (2012) Animation in Paleolithic art: A pre-echo of cinema, *Antiquity*, 86, 316

Baldwin, J M (1896) A New Factor in Evolution, *The American Naturalist*, 30(355), 536–53

Boesch, C (1991) Teaching among wild chimpanzees, *Animal Behaviour*, 41(3), 530–32

Clark, D (2020) *Artificial Intelligence for Learning: How to use AI to support employee development*, Kogan Page Publishers, London

Dennett, D C (1991) *Consciousness Explained*, Little, Brown and Co, Boston MA

Dennett, D C (1995) *Darwin's Dangerous Idea: Evolution and the meanings of life*, Simon and Schuster, New York

Geary, D C (2005) *The Origin of Mind: Evolution of brain, cognition, and general intelligence*, American Psychological Association, Washington, DC

Gowlett, J (1993) *Ascent to Civilization: The archaeology of early humans*, McGraw-Hill, New York

Gowlett, J A J (2016) The discovery of fire by humans: a long and convoluted process, *Philosophical Transactions of the Royal Society B*, 5 June 2016, 371

Hinton, G E and Nowlan, S J (1987) How learning can guide evolution, *Complex Systems*, 1(3), 495–502

Hinton, G E and Nowlan, S J (1996) How learning can guide evolution. In R K Belew and M Mitchell (eds), *Adaptive Individuals in Evolving Populations*, 447–54, Addison-Wesley, Reading, MA

Kohn M (1999) *As We Know It: Coming to terms with an evolved mind*, Granta, London

Lewis-Williams, J D (2002) *The Mind in the Cave: Consciousness and the origins of art*, Thames & Hudson, New York

Lubbock, J (1865) *Pre-Historic Times as Illustrated by Ancient Remains and the Manners and Customs of Modern Savages*, William & Norgate, London

Richards, R (1987) *Darwin and the Emergence of Evolutionary Theories of Mind and Behavior*, University of Chicago Press, Chicago

Rutherford, A (2018) *Book of Humans*, Weidenfeld & Nicolson, London

Shea, J (2018) Tool Use and Evolution: Behavioral modernity vs. complexity: What stone tools teach us (online video), 5 December 2018 www.youtube.com/watch?v=Zw5KoDqK5H8 (archived at https://perma.cc/FLU5-47PE)

Weber, B H and Depew, D J (eds) (2003) *Evolution and Learning: The Baldwin effect reconsidered*, MIT Press, Cambridge, MA

Wrangham, R (2009) *Catching Fire: How Cooking Made Us Human,* Basic Books, New York

03

Writing

The ability to make our mark has been around for at least 500,000 years, since our ancestors made the first deliberate marks on shells. Subsequent scribbling, in one form or another, went on to create civilizations. Whether by stylus, pencil, pen or keyboard, writing remains a primary learning technology. It is not something we just use, it is part of us and we would not be where we are without it.

I, Pencil (1958), the famous essay by Leonard E Read, starts with a simple sentence, 'I am a lead pencil—the ordinary wooden pencil familiar to all boys and girls and adults who can read and write.' It is written in the first person from a pencil's point of view and although 'seemingly so simple', the pencil claims that not a single person knows how to make a pencil.

What follows is the extraordinary complexity in the manufacture of a pencil, starting with the tree, logging, sawing and kiln drying. Quite separately, there is the mined graphite, ground and mixed with many other substances, extruded like a very thin sausage and baked. Then six coats of yellow lacquer, made from castor oil and other dyes. A brass collar, the ferrule, from mined zinc and copper, milled and cut, holding the crowning glory that is the eraser, not made of rubber but rapeseed oil from Indonesia with sulfur chloride and many vulcanizing and accelerating agents, along with pumice from Italy, its pigment is cadmium sulfide.

The pencil is a complex combination that, when reflected upon, is a wondrous thing, yet we treat it with almost disposable disdain. The pencil quotes G. K. Chesterton: 'We are perishing for want of wonder, not for want of wonders', a quote that one can apply to much of learning technology. These wonders often go under the radar, like the pencil and other scribing instruments, consigned to just being there without reflection or assessment of their importance, as the technology that has been delivering teaching and learning for over 5,000 years. Of course, the pencil is just one example of that huge event in learning technology – *writing*.

Writing: the Big Bang of learning technology

Thomas Hobbes made the claim that 'The invention of printing, though ingenious, compared with the invention of letters is no great matter', and the invention of writing is indeed the Big Bang of learning technology. It is writing that fed learning and cultural transmission for centuries. It allowed us to transcend memory, to create and store written content which others could distribute, retrieve, access, read, communicate and search. It is both the external expression of our ideas and through reading, the shared memory of our species. Commerce, religion through scripture, literature through books and science through publication, writing is the wellspring of knowledge and communications. Without it, even technological advance itself would be impossible. Arguably the most important piece of technology ever invented, writing has both generated and shaped our culture.

Early writing

Writing was invented, independently, only four times; first in Mesopotamia and in Egypt at around the same time in 3200 BC, then in China around 1700 BC and finally in Mesoamerica around 900 BC. As information or software, it required hardware for its production and distribution: reed pens pressed into wet clay in Mesopotamia, brush pens ostraca and papyrus in Egypt, flat oracle bones in China and on bark in Mesoamerica.

This breakthrough, especially by the Sumerians in Mesopotamia, allowed humans to store and use information outside of our brains, not just writing but also mathematics. Writing is a technology, fundamentally the software of thought, but it also involves the hardware of production and distribution. Writing started with the accounting of objects, so we have pictures of objects which quickly became more simplified, stylized and symbolic. The first scribing devices were scraped across the surface of the clay, then written by pressing a sharpened reed into damp clay to produce neat rows of precise cuneiform, with its echoes of printing. Clay and reeds were natural, cheap and plentiful, allowing knowledge to be recorded at little cost The clay was shaped into pillow-shaped tablets or cylinders that could be stored, making it useful for contracts and agreements. It was even placed inside clay envelopes to preserve privacy for posting.

The Egyptians invented their script around the same time but used papyrus in the Royal Court, again for administration. Papyrus was easy to flatten, could be stuck together into a scroll and was lighter and more portable than clay. Reeds, chewed at one end, were used as brushes as well as sharper reed pens. These brushes and pens could also be used to write quickly. The Egyptian system used a hybrid of picture signs representing sounds alongside pictures of objects, mostly on papyrus, using red ink for headings, emphasis and deficits (hence 'being in the red'). Writing in Egypt was an instrument of power and prestige, not the masses.

Chinese writing started with oracle bones around 1700 BC, which were used for divination. The Chinese took the shoulder blade of an ox and created holes and cracks with a poker. Alongside these marks are characters written by the diviners. They provide a record of people and events in Chinese history. The Chinese also used strips of bamboo, wood and even silk for writing. Note also that paper was invented in China in the 1st century BC by the eunuch Cai Lun, and by the 9th century the Chinese were block printing books on paper. Moveable type was also invented there in 1100 AD but never flourished due to the pictorial nature of the written language, such is the close tie between hardware and software in learning technology. Once again writing was used mainly for bureaucracy, until Confucius in the late 6th century BC, when it started to be used for learning.

Wax tablets were used in Greek and Roman times and into the Medieval age. The wax was poured into a frame and when solid could be inscribed with a spatula. Inscriptions could be erased by heating and wiping with the same spatula.

Writing technology

Early writing has led to a remarkable range of technology for writing and reading, developed over 5,000 years. Cheap, easy and quick to use, this technology has included reeds, brushes, styli, pencils, pens and typewriters and now keyboards, touch screens, eye movements, gestures and speech-to-text software aid the process of writing. Materials including clay, stone, wood, silk, papyrus, vellum, paper, screens, touch screens and text-to-speech software have all provided suitable reading technology. Teaching technology to display writing has also emerged, such as chalkboards, overhead projectors and whiteboards.

Writing also led to mathematics. The Sumerians had a sexagesimal (base 60) system, which is still used for measuring time and is the reason we still have one-hour lectures and periods in education. This mathematics was surprisingly sophisticated and only discovered in the late 19th century. The

Greeks, Indians and Arabs all made advances that relied on a growing symbolic system that, as a form of technology, would go on to create computers and the internet.

Writing and reading are skills that have to be mastered, so wherever there is writing, there must be formal teaching and learning. The many Sumerian and Babylonian cuneiform 'exercise' tablets illustrate the intensity of teaching and practice. The discovery of schools for scribes, where these skills were taught, contain evidence of clay tablets with exercises completed by learners in writing and calculations.

The same phenomena can be seen in Egypt on shards of limestone and pottery. In Deir-el-Medina, the workers' village near the Valley of the Kings, lies an abundance of these shards of stone and ostraca. Writing on these robust materials put knowledge beyond the ravages of time so that even now, over 3,500 years later, we can read their attempts, mistakes and corrections in writing and mathematics.

Reading and writing

Reading and writing remain the most important form of learning technology as they are profoundly learner centric. Writing records thoughts, but is also a generative activity and a powerful method of learning. As a learning technology, writing is flexible in its range of structured expression in fiction, non-fiction, encyclopedias, academic papers, textbooks and on social media. It allows learners to access indexes, glossaries, lists and menus. Easy to update, especially in digital format, it can be cut and pasted with tools such as spell checkers, grammar checkers and pre-formatted citations. It is also, when digital, searchable and usable as a corpus of data for training AI.

Reading, the corollary of writing, is even more important, as it gives access to the collective knowledge and intelligence of our entire species. We read much faster than we speak, and written text is more complex and compressed than speech. Just as important is the simple fact that learners can read at their own pace, which is important in comprehension and retention, as we control our pace to focus on meaning and reflection, as well as wedding new knowledge to existing knowledge and constructing internal models.

Reading and writing are now widespread skills that give learners access to immense amounts of quality learning. Continuous media, such as audio and video, suffer from the transience effect, where we as learners do not have time to digest and remember what we experience. Writing suffers less from this effect, although Plato's *Republic* warned us of the dangers of reading and writing, inhibiting oral skills and making us less reliant on memory. This is echoed in contemporary claims about it being too easy to Google content, weakening our reliance on learning.

It is not that writing freed us from superstition, dogma or fixed thought, controlled by elites. Texts, whether mythical or scriptural, became fixed for centuries, especially in the Abrahamic religions of Judaism, Christianity and Islam, where scholarship and learning was locked into the reading, recitation and remembering of a few sacred books. One cannot underestimate the force of the Torah, Bible, Quran and Buddhist works that led to formal schooling, teaching and learning. We should also be aware of the simple fact that the past is represented largely in writing and that literate societies tend to write history and make claims that others could not deny.

Writing gave religions proselytizing power. The Codex Sinaiticus, the earliest complete copy of the Greek New Testament, was written in the 4th century on parchment, and 'fixes' the canon of Christian scripture. Christians like St Paul wanted to pull together all of their works and the book provided the unity and the authority of the Gospels. The Quran was put into writing in the 7th century, with scribes literally copying the words of God voiced by Mohammed, sent by God as 'writing'. Kufic scripts arose in the 8th century, with small books being used on the move. Buddhist texts, printed in 868 AD China, are the world's earliest dated printed texts. In Buddhism, repeated reading is a method of gaining merit, which affects reincarnation, so books made religious sense. This embedded reading and writing in all of these cultures, even if for many they were only able to listen to someone reading aloud.

When writing was eventually replicated in print and then in digital technology, it could be created, corrected and reproduced perfectly at almost no cost. This has had profound consequences for learning, as technology-based learning has continued to take more and more of a share in learning. The rise of the textbook is an obvious example, as well as Wikipedia, which has replaced encyclopedias with a more accessible, searchable, editable and distributable knowledge base. Through digital devices and especially smartphones, we are seeing a massive amount of writing, in direct communication, comments, posts, blogs and social media. Never have so many people written so much, so often and read by so many.

Around 5,000 years ago, writing lifted us out of the oral tradition that limited cultural transmission to the fallible memories of individuals and those they spoke to. We were freed from the limitations of memory and personal transmission. Writing is the greatest of all learning technologies. It created the modern world and has had a profound and lasting influence.

Alphabets – simplified writing and turbo charged learning

Early alphabets

Standing on a small hill, in Ugarit, is to stand in the place that the earliest alphabet, as we know it in the West, was found. It is now a small, deserted, coastal hill in Syria, far from the sea, razed and burnt around 1200 BC by the Sea Peoples. Excavations in the 1920s found cuneiform clay tablets, and as clay is merely baked by heat, this preserved the tablets. Travelling south, I had to lean down to peer through a small glass window in the Damascus Museum to see its most fascinating exhibit, a small clay tablet with the world's earliest alphabet pressed into its surface by a reed pen. It heralds a design change in a writing system that proved superior to previous systems; so superior and efficient that it quickly became the Phoenician, Greek then Latin alphabets. It literally provided the lettered foundation for Western culture.

Alphabetic writing resulted in the flourishing of Greek culture. Written down around 750 BC, from an older oral tradition, the Odyssey and Iliad tell of the Heroic Age. Histories also emerged along with science, philosophy and drama. Hippocratic texts appear in 600 BC in Greece, most likely produced for teaching. Plato gave us philosophy. Aristotle's works were deeply and profoundly scientific. Both produced works on learning theory. This is consolidated in Alexandria with further science, mathematics, astronomy and literary criticism.

The very word 'alphabet' comes from Alpha and Beta, the first two letters of the Greek alphabet. What is often overlooked is its implications for teaching and learning. Learning to read and write was reduced from several thousand to just a couple of dozen symbols. The Greeks were then able to take the idea of an alphabet from the Phoenicians and adapt it to become their own, with signs for sounds making it a fully phonetic script. A phonetic alphabet simplifies and therefore supercharges writing, reading and also learning. This was a huge breakthrough.

Reforms to alphabets

There have been many other improvements to make writing and reading easier. Take upper and lower case. All phonetic alphabets were in one case but as brushes and styli started to be used, writing became more fluid and cursive. Letters following the first letter in words were run together and got smaller, so lower case evolved. This move to the cursive improved the speed of writing and legibility for reading. In general, lower-case letters are not found in European languages before 1300 and even then, there were no fixed rules for capitalization until the early 18th century. In English, capital letters indicated proper names, abbreviations, personal pronoun 'I' and the start of sentences. In German, all nouns are capitalized. Arabic and Hebrew still have only one 'case' and therefore no capital letters, whereas Latin, Cyrillic and Greek alphabets have two cases. The words 'uppercase' and 'lowercase' are actually named after the 'cases' in which printers' stored their moveable type. In an interesting twist, CAPITAL LETTERS have come to indicate 'shouting' when used in emails and texting. Writing evolves and is still evolving.

Alphabets accelerate literacy, not only making reading and writing easier but making learning how to write and read easier. Languages that have more irregular spellings and complex grammar are more difficult to learn than others. So despite the obvious advantages of an alphabet for learning, there are differences across languages on the degree to which letters represent sounds. Finnish, Turkish, Serbo-Croat and Bulgarian have nearly one-to-one correspondence between letters and spoken words, making spelling easier to learn. English, however, has lots of mismatches, as it is highly irregular with silent letters, double letters and so on. This is because it went through a historic vowel shift and has absorbed many words from other languages. English is, by consequence, more difficult to learn. The good news is that it has a simpler grammar, with no gender differences, and this irregularity gives English breadth of expression over a wide range of dialects.

Ease of learning has led to the search for and attempts at reform in writing. Children learn to read and write faster in countries where letters match sounds, so why not reform language to make life easier for us all? English spelling is only about 20 per cent predictable, whereas with truly phonetic alphabets it rises to nearly 100 per cent. This pedagogic problem has led to attempts to reform writing.

Benjamin Franklin recognized, or should that be recognised, that English's irregular spelling made it more difficult to learn, so advocated for alphabet reform. He published his new alphabet and reformed spelling scheme in *Political, Miscellaneous and Philosophical Pieces* (1779), eliminating c, j, q, w, x and y as superfluous but adding six new letters for sounds he thought were not represented. It never took off and he lost interest in the project. Andrew Carnegie tried again to reform spelling with simplifications and got some support from President Roosevelt. Examples include: 'bizness' for business, 'enuf' for enough, 'fether' for feather, 'mesure' for measure and so on, but again it failed. Mark Twain (1906) doubted that large scale spelling reform would work but did want to simplify the 'drunken old alphabet' and its 'rotten spelling'. Twain and George Bernard Shaw wanted complete and radical alphabet reform and Shaw proposed a 48-letter alphabet that matched the actual sounds of English, 36 brand new letters and 12 combinations. American English, in the end, did benefit from this simplification.

That is not to say that writing reform is impossible. Turkey reformed its alphabet in the 20th century in response to western oriented Turkish nationalism, against Ottoman resistance to printing. This new alphabet was more suited to Turkish than Arabic, which had been used for over a thousand years and, although consonant rich, lacks the vowels commonly used in Turkish. Ataturk promoted the project on the basis of it being easier to learn, with the promise of higher rates of literacy. The literacy rate did indeed rise from 20 per cent to over 90 per cent. This was an interesting attempt to use alphabet reform to push a country into the modern age by breaking with its religious past, a cultural, historical, linguistic and pedagogic break.

Neil Postman was right to note that few could tell when the alphabet was invented and that most would be puzzled by the question. Yet alphabets are fundamental in the currency of writing, especially when they phonetically match sounds and accelerate literacy and learning. What alphabets did was make both reading and writing easier, not only to teach and learn but practice. They have had an inestimable impact on learning, accelerating both the production and consumption of text.

Scribing devices

The pen, as they say, is mightier than the sword, and it is true that the great works of literature, religion, science, philosophy, politics and law are all products of the invention of the technology of writing. The civilizations of Greece and Rome, the Renaissance, Reformation and the Enlightenment were all driven by the ability of minds to put stylus to papyrus or pen to paper. Yet we overlook the technology of these scribing devices that have always been cheap, light and easy to use, putting writing in the hands of teachers and learners. As a learner-centric piece of technology, the stylus, in its many forms, remains a mainstay of learning.

Stylus and brush

To write one needs something to hold in the hand which makes a mark. Scribing devices have been used for over 430,000 years, the earliest known being zig-zags engraved on fossilized shells from Indonesia. Much later, cave painters used sharpened objects to inscribe on rock.

The writing stylus, however, is a small, pointed inscribing instrument made of plant, bone or metal. It has been used for millennia. First used for writing in Mesopotamia and made of reed, it had a trapezoidal point that could be pressed into clay. Cuneiform literally refers to the wedge-shaped impression made by the plentiful reeds found alongside rivers.

In Egypt, brushes to make marks on limestone flakes, pot shards or papyrus were more common. These were rush plants, cut to length, then chewed or hammered at one end to hold the ink, which was made from carbon and bound by gum. Red ink was also used, made from oxides. The hieroglyph for scribe was a brush, bag (for powdered pigments) and palette. Cakes of ink were developed later.

The use of the metal stylus in Greece was in part driven by a ban on the export of papyrus from Egypt. The Greeks, fortunately, were enthusiastic beekeepers, so had a plentiful supply of wax for tablets, upon which they used a stylus. This writing on wax tablets with styluses lasted well into the Middle Ages. The stylus was also used to inscribe lines on parchment to guide the subsequent writing.

Styluses are quite common in the archeological record as they are usually made of materials that do not decay, unlike the wood and wax of tablets. Some styluses had separate stone scribing tips and many had a flattened shape at the other end to erase letters or flatten the wax on tablets. The flattened end was heated and then run over the mistake or whole tablet to start again. This combination of writing and erasure made the tablet and stylus ideal teaching and learning technologies. There was often a groove or place in the tablet to hold the stylus.

The stylus survives to this day as a computer stylus, used for handwriting on tablets and screens. It provides a degree of precision on graphics production, for example, that is superior to other input devices.

Pens

Several countries, including Germany, the United States, France and England, claim to have invented the pen. James Perry produced the Patent Perryman

Pens (1824) in Birmingham; these were split nibbed pens that took advantage of newer quality smooth paper and rising literacy. Steam engines stamped them out from metal sheets in such numbers that the price fell from 2d each to 2d per gross. By the end of the 19th century hundreds of millions of metal nibbed pens were being produced in huge factories in Birmingham. The Industrial Revolution had provided the means to produce cheap, elegant and efficient learning technology.

Learning technology often arises because there is a need or demand. The industrial age was one of self-improvement, bookkeeping, contracts and mass education. There were innumerable education programmes on handwriting with products matched to school curricula, but professional scriveners or clerks still held sway in the law, as they were paid to write contracts and other documents.

New inks which were non-corrosive and just the right viscosity to run freely without blotting also had to be developed, while the inkwell was a standard feature of school desks until the 1960s.

One huge technological breakthrough was the patenting of the ballpoint pen in 1938 by Laslo Biro, a Hungarian journalist. It delivered ink evenly and smoothly as the ball rolled across the paper and dried quickly. It was a massive success and is still used in most pens to this day. Biro sold the patent to the British Government in 1943, but never took out a patent in the United States.

Learning technologies always have pedagogic consequences and pens have a pedagogic weakness, as ink is easy to smudge and almost impossible to erase. Using a pen for creative and critical writing is inefficient and difficult, as editing, redrafting and reordering are difficult. In exams, the pen encourages the regurgitation of pre-prepared, memorized answers. A pencil is superior as it can be erased, and a computer keyboard better still in terms of deletion, insertion, cutting and pasting. This begs an obvious question: Why do many education systems, in examinations that ask for critical thinking and creativity, still require pen work, when students rarely use them, and they don't encourage the skills that are being assessed?

Pencils

Who does not enjoy that feeling of freedom of flow in writing or drawing with a pencil? The pencil, that humble and wondrous piece of learning technology we introduced at the start of this chapter, has been used by almost every learner at some stage in their lives. It is also a fine drawing instrument as it can create lines of different width, texture and shading. It is its ability to erase work that makes the pencil such a flexible piece of learning technology.

Referred to as 'lead pencils' as graphite was thought to be a lead ore in the early days of chemistry, in fact the graphite and clay mixture contains no lead. Only the paint on the wooden casing of the pencil contained lead, up until the middle of the 20th century, when it was recognized as a health risk.

In the middle of the 16th century, Italians Simonio and Lyndiana Bernacotti were the first to insert a graphite rod within a hand-held wooden case, with the two wooden halves stuck together with glue.

But the person usually identified as the inventor of the manufactured modern pencil was Nicholas Jacques Conte in the late 18th century. An officer in Napoleon's army, he distinguished himself by demonstrating a flying balloon on the Egyptian campaign, but he is now better remembered as the inventor of the pencil. The only known source of solid graphite in the world was in Cumbria, England, where solid graphite pencils were cut straight from blocks. As France went to war against Britain, they could no longer import graphite. In 1795, the ever-ingenious Conte came up with a solution. He found that ground graphite mixed with clay could be shaped into thin sticks, then baked hard in a kiln. These thin sticks could then be placed between the two wooden halves of a pencil and glued together, and so the modern pencil was born.

Let us not forget the pencil sharpener, too, that cleverly shaves and saves the shavings into a tiny box. Larger versions were attached to the teacher's desk, originally hand-cranked, then electric. Other writing devices include coloured chalk pieces, wax crayons, coloured pencils and brushes, all used in art and for diagrams and graphics. For precision in geometry, drawing shapes was aided by geometry sets that included a protractor, setsquare and compass.

There are clear pedagogic differences when comparing the technology of the pencil with the pen. It is perhaps more difficult to draw with a pen and the pencil gives more freedom of movement, flow and a huge range of line width and shading. There is a myth that NASA spent millions developing a gravity free pen, while the Russians simply used pencils. In fact, both the United States and Russia used pencils in early space flights, but they are flammable and the tips could break off and be dangerous. It was the Fisher Pen Company that developed an ingenious pen that could work upside-down and in very hot or freezing conditions. More than this, it used a pressurized nitrogen cartridge to push gel ink to a tungsten carbide ball. The gel doesn't evaporate or oxidize because of the nitrogen.

But there is one clear advantage of the pencil over the pen – erasure.

Erasers

To err is human, to erase divine. Learning is about repeated but useful failure, correcting mistakes, so erasure has been necessary for learners and writers since the invention of writing. From the earliest clay tablets to the wax tablets used by the Greeks and Romans, spatula-like scrapers, often on the opposite end of the stylus, or melting, was used to erase unwanted marks or mistakes on clay or wax.

Even when ink was used in beautiful and carefully crafted medieval manuscripts, there was on average one error per page. These mistakes in writing and copying were erased using a scraper, piece of stone or pumice. Slates were erasable using nothing more than a little spit, cloth or sponge.

Then along came the eraser. Small and simple, first as a separate object, then on the end of the pencil, the eraser is a superbly convenient piece of learning technology. It was developed by Edward Nairne in 1770. Joseph Priestly describes using a 'rubber' 'sold by Mr Nairne' for correcting writing in 1770. Vulcanization boosted their use in the mid-19th century as it gave 'rubbers' a longer life. Before this, they were perishable.

The next simple but clever step was to place them on the end of pencils. A patent by Hymen Lipman in 1858 failed, as it was felt to be a composite device, not something separate, However, from that point on, it became common in the United States for pencils to have erasers on the end of pencils. Pencil erasers then came in a massive range of forms from the classic sharp, rectangular block, still popular for fine corrections, to eraser pencils with rubber rather than graphite. We now have novelty erasers in every imaginable shape and colour.

Teachers have also used erasers, especially after the widespread adoption of blackboards, or chalkboards, in the early 19th century. Some put the success of the blackboard largely down to the fact that content, especially in the symbolic teaching of mathematics or physics, can be erased with a deft swipe with a felt pad. Sewall Wright, geneticist and legendary absent-minded professor, was said to have taken live erasure too far during a lecture, when he mistakenly picked up and used one of his experimental guinea pigs on his blackboard! The felt eraser is also used on whiteboards, although who hasn't fallen foul of the permanent marker?

Erasure, the ability to correct mistakes, is a potent learning technique, as failure is an integral part of learning. Writing is a tricky skill to master. We forget how, as children, it was difficult to hold and manipulate a pencil to create letter formations which we had to repeat until our hands hurt. Then there was writing in a straight line, capitalization, the alignment of lines one below the other and many other degrees of skill that result in competent writing. Spelling is also a lifelong, learning task. Few adults feel confident in writing prose without a dictionary or spellchecker. This constant lifelong learning from failure goes way beyond spelling, to word order, sentence construction and the general structure of pieces of written prose. Even if one has mastered clear writing and spelling, good writing is achieved by constant rewriting. Erasure, whatever technology is used, is therefore an essential feature of good writing. No erasure, no learning – there's the rub!

Typewriter

Terms such as return, backspace and shift, as well as the QWERTY keyboard layout, are legacy terms from typewriter technology. This is the moment that writing hits machine technology. The typewriter used the hardware of moveable type combined with the software of a small alphabet, to produce a popular and efficient mechanical writing machine. Until then, writing was handwritten using pens and pencils. The problem with written text is the legibility (or not) of the writer. With a typewriter, the characters are mechanically propelled onto the paper to leave indelible marks. The other innovation was the moving cartridge that provided accurate lines and letter spacing. Carbon paper could also provide copies.

There is evidence of an early typewriter having been patented and built in 1714, but the modern version is recognized as having been invented in the 1860s. Interestingly, many early versions were attempts to build a machine that could allow the blind to type. The first commercially successful machine was sold in 1868 and had the now-famous QWERTY keyboard.

Typewriter technology literally put publishing type into the hands of writers. Neat books, papers, articles and letters could be written in a format close to what looked like a printed version, almost ready for publishing. Early adopters included Nietzsche and Mark Twain. Kerouac famously typed his entire novel *On The Road* on a single roll of paper. Even in the age of word processors, authors such as Cormac McCarthy continue to use typewriters.

Technology is not always as liberating as we imagine. It invariably has limits and downsides that are not always apparent. Although they do not require power or batteries (unless a later electric model), typewriters were prone to jams and failure, require ribbons and make text difficult to erase, so are not conducive to editing and redrafting.

The mechanical nature of the typewriter also meant that the writer had to be slowed down, as the keys would clash and jam. The solution was the QWERTY keyboard, where letters are deliberately spaced far apart to prevent jamming. This keyboard format, a relic from the mechanical past, still dominates the digital future and is a classic example of technology locking in a standard practice. The word 'typewriter' it is said, is the longest word you can type from one row of letters on a QWERTY keyboard. Despite its limitations, the typewriter was hugely successful. The first typewriters were marketed as machines at which female 'typists' would take dictation from male managers. Indeed, the term 'typist' was a standard job description for decades and the 'typing pool' a sizeable department.

Typewriter technology was a temporary bridge from handwritten writing to word processing. Made rapidly redundant by word processing, with its superior editing and ability to produce digital files, it is now no more than a curious, historic relic, a lesson in how quickly human learning technology can change.

Computer keyboards

The radical shifts in learning technologies, from pen and pencil to the keyboard on a typewriter and then on a computer and smartphone, raises some key issues for teaching and learning. Like gear changes, they brought an increase in access, speed and efficiency.

As new forms of electronic, written communication technology emerged, new forms of writing skill (email, texts, tweets, posts and blogs) have developed. Using a keyboard, whether physical or on a touch screen, is a skill in itself. It is surprising that keyboard skills are not taught more widely, since almost all useful text is now produced via keyboards, and it would result in significant increases in productivity.

Today, writing has moved from being a deliberate, formal activity to an ambient, everyday activity. Although there has been a renaissance in writing, in the eyes of educators especially, it is the 'wrong type of writing'. This shift from long- to short-form expression through writing is significant and points towards an irreversible change in our writing and reading habits and culture.

As writing has become more common, a much greater range of genres and styles have emerged. In terms of size, we now have everything from tiny texts (lol), 140-character tweets, posts on Facebook/other social media sites to email. Far from being illiterate, many of us have developed strong skills in short-form writing, such as being concise.

The smartphone brought touchscreens to the fore, and this led to short-form writing including email, texts, messenger, blog posts and so on. These skills were immediately apparent, and who has not wondered at the speed at which some people can text? Consumer demand for smartphones led to the massive use of communication tools and social media such as Facebook, Twitter, LinkedIn, Instagram and TikTok. Even in work, social systems such as email, Slack, Teams and chat on webinar software has led to a more intense use of short-form writing in the workplace. This is not to say that long-form writing has waned or is unimportant. Reports, well-argued essays, articles and books still have to be written, but demand for this form of expression may be falling. These formats are, arguably, becoming less important for the majority of people than short-form writing.

The writing technology of keyboards and word processors have clearly revolutionized long- and short-form writing, allowing deletion, insertion and cut and paste, as well as useful writing support tools. Writers no longer have a dictionary and thesaurus by their side as sidekick technology bring these automatically when needed. Technology is moving towards doing much of the writing for us.

Writing mediums

Just as the technologies that help us to write have evolved, so has the media upon which writing appears. They are yin and yang technologies, one side necessary for the existence of the other. We write to be read and the learning technology required for us to physically make our mark is more complex than most realize.

To write and be read, one needs a medium for display and distribution. Significant technological leaps from readily available natural surfaces such as bones, clay, pottery, stone, wood and bark, to the physical manufacture of papyrus, vellum, slates and paper, laid the ground for scaling from simply copying manuscripts to single page printing presses and rolling presses. This was scaling of physical processes using physical and mechanical technology. The leap to digital meant that replication on screens was unlimited – scale was no longer a problem.

Tablets

Wooden tablets dating back 3,500 years have been found, the earliest from a shipwreck off Turkey. But they became common among the neo-Assyrians from the 8th century BC onwards. They were sometimes covered with a film of white plaster, as an alternative to papyrus in Egypt. Considerable quantities have been found on Roman sites, such as Vindolanda in the north of England, written upon using pens and brushes. There are many examples of wooden tablets surviving as teacher notebooks and student homework.

Wax tablets were also widely used, as wax is a material that can be melted and spread smoothly. Specific soft woods such as cypress or boxwood were used to create a rectangular box, which was filled with a puddle of wax, widely available from beekeeping. The wax was often black or coloured so that the wood or a white surface would show through.

The earliest recorded wax tablets are from the Etruscans in the 7th century BC, while the British Library contains two 2nd century AD wax tablets that would have been bound together. Although found in Egypt, they show Greek homework, with two lines inscribed by the teacher at the top, which the student has copied out twice below. The learner missed a letter on the first try, so tried again. On the opposite side the teacher has written a multiplication table. There is also some phonics teaching, with words starting with 'th' written by the learner. We see here the emergence of teaching and learning techniques. It is a marvelous object, as it has three major pedagogical techniques inscribed into the wax – literacy, numeracy and handwriting exercises. Effortful learning around literacy, mathematics and other subjects could be attempted by the learner using a wax tablet.

Papyrus

Papyrus was invented and used in Egypt, as well as being exported to Greece and Rome. It is the heraldic plant of Lower Egypt, often seen alongside the lotus as a sign of the unification of Upper and Lower Egypt. Papyrus was used for all sorts of purposes, including rope, baskets, sandals, boats, rafts and sails. More famously, it was used by elite scribes for writing since around 3200 BC.

Cut into strips, papyrus was laid out in two layers (one vertical, the other horizontal), then moistened and beaten together into a single sheet and finally polished with a smooth stone. The sheets were quite small at around 18 inches. They were trimmed, then stuck together with starch paste to form rolls, commonly of 20 sheets but they could be huge, up to 130 feet long, with a holding stick in the last sheet.

The medium used to record writing sometimes has powerful pedagogic consequences. Moving from clay to papyrus was significant as it was lighter, easier to flatten out and sheets could be glued together to form long scrolls. Brushes and pens could also be used, as it was easier to write on and produce faster, cursive writing. Unfortunately, supply was limited largely to producers in the Nile Delta in Egypt, who kept the method of manufacture a secret, making it expensive. One other flaw was that it could only be used on one side, as it had a vertical and horizontal grain.

Despite the advance from clay to papyrus, the 'software' of Egyptian writing failed to abandon pictures to develop a full phonetic alphabet. The abundance of space on papyrus may in fact have restricted innovation, as we know, for example, that Sumerian writing had to become efficient as clay tablets were small. However, the Egyptians were the first to introduce fluid, cursive writing as they used the technology of the brush and pen.

There were schools for scribes, where copying huge amounts of existing text was controlled, as was the papyrus trade, by the ruling class. The fact that papyrus was sometimes reused by wiping the ink clean and the abundance of pottery shards and limestone flakes for practice, show that writing was expensive and still relatively rare in the general population. Yet even those who were illiterate were keen to include a written Book of the Dead in their tombs. Despite their thousands of years of writing, it is surprising that the Egytians did not move towards a phonetic alphabet or develop a culture of writing beyond the fixed texts. It shows that writing, and writing technology, no matter how sophisticated, does not necessarily lead to high levels of literacy or produce a culture in which writing flourishes.

Parchment

Parchment for writing, namely animal skins, started to appear in Pergamum, in modern Turkey, in the 1st century AD but soon spread. Damp conditions in Europe meant that papyrus rotted, so parchments were more durable. They could also be written on both sides, scraped clean to be used again, folded, stitched together into a codex (manuscript) and bound. Yet parchment was difficult to make and therefore remained expensive. One bible could take hundreds of calf skins (vellum) selected from thousands of blemished skins.

The Romans brought writing to Britain in the 1st century BC, and evidence refers to pocket versions of texts, so some sort of book was around from then. These codices made from parchment had pages and were sewn and cased in a binding. The earliest intact book in the world is St Cuthbert's Gospel, a hand-sized copy of St John's Gospel from the 7th century AD which was made in Jarrow in the north of England. It comes from his coffin and was found in 1104. Pocket gospels suited mobile monks.

The medieval, monastic scribe used a lined parchment, where a plumb line and stylus was used to inscribe parallel lines. The scribe sat in a position next to a window, where light could illuminate the writing surface that sat on a lectern, at an angle to control the flow of ink. He held a quill pen and a knife for both scraping away errors and sharpening the quill. At only three to four pages per day, it was painstaking work and even the best scribe made a mistake per page, erased by scraping with a knife or pumice stone.

These illustrated manuscripts are much admired by book lovers, but what effect did they have on the dissemination of knowledge and learning? 'Manuscript' literally means written by hand, but this meant that books were scarce and existed in a culture of fixed knowledge and deference. Limited to small libraries that were often controlled by religious institutions, learning was not only severely restricted in terms of the nature of the content but also access and distribution. As most manuscripts were written in esoteric languages, most notably Latin, even greater limitations on content and access were present.

What did happen was the copying of ancient Greek and Roman texts, often via Arab scholars. This, at least, created a corpus of non-religious texts in philosophy, history, drama and mathematics, from Greece and other sources. The flame of learnt texts and learning, although for the few, was kept burning, albeit on a slow-burning wick.

In Britain, literacy plummeted at the end of the Roman era, meaning that for over a thousand years the culture of writing and reading was confined to a small number of scribes using an expensive medium available only to elites. Incredibly expensive to produce and therefore scarce, they were treasured by church and monarchy. Print was power and politics, an expression of religious certainty, conviction, conversion, dogma, flattery, preferment, a claim to legitimacy and the rights of kings, a contract and a confirmation of status. This had as much to do with control as learning. Illustrated manuscripts were very much the luxury goods of religion and royalty.

Yet the church played such an important role in schooling in the Middle Ages that Shakespeare in *Twelfth Night* could write about the 'pedant that keeps a school i' th' church.' Latin Psalters were used throughout the Middle

Ages to teach children to read, and in the 13th century the 'Primer' or 'First book' contained prayers and perhaps an alphabet so that parents could teach their children to read.

Writing became the medium of the 'book' religions, helping to spread and proselytize Buddhism in China and Asia and Judaism, Christianity and Islam in the Middle East and Europe. Manuscripts were not objects for open learning, but texts to be read aloud, learnt by rote and believed.

However, manuscript culture did create an interesting and significant shift from reading aloud to devotional silent reading. More sophistication in the design and format of the text appeared, with spaces between words, punctuation, paragraphs, capitalization, page numbers, contents pages and indexes. These all helped the individual to read alone. Latin inscriptions tend not to have spaces but the Irish, for whom Latin was new, in the 5th century, broke up the words with spaces.

As largely objects of religious belief, manuscripts were the enemy of learning in the sense of new ideas and critical analysis. Many early writers were burnt alive for their heretical writings and Jean-Paul Sartre, Simone de Beauvoir, Voltaire, Victor Hugo, Jean-Jacques Rousseau, Immanuel Kant, David Hume, René Descartes, Francis Bacon, John Milton, John Locke, Galileo Galilei and Blaise Pascal were among those on the Catholic Church's prohibited books list until 1966.

Mesoamerica, one of the four civilizations that invented writing, had its entire literary output burnt by the Spanish conquistadors in 1562. Despite its rich tradition of religious, astronomical and other literature, Bishop Diego de Landa ordered the collection and destruction of all Mayan manuscripts. Only a few survived.

Yet for all of these failings, many magnificent manuscripts give us beautiful insight into the past. The *Book of Kells*, with its intricate details and illustrations, is a masterpiece. Matthew Paris was a 13th-century monk, whose intriguing strip map of a journey to Palestine and the Holy Land is wonderful, even though he almost certainly never made the journey himself.

This was not, therefore, a golden age for books and learning. Manuscript culture placed strict limits on learning. Fixed in a pattern of copying, scarcity and repetition, manuscripts fossilized knowledge and kept it firmly in the hands of church and rulers. The saving grace was that meticulous copying was also a conduit for saving secular knowledge from antiquity and that was to have a huge and enduring impact on our culture. It saved a corpus of books, waiting to be unleashed by Gutenberg, Caxton and others, in a print revolution that we will examine in the next chapter.

Paper

Invented by the Chinese around 105 AD, rags, hemp, bark and meshed fishing nets were used to produce the first dried and bleached paper. It moved beyond China around the 7th century, travelling westward towards the Arab world. Arabic scholars used paper books made from pulped rags, and in 870 AD there were around 100 bookshops in Baghdad. Paper only reached Europe via Islamic Spain in the 11th century. By the 12th century the Italians were renowned as paper makers, and from the 14th century, papermaking spread to other European countries.

Paper is light, making books easy to carry and transport. Another important physical point is that manuscripts were stored flat under lecterns, in libraries with not more than about 200 books. When printing became possible, libraries of several thousand books became common. Books were also stored upright, and so libraries were built with increasingly higher shelves.

Cheap paper makes printing on a large scale possible. When paper manufacture became much cheaper in the 19th century, Fourdrinier (1799) and Gilpin (1816) invented machines that output paper in massive, wide rolls. By the 1860s paper was produced from wood pulp, not rags, and the price plummeted. The price of books fell by a massive 50 per cent and the demand for clean white pages led to the use of chlorine for bleaching. Cheap paper could be printed and distributed on the new rail networks, so newspapers flourished, while postal services led to mass letter writing.

Cheap paper also put mass writing in the hands of learners, through books and textbooks but also notebooks and exercise books for students to take notes and complete exercises. Paper freed the learner to write and, of course, to read more, from books, newspapers, letters and pamphlets.

Although it has been a transformative material, paper is also unstable and decays. The acid which forms in paper was to prove fatal for many books as they decayed while in storage. This has encouraged mass digitization of print books and newspapers, a process that has the added advantage of making the contents accessible and searchable on the web. After its thousand year run, paper is increasingly being challenged by digital storage and access.

Slates

Writing slates were mentioned as far back as the early 11th century in *Alberuni's Indica*. In the 14th century, Chaucer mentions them frequently, used with slate pens and scored (lined) for writing. Their popularity in education, however, came with the rise of mass schooling in the early 19th century. A variety of slate types existed, usually with a wooden frame, in two sizes, typically 4 x 6 inches or 7 x 10 inches, with double slates that could be opened like a book and quiet slates bound in leather that didn't make a noise when put down.

Joseph Lancaster's 'Lancastrian system' laid down specific teaching methods using slates and slate pencils, within a defined system of teaching and learning. Lancaster saw slates as the key learning technology for the 3Rs – reading, writing and arithmetic. Within his systematic set of teaching practices, slates placed the power of learning into the hands of learners and encouraged practice and attention. Surprisingly, they also allowed supervision of a large class by the teacher.

Slates were much cheaper than paper. Indeed, Lancaster provided detailed return on investment calculations to show that they were many times cheaper than pen and paper. There was less waste, and they were very durable. Similarly with slate pencils. Slate was readily available and a recommendation for local schools was to reuse and polish roof slates from demolished buildings.

'Wiping the slate clean' possibly originates from the fact that students had to wipe their slates clean at the start of every class and frequently during lessons, at first using their own spit but cloths and sponges started to appear when it became known that germs were harmful. This meant that mistakes could also be erased with much greater ease than ink on paper, a huge advantage when learning to write. As efficient mobile learning devices, they were cheap, easy to use and reuse.

'To slate someone' also comes from the use of slates. They were used by school monitors to record absence or bad behaviour on their monitors' slates. With classes that frequently topped a hundred, control and assessment was a problem. Lancaster recommended that students hold up their slates and turn them towards the teacher for whole class assessment. In his system, classes were based on competence, not age, with constant movement, so this form of continuous assessment was necessary.

Slates had their heyday in the 19th century and into the mid-20th century, as the need for universal schooling demanded cheap learning technology. The moment cheap paper became available, they were doomed. Looking back, they were the affordable tablets of their day and provided a more sophisticated role in teaching and learning than many imagine, improving the literacy and numeracy of generations of children.

Screens

The use of paper has existed for over a thousand years, but is now challenged by electronic screens. We have huge ones in stadiums, large ones in our homes, medium-sized portable ones in laptops and tablets on our desks and small ones in our pockets. They even exist to deal with stereoscopic vision and 3D in virtual reality. There is a screen for every environment and occasion. We interact with them, touch them, use trackers and mice to do things on them.

Their ability to display high-definition text and images, scroll, zoom, display any colour, develop interfaces, deliver personalized tiled interfaces and display knowledge and learning to anyone, anywhere, at any time, has freed writing from the fixed dimensions of printing on paper. Writing and all other media are literally printed to screens. Screens are now so familiar to us that we barely see them as technology at all, yet they dominate our interface with technology.

Writing becomes much more flexible and dynamic on a screen. A screen allows hyperlinking, writing and spreadsheets to be displayed. Digital formats allow for editing by the writer, shared writing on documents and even reader updates in wikis. Your writing can receive feedback via spell-checking, predictive text and grammar checking, while a new generation of software will be teacher-like as it helps with style and structure.

Computer technology has profoundly reshaped and even wiped out some traditional paper technologies and products. Just as the railways were partially destroyed by the automobile because their owners did not recognize that they were in the transport business, not the railway business, so newspapers have been transformed by the internet, as they forgot that they were in the news business, rather than the newspaper business. So deeply attached were newspapers to paper and physical printing that they at first refused to believe that this new kid on the block, screen-based writing, would survive. Grudging acceptance led to newspapers eventually adopting its ways.

A simple piece of software, the wiki, devastated that most paper-based medium, the encyclopedia. It literally wiped out the physical competition as knowledge moved to screens. The centuries-old tradition of capturing all that we know in volumes on paper to be held in a library, was brought to a shuddering halt and then collapse by a combination of smart software known as the wiki. Once again, publishers saw themselves as being in the book business, not the knowledge business. Wikipedia has trounced the traditional paper encyclopedias on every front with its free, searchable articles which are updatable, and copes with disputed knowledge on the edge of the less volatile content.

Amazon reshaped the book business, with its online 'one click' ordering and delivery. Its vast stock, low prices, smart use of scalable web technology and ease of use, propelled it to a dominant position very quickly. Then came book readers such as the Kindle, really a screen for books, that started to reshape the very nature of the book. You could carry as many weightless books as you wanted, especially when travelling, and it had a long battery life.

None of the learning and other traditionalists realized that their true core business was not in the delivery of paper but the delivery of text, graphics, audio and video. They delivered atoms not bits. But atoms are expensive to produce, distribute and store, whereas bits are all but free to replicate, distribute and store. This has had a profound impact on learning.

Conclusion

As the physical manifestation of language, writing is of inestimable importance as a learning technology, enabling cultural capital to be captured, nurtured and carried into the future. It allowed civilizations to grow, empires to be administered, religions to spread, art to flourish and stories to be told. None of this was possible without seeing writing itself as a technology – the means by which we can write and that which is written upon. We learn to read and write and it in turn helps us to learn, know, understand and move forward. Writing is a physical act, using physical technology, but it is also the software that propelled history. It feels like a natural extension of our bodies and minds. The next step in the advance of civilization was something that made writing far more potent, through the technology of mass replication – printing.

References

Callaway, E (2014) *Homo erectus* made world's oldest doodle 500,000 years ago, *Nature*, 3 December, https://doi.org/10.1038/nature.2014.16477 (archived at https://perma.cc/53EP-GSRU)
Dani, A H (1973) *Alberuni's Indica: A record of the cultural history of South Asia about AD 1030,* University of Islamabad Press, Islamabad

Franklin, B (1779) Political, miscellaneous and philosophical pieces, 17 December, *Founders Online*, National Archives, https://founders.archives.gov/documents/Franklin/01-31-02-0134 (archived at https://perma.cc/H2QU-PREP)

Jackson, D (1981) *The Story of Writing*, Studio Vista, London

Kolak, D and Missner, M (ed) (2016) *Thomas Hobbes: Leviathan,* Longman Library of Primary Sources in Philosophy, Routledge, New York

Lancaster, J (2014) [1807] *Improvements in Education, as it Respects the Industrious Classes of the Community*, Cambridge University Press, Cambridge

Orme, N (2021) *Going to Church in Medieval England*, Yale University Press, New Haven

Postman, N (1985) *Amusing Ourselves to Death*, Penguin, New York

Read, L E (1958) I, Pencil 1958, *Freeman*, 8(12), 32–37

Shakespeare, W (2008) [1601] *Twelfth Night*, Act 3, Scene 2, Arden Shakespeare: Third Series, Bloomsbury Publishing, London

Tune, N W (ed) (1950) George Bernard Shaw, §9 Spelling in relation to reading, writing, phonetics, *Spelling Reform Anthology*

Twain, M (2010) [1899] *A Simplified Alphabet. What is man? And other essays*, The Floating Press, Auckland

04

Printing and books

Printing allows us to learn about the whole of known history, across the entire globe, and its accumulated knowledge. With science we can also discover prehistory and all that has happened since the beginning of time. It is learning technology that enables this.

If writing was the Big Bang of learning technologies, printing was its amplification, echoing down the ages. The last 500 years have seen the evolution of printing, from the manual press to automated press and now the internet, which 'prints' text to our screens. Printing unleashed and democratized learning culture by removing the control of knowledge by elites in the church and state. It became accessible to all, instead of just being used to convey knowledge to the few. Printing gave much of the world we now know, one of personal freedom, possibilities, technology and innovation. Learning came out of the church and schoolroom into the hands of individual learners. According to Eisenstein (1979), printed texts set imaginations on fire and gave us the Reformation, Scientific Revolution, Industrial Revolution and the modern world. It also allowed us to see technology as fundamental to progress. Science and technology were different domains prior to 1500. Francis Bacon joined them together in *The New Instrument* (1620), and this led to several centuries of technological innovation tied to mathematics and science.

This chapter looks at the history of printing and how it has been used to advance learning through the creation of books. It looks at the evolution of printing from Gutenberg's moveable type to the modern day and examines the role that books have played in history, particularly in learning.

Printing technology

The printing press was not invented by Gutenberg, nor was it a single technology. Although the Chinese invented paper, block printing and even moveable type, their character-based language made Gutenberg-type presses impractical. It was the existence of another piece of technology, the Roman alphabet, that made the printing press practical. This is yet another example of how software can be the real driver behind a technological advance.

Early printing technology

Brian Arthur (2009) shows that technology is often an accumulation and convergence of previous technologies. Printing with moveable type was being experimented with from the 1430s onwards, with Gutenberg developing moveable type, alloys for type and reusable type, modelled on existing screw presses. Together with the development of indelible ink and cheap paper, this combination of technologies enabled Gutenberg to create his famous Bible.

The core technology in the 15th century was moveable type. The compositor set each letter, in reverse, on sticks, bedded it down and adjusted as necessary, with each page being separately printed. This was not easy, and just like manuscript writing, errors were easy to make. The initial investment needed was quite high and if sales were better than expected the whole process had to be repeated in order to produce more copies. Paper remained a problem even after the printing press was developed, as it was so expensive. Gutenberg got into deep debt and had to pass his workshop over to his investor. One of his first books, the Gutenberg Bible, took two years to typeset and print.

What the printing press did was scale production and distribution. The number of books available increased significantly, prices plummeted and the idea of writing new works to be printed, as opposed to just reading fixed texts, took hold. It was a technology (or set of technologies) that was to cause irreversible change in the world.

The Bible was, of course, the first book to be printed, along with indulgences by the Catholic Church, the misuse of which led to Luther's Protestant Reformation and his best-selling, vernacular German Bible (200,000 in his lifetime). The boost to science was also considerable, as findings, criticism and commentaries could be written, printed and disseminated at speed.

Scalability of knowledge

Printing technology allowed knowledge to be made, distributed and stored more easily and on scale. It was not a process of replacement, as printing extended the reading of classical and medieval texts. Neither was it wholly secular or humanist.

Just as importantly, previously preserved written texts could now be printed, saving original texts from the possibility of destruction and damage. Most of the works by the pre-Socratic philosophers such as Plato and Aristotle, and most of the output from Greek dramatists, had been lost. Printing preserved what we have, its scale preventing the losses inherent in scarce written texts.

Printing also brought a degree of standardization of written language. Interestingly, some printers added letters to pad out lines to the right-hand margin, such as an extra 'e' on the end of words. In its own way, printing also selected and to a degree determined and controlled literature and knowledge. Technology, once again, became the underlying driver behind cultural expansion.

Before the invention of the printing press, academic learning was oral and involved listening to an expert, who often read from a book. Until the 14th century, the word 'lecture' meant 'to read', so students were likely to simply hear portions of books being read aloud. It was printing that put reading and learning literally into the hands of learners.

Print meant relatively large batches (200–1,000) of identical texts. A printer could make more books in a month than a scribe in a lifetime. The printed book, like the modern mobile, was portable, personal and could be read at any time and in any place. It was no longer necessary to listen to someone transmit knowledge at a particular time or place. It also meant the democratization of knowledge, and therefore learning, as scalability through the replication of books enabled the many, not just the few, to learn. Indeed, scholars expanded in number but, more importantly, so did readers. Reading became far more common. Note also that the Reformation, itself a product of printing, promoted personal development through education, especially for the poor. It was not until then that mass reading and universal schooling got underway.

In the 19th century, printing was further transformed by faster and more efficient steam-driven cylinder and rotary presses and much cheaper paper produced from wood pulp that was manufactured in huge rolls. In the 20th century, the photocopier and computer printer took printing into the high street, businesses and the home.

So Gutenberg's printing press, with moveable type, changed the course of knowledge production, dissemination and therefore learning. It led to a radical shift in how, what, where and when we could learn.

With the super-printer that is the internet and world wide web, an age of digital abundance is flourishing, similar to that of the post-Gutenberg era. At first the availability of books in that huge bookshop, Amazon, changed access to books forever. The shift from atoms to bits also meant that print was not only infinitely replicable but also cheap and easy to distribute. In a sense it is our own devices that 'print' text to our screens. We have control over the font size of text and can annotate and search it. The world of print has changed irrevocably. The digital genie is out of the bottle.

Printing and literacy

Printing has had a profound effect on both formal and informal learning. Its effect on formal learning, which became the springboard for the ages of enlightenment, science, innovation and industrial revolutions, had a deeper cause – literacy. We learn unconsciously to speak and listen, whereas reading and writing – literacy – needs to be taught.

Literacy certainly increased with the availability of printed texts. Printing also had the advantage of people being taught in and learning from texts in their own first language. Language also became more standardized in its written form, with a larger vocabulary of more technical terms. From new bibles and prayer books in local languages to a wide selection of secular works, by the 1500s printing was well established in England, with many texts being imported from Europe. Around 1500, the teaching of Latin changed from Medieval Latin to Classical Latin and the Classical scholars were taught instead of sacred texts. This led eventually to a Reformation in instruction, by Henry VIII, in 1536, to have both English and Latin bibles in churches and to teach children to pray in English. Schools were quick to adopt this convention (Orme, 2021). The print revolution resulted in an increasingly literate population and led to a flourishing pamphlet and book culture.

Products of print

We have seen how printing marked a change in the scale and reach of the written word. We can now look at the impact this had in terms of science and culture. As a learning technology, printing literally created what we know as the modern world. From Gutenberg in Germany, printing technology quickly spread across Europe, while William Caxton is thought to have been the first to introduce a printing press into England in 1476. That same year, Caxton is noted for printing the first edition of Geoffrey Chaucer's *Canterbury Tales*, which was written between 1387 and 1400. The second edition printed by Caxton was illustrated with woodblock prints, in 1483.

Before 1501, 77 per cent of all books were in Latin, but the Protestant Reformation reversed this. Luther's 1534 Bible, written in German, and his rebellion against the Catholic Church resulted in a pamphlet war between Reformation and Counter-reformation publishers. The Protestant Revolution also created a counter-revolution and censorship, with the Catholic Church placing many scientific works on its Index of Prohibited Works. The path to enlightenment through printing was never easy.

Monarchies also feared freedom of thought and made efforts to suppress printed works. In 1543, Henry VIII passed an Act that banned the reading of the Bible in English by women, apprentices and the peasant and working classes. In 1559, Elizabeth I granted the Company of Stationers a monopoly on book production, with the intention of suppressing Catholicism. It failed, as books were simply imported from abroad. Indeed, the Low Countries became the source of both the business of book printing and distribution.

Science and knowledge

In science, it was not long before the works of astronomers appeared. Nicolaus Copernicus turned the world on its head with his *De Revolutionibus* (1543), which offered an alternative model of the universe, contrary to the accepted theory of the time. In the 17th century, printed works by Johannes Kepler (mathematician, astronomer and natural philosopher), Galileo (astronomer, physicist and engineer) and Sir Isaac Newton (scientist and mathematician) accelerated the Scientific Revolution, providing examples of how writing allowed the human mind to make great leaps of imagination and science. Printing technology could extend memory and store numbers, results of experiments, data, diagrams and facts. Written patents also began in the 17th century, which protected inventions and helped to drive techno-logical change that would eventually lead to the Industrial Revolution.

Astronomical data was particularly important for navigation. Printed atlases and maps allowed European explorers to conquer the globe in a golden age of exploration. The first modern atlas appeared in Antwerp in 1570. Maps evolved as places were explored and mapped, while many were also copied from previous maps, thereby perpetuating errors and the inclu-sion of fantastical creatures.

Encyclopedia Britannica was created by a private publisher and first published in three volumes from 1768 to 1771. It continued to be published by private companies for nearly 250 years, until Wikipedia led to its demise.

Newspapers and pamphlets

The term 'newspaper' came into existence in the 17th century. The first news books or pamphlets distributed mainly foreign news, while the first newspaper appeared in England in 1665. Newspapers made writing a popular, dynamic medium.

Censorship

Censorship was not only the preserve of the church and English monarchy. In France, the writer Voltaire was imprisoned in 1711 and again in 1726 for criticizing the French government, while Rousseau was threatened with imprisonment after publishing *Emile* in 1762. Napoleon also implemented strict censorship in 1811 with all books having to be approved before publication, and only 80 publishers and four newspapers were approved. Of course, this led to a clandestine trade in banned books. We can see echoes here of attempts to control social media and the internet.

Fiction

In the 17th and 18th centuries, there were landmark successes with the printing of fiction, including Miguel de Cervantes' *Don Quixote* (1620) and Daniel Defoe's *Robinson Crusoe* (1719). As literacy levels rose dramatically in the west, Sir Walter Scott enjoyed commercial success with his romantic novels in the early 19th century. By the 1890s, fiction had become widely popular in the United States, UK, Europe and Australia.

Children's books

Since medieval times, children had been taught to read from 'horn books', a wooden frame with a short handle holding a single sheet of paper showing the alphabet, a few phonemes and the Lord's Prayer. It was protected by a sheet of horn (hence the name) and designed to be used in the home rather than school. It was not until the 19th century that children's books emerged as a genre. Hans Christian Anderson's *Fairy Tales* (1834–45), Lewis Carroll's

Alice's Adventures in Wonderland (1865), Robert Louis Stephenson's *Treasure Island* (1883) and Carlo Collodi's *Pinocchio* (1886) were some of the first to be published. Today, children's books have expanded into several genres and the success of JK Rowling's *Harry Potter* series (1997–2007) demonstrate they still have a powerful impact on the minds of children.

Book presentation

As literature progressed, so did the underlying presentation technology that made books easier to read. Paragraph breaks came in the 16th century, when standardization and even errata slips began to appear. Engraved frontispieces started to appear in the 17th century, along with the date of publication, table of contents and page numbers. Printing, despite creating a new future, also looked to the past. Classical texts were revived and widely read. Texts from Plato, Aristotle and others became popular, and *italics* were introduced in these texts to indicate 'classical Italy'. A battle of the fonts, between the classical, Renaissance Roman fonts versus Gothic fonts emerged, with Reformation printers preferring Gothic, a trend that continued into the 20th century in Germany. Some newspapers, such as France's *Le Monde*, still have Gothic mastheads.

Printed works as learning technology

The printed book is arguably the most successful physical piece of learning technology ever invented. It is practical, portable and potent. Some books have changed the world and books have played a pivotal role in history, to administer, record, inform, spread ideas and effect change. Above all they have been used to educate, both formally and informally.

The book has gone through several transformations, starting with the codex, which was the basic idea that pages could be bound in such a way that they could be turned into a book, a shape that has lasted for two millennia. The book, in this form, was invented in the 2nd century AD by early Christians. It is thought that they were keen to distinguish the physical form of their holy book from that of the Jewish Torah, which remains loyal to the scrolled format. The scroll was, generally, the dominant form for writing, but it had its weaknesses. For example, it had to be held in both hands, was difficult to unroll, rolls away on a flat surface, is difficult to carry and store, is written only on one side and is difficult to search to a specific place.

The nature of books

It is useful to separate the hardware and software components of books, as the word 'book' has two meanings – first, the whole physical object of paper and text; second, just the text. Authors don't write books, they write texts. It is publishers who package texts into books by commissioning covers, paper type and weight, font and other features.

A book, as hardware, is light, portable and never runs out of battery. It is undoubtedly an attractive object that doesn't break when dropped and is easy to carry and hold for reading. Even its flexibility makes it comfortable to hold or lie on one's lap when read. Paper, as a reflective medium, is also eminently readable. The physical pages can be written on both sides. It is easy to see where you are in a book and how much you have completed. Block shaped books also make them easy to store upright on shelves. There can be no doubt that the physicality of the book contributes to its appeal.

However, the most useful part of a book is, of course, its software, or text. We think of the book as a single text, but early books tended to contain a miscellaneous mixture of different texts on different subjects, often in different languages by different authors. Paged books encouraged the development of readable content, because texts were chunked into chapters and paragraphs with spaced (words and sentences), punctuated to aid reading, capitalized for sentences and emphasis, given page numbers, listed by contents and indexed, with appendices and bibliographies. These features all aid navigation. However, all of this took centuries of slow incremental progress. Note that these are features of the text, not the physical book; in other words, this is the software, not the hardware. The technological advances in books were both in the process of production (printing, ink and paper) and software improvements.

The scroll versus page technology continues today in learning technology, where horizontal and window-based web pages live alongside vertical scrolling. We can see this in Wikipedia, with its page structure for entries and scrolling for reading.

A further period of note was the rise of silent reading. Originally manuscripts were read aloud, but in the Middle Ages, monks began to read in silence as a form of devotion, which led to more structured presentation in the text and punctuation. Incidentally, it also allowed texts to be read out more easily. This is a significant shift, as it is precisely what we do when using books to learn. The 'reading revolution' of the late 18th century, when reading became a mass pastime, was a silent revolution.

It is in the second half of the 19th century that writers, publishers, printers and distributors, with royalties for authors, created the ecosystem for book publishing that exists to this day. It is a complex world, and this book you are reading involved an author, editor, proofreader, graphic artist, publisher, printer, warehousing and distribution, both physical and electronic. There is also you, the reader, with your expectations about books.

Books have a special status in western culture as 'almost objects of worship' while non-readers may be stigmatized. Yet reading is often non-reading, as we forget most of what we read almost as quickly as it is read. As we move forward, content is forgotten in the wake of memory. Most reading is forgetting, yet it is almost taboo to underline or mark books and blasphemous to tear out a page or chapter! Life is short, and books are long, so it may be fine to skim. For many, the fact that most of what is read will be forgotten means reading just a summary may be adequate.

In *How to Talk About Books You Haven't Read* (2007), Professor Pierre Bayard throws the book at books. He provides a deep analysis of the ambiguous role of readers and books, and suggests we take books too seriously, forgetting that many are bought and not read, skimmed or talked about as if they had been read, and most are forgotten. As an academic, he describes a world he knows well, where academics discuss books they may not have read and students respond by pretending to read long reading lists. Shortcuts are taken by all. It is a game where reading is the facade and non-reading the reality.

Bayard quotes many writers, including Oscar Wilde, Graham Green, Montaigne, William Shakespeare, James Joyce and Marcel Proust, to build a case, not against books, but against the bogus idea of books as pure and sacrosanct. You can't judge a book by its lover, so reading, and the culture of reading, is not as simple as we think it is. It can be full of deceit, snobbery and false claims.

New media and self-publishing are also tearing apart the myth that reading is synonymous with books. In many ways, reading has freed itself from the tyranny of books. The digital revolution has been by far the biggest change to the concept of a book as it has eliminated its physical form. The book lives on with page turning and a recognizable layout, but other forms of online writing have shattered the format into tweets, posts, comments and blogs, alongside other media such as images and video.

Libraries

There is a problem with books as a learning technology. How do you store and catalogue them for efficient access to learning, research or pleasure? Early libraries such as the one in Alexandria, Egypt not only collected and contained a huge number of scrolls, but they also became centres of learning and prototype universities. While small, private libraries allowed many classical texts to survive and be passed down through the ages, larger libraries have often been a target in times of political turmoil. From the Spanish conquistadors in Mesoamerica in the 16th century to the Nazis, Chairman Mao and the Balkans conflict in the 20th century, books have been looted and burnt throughout history.

Despite this, libraries grew alongside universities across Europe and books remain a mainstay of learning in education. Today we have public, school and university libraries, but the few libraries that attempt to store all published books struggle with space and the inevitable decay of their books.

Cataloguing started with labelling on baskets of clay tablets. Codices were not only easier to store, the alphabet and Arabic numerals could be used to catalogue them. There was always an uneasy relationship between quantified cataloguing and rational category-based cataloguing. The Dewey Decimal System was invented by Melvin Dewey in 1876, although many large storage libraries, where space is at a premium, now store by size and catalogue separately.

The idea of storing texts in miniature through photography was first suggested in the late 19th century. It was the Pigeon Post in Paris during the Franco-Prussian War of 1870–71 that pushed this idea further, with the need for miniature texts that could be carried by pigeons. This in turn led to the use of scaled-down microforms, while the development of both microfilm (reels) and microfiche (flat sheets) came into widespread use in libraries from the 1920s.

Over the centuries, millions of books have been published in dozens of languages. Libraries preserve books that are no longer in print, allowing them to be accessed for generations to come. However, paper production is expensive, polluting and contributes to global warming, while books disintegrate and are expensive to store. Books are also going out of print faster than ever before, due to the business practices of publishers, which can mean books are becoming less available than ever before. Libraries as a place to conduct research are now facing the challenge of technology. Researching individual books is much slower than using a search engine; inter-library loans are expensive, and the researcher cannot gauge a book's worth prior to ordering. Maintaining stocks of books and preserving those at risk of deterioration adds to the burden placed on libraries.

In the 21st century, computer and internet technologies have, of course, revolutionized how libraries store, manage and deliver their services. Sizeable funding from Google and others has allowed vast numbers of out-of-print books to be uploaded to the web. This has led to the digital publication of the largest repository of human knowledge ever, making it available and searchable online and ensuring the internet is truly useful in advancing knowledge and research.

Textbooks

The textbook is a hugely successful piece of learning technology. Mediating between the teacher and learner, textbooks deliver learning at every level and on every educational subject.

Early textbooks

Textbooks have evolved over time to match the cultural context, from the classical tradition of reading Homer to the religious imperatives of reading and studying religious texts such as the Quran and Christian scripture, through the rise of literature, mathematics and science in more secular times. For a long time, textbooks were largely written in Latin, the language of the Church, as that was the language of teaching and instruction.

Unsurprisingly, textbooks as we know them today have their origins in books that taught children to read and write. These early textbooks were a mixture of alphabets, phonetic instructions and maxims. They were primarily religious in intent, allowing one to learn to read scripture, while some were catechisms with questions and answers both found in the text. They first appeared in the 1st century AD and were still prominent in the 19th century. These were popular, as schooling mainly involved reciting back to the teacher, with questions from set texts demanding set answers. Such textbooks also provided knowledge of a subject which the teacher may not themselves have possessed, enabling relatively untrained teachers to teach.

The Reformation saw an entirely different type of textbook. John Amos Comenius (1673) was a Czech educator who promoted 'universal education' to solve the problem of human and religious conflict. After the Lutheran Reformation in 1517, the idea of education for all took root. Comenius was a bridge between the reforming zeal of the post-print Reformation and the universal values of the Enlightenment. He was also a proponent of the Scientific Revolution, represented by the dedication of his book *The Way of Light* (1642), written in England and dedicated to The Royal Society, which posited the idea of a universal college and network of schools working towards universal knowledge.

Comenius' Reformation spirit led him to imagine a 'pansophism', a universal wisdom, which teaches a unified knowledge through a unified system of education, covering a wide range of knowledge which is used to understand God's world. Moving away from the classics and an obsession with grammar and rote learning to content that was sensitive to the motivation and interests of the learner, Comenius saw print as the medium through which this could be achieved. His approach encouraged parents and teachers to constantly observe and explain the world to children but also to continue to learn themselves, making him an early proponent in lifelong learning. An important dimension of his pansophism was his desire to see *access* to learning for the whole human race – rich, poor, male, female, rural, urban and importantly, those with disabilities.

Comenius' *The Door of Languages Unlocked* or *Janua Linguarum Reserata* (1631) was the first of a number of textbooks that were revolutionary as short encyclopedias for children, providing an alternative to the traditional learning of Latin through grammar, rote learning and memorization. It was one of the first 'textbooks' to teach language through a knowledge of the world, and became a bestseller.

His *Orbis Pictus* (1658) was the first textbook to use pictures to illustrate the content, connecting words to things. First published in German and Latin, it was subsequently published in many languages. Comenius explains its pedagogic approach in the Preface and its 150 chapters start with the phonetics of language (surprisingly modern) to aid reading, then inanimate objects, botany, zoology, religion, humans and human activity. He recognized that pictures mattered, in this case woodcuts, to retain the child's attention. It is a truly remarkable and forward-looking textbook.

Impact of mass teaching

The rise of universal schooling and the need to teach entire populations how to read and write created an enormous demand for textbook production. As the profession of teaching developed, along with more formal teacher training, the textbook adapted to this need. Changes in teaching methods and training were also mirrored in the shift from primers and readers to covering the knowledge of a defined curriculum. With the rise in alternative learning theories in the 19th century, a more sophisticated enquiry approach developed in classrooms, with increased focus on understanding, which was mirrored in published textbooks. Textbooks began to include more exercises and inductive questions. Illustrations, diagrams and graphs were also more common as printing and colour printing developed.

Once textbooks gained the status of a learning technology in themselves, they began to sell in the tens of millions. The market was huge as universal schooling grew in terms of total numbers of learners as well as the number of years children spent in school. Today, textbooks have evolved into being written specifically to match school curricula, by global specialist publishers.

Despite the shift to enquiry-based learning, direct instruction from textbooks is still popular. Some argue that teaching can be inhibited by too strict adherence to textbooks and that they are an aid to teaching rather than a programme of learning. As they take a great deal of time and money to create and publish, with input from subject matter experts, students, teachers, parents, curriculum planners and educational boards, publishers need to have a return on investment and so their textbooks may 'lock down' teaching and learning for 3–4 years and possibly longer.

Future of textbooks

As a huge multi-billion-dollar market and a considerable cost to schools, parents and students, printed textbooks are now undergoing a massive and significant technological transformation, as the nature of how they are produced, sold, bought, borrowed and shared is changing rapidly.

Digital technology means that the role of the traditional textbook is waning, as screen-based learning technology replaces, by degree, the need for the printed book. The development of textbooks under creative commons licenses allows them to be used for free, in an interesting combination of technology and print or screen. However, online textbooks give access to a wider range of teaching and learning tools, resources and media types, that are perhaps more suited to 21st century needs. Some textbooks are simply published as ebooks, with minor enhancements such as links to other resources and different media types. Others offer formative assessment, remedial branching, adaptivity and personalization, moving away from the traditional textbook to become online learning platforms. The printed text-book will become rarer as time passes and new technology proves more efficacious.

The printed textbook was a learning technology of huge significance but is now giving way to digital alternatives. It is clear that technology itself is the driver, along with a recognition that 'text' needs to expand across a more flexible range of different media types such as audio, animation, video, AR and VR. The word 'book' also seems to be increasingly redundant as the physical object gives way to learning experiences delivered by smart technology.

Distribution

At its simplest, printing can be viewed as just mass manufacturing. The real benefits of printing come from distribution. Without distribution to book-shops, libraries and now online, the fruits of printed material are not realized.

Early distribution of books

Libraries may have existed for centuries, but where did they get their books? In Ancient Rome, for instance, there was a specific street of booksellers called the Argiletum.

Islam was a conduit for many ancient texts but its adherence to the idea of 'written' and copied texts, rather than printed, meant it remained in the 'manuscript written by hand' age well into the 19th century. In the 15th century printing was banned completely across the Ottoman Empire, and it wasn't until 1727 that this law was repealed, and even then only for secular books. This had a devastating effect on the Islamic world's contribution to knowledge, science and learning, and it wasn't until the second half of the 19th century that printing became commonplace. Nevertheless, the Middle East had sophisticated systems of distribution and thriving bookstores. It is said that 'Books are written in Cairo, published in Beirut, and read in Baghdad.'

In the 16th century, the distribution and selling of books through book-stores began to thrive. In Europe, the oldest bookstore (which is still open) is in the Librairie Nouvelle d'Orléans in France. Wholesale booksellers emerged through demand for printed books in the 19th century, but it is the internet that was to provide the real revolution in distribution.

Amazon and distribution

Jeff Bezos had the vision to not only remove the need for intermediaries between publishers and purchasers of printed books, he went on to create the market for electronic books (ebooks), removing our reliance on traditional printed books. Bezos is a talented programmer, but more than that he is an entrepreneur with a single-minded vision: Bezos was born to sell books. He took a course on bookselling just 10 months prior to setting up Amazon where he learnt that customer service is the vital ingredient. But customer service is not just about people; it is also about brand, reliability, finding what you want quickly, ordering quickly, price, ease of use, personalization and the ability to communicate quickly via email. Busy people want to browse, but they also want transactions that are simple, fast and intuitive.

What Bezos saw was that the book is the text, not the binding and cover, which were added by the publisher. 'You can't ever out-book the book', he says, 'so you have to give added value such as font size, lightness, dictionary, quick downloads...' (Brandt, 2011). Bezos quite literally sees himself as having ended the '500-year run' of the book and its associated, expensive distribution. And he has done this by creating the biggest bookstore on earth with its famous '1-click' button. Amazon's contribution to the dissemination of knowledge, whatever one's view of its commercial dominance, is considerable.

A lot is made of 'personalized learning' but Amazon gives it substance. Beyond the simple buying (or selling) of books lies the cleverness of the recommendation engine. Users have access to customer reviews as well as lists of recommended books under specific topics and personal recommendations tailored to their interests, based on data gathered from past purchases. Some argue that this leads to an expansion of reading and interests, as the buyer is given information about books that encourages them to buy more books. Amazon offers the option to 'Look Inside' a book – a selection of pages that can be previewed before purchase.

Online access to books has also given us the ability to search, browse and buy a larger range of books than was ever possible through traditional bookshops, often at cheaper prices. However, it is clear that Amazon has led to the demise of many traditional booksellers, both large chains and small independent bookshops. Like music stores and video rental stores, they have been disintermediated. On the positive side, it has never been easier for those with little or no access to traditional bookstores to buy from the biggest bookstore in the world.

Chris Anderson (2006) points to Amazon as the prime example of how technology plays to 'long tail' selling. In a typical bookshop, stock will be limited and often controlled by behind-the-scenes deals with publishers. On Amazon, it is possible to find almost any book, no matter how obscure. The long tail has also been extended by allowing small book sellers and authors to print and sell their work through Amazon. This is clearly a boon to learning, as it provides depth and breadth of access to learners, students and academics, who were often limited by the contents of their local or institutional library.

Amazon has proved to be a huge global success. Many of us love tearing open that cardboard package and seeing our books (and other goodies) appear. In terms of learning, Amazon has increased access, lowered prices and provided access to both popular and obscure titles, resulting in more, not less, learning. If learning must be more responsive to need – faster, cheaper, easier to access, responsive to user data and online – then surely the days of the traditional printed book are numbered?

Screen technology

Just as the printed book was a hardware improvement on the technology of the vellum codex, manuscript and scroll, so screen technology is in some ways an improvement on the hardware of the physical book. Books destroy trees, require complex and polluting processes and are expensive to transport and store. By turning atoms into bits, books become weightless, and distribution and the problem of storage become trivial.

Although the book, as a physical technology, has developed over nearly 2,000 years into a finely-honed, much-loved object, that technology is being challenged by screen-based reading and writing. There has been an explosion of publishing, writing and reading on screens, aided by the internet. This has been boosted by good quality, readable screen technology, mobile devices and inexpensive ebook readers.

Traditionalists may wave their reading glasses in horror, but to turn books into a fetish may be to deny the inevitable. Paper books are great but let us not confuse the medium with the content, or hardware with software; namely, books with texts. Just as journalists and newspaper owners fail to realize they are in the 'news' not the 'newspaper' business, so book fans and publishers sometimes fail to realize that writing and reading are at the centre, not books. Screen-based delivery also puts books in the realm of software control, making them easier to download, store, search, hyperlink, change font and size and highlight. Ultimately, books are simply a piece of technology, first enabled by printing and now, by more modern technology in the form of the internet.

We can now see where this leads us in improving learning. Why lock up knowledge and the ability to learn in libraries, schools and physical books, when we can use the technology of the internet to publish and distribute it at marginal cost to everyone?

Conclusion

The book (codex) was a superior technology to the scroll, and in the form of handwritten manuscripts had a lifespan of around 1,200 years. The printing press scaled up the process of replication and has been around for around 500 years. Building on this, screen-based reading has given us another massive boost in scalability, making printed books and documents weight-less, easy to distribute and searchable.

What we are witnessing is not the death of the book but its electronic replacement as the dominant form of written and learning expression. Wikipedia is not really a book in the sense that the Encyclopedia Britannica was a book or large set of books. A much wider range of writing, images, audio and video have emerged. Texting, posting, commenting and blogging are challenging the long-form book as the writing and reading medium of choice. Books themselves are being seen as just one form of expression among many.

Another form of printing that emerged during the 20th century was broadcast media. This was recorded audio and video which was literally printed onto magnetic tape (and later produced in a digital form), then broadcast. In many ways the next chapter is about printing for media that can be watched or listened to, rather than read. One can see this analogue then digital technology as a form of media printing – broadcast media.

References

Anderson, C (2006) *The Long Tail: Why the future of business is selling less of more*, Hyperion, New York

Arthur, W B (2009) *The Nature of Technology: What it is and how it evolves*, Simon & Schuster, New York

Bacon, F (1960) [1620] *The New Organon and Related Writings*, F H Anderson (ed) Issue 97 of Library of Liberal Arts, Bobbs-Merrill, Michigan, MI

Bayard, P (2007) *How to Talk About Books You Haven't Read*, Bloomsbury Publishing New York

Brandt, R L (2011) *One Click: Jeff Bezos and the Rise of Amazon.com*, Penguin, London

Chaucer, G (2012) *The Canterbury Tales*, R Boenig and A Taylor (eds), Broadview Press, Peterborough, Ontario

Comenius, J A (1673) *The Door of Languages Unlocked, or A Seed-Plot of All Arts and Tongues: Containing a ready way to learn the Latine and English tongue*, Printed by TR and NT for the Company of Stationers, London

Comenius, J A (1968) *The Orbis Pictus of John Amos Comenius,* Singing Tree Press, Detroit, MI

Copernicus, N (1854) [1543] *De revolutionibus orbium cœlestium*: *libri VI Norimbergae, I Petreium*, Culture et Civilisation

Eisenstein, E L (1979) *The Printing Press as an Agent of Change: Communications and cultural transformations in early-modern Europe*, Cambridge University Press, Cambridge

Keatinge, M W (ed) (1967) *The Great Didactic of John Amos Comenius: Now for the first time Englished,* Russell and Russell, New York

Orme, N (2021) *Going to Church in Medieval England*, Yale University Press, New Haven, CT

05

Broadcast and media

The broadcast media of radio and television are unusual forms of learning technologies because they are one way. For nearly a century, their role has been to inform and educate huge numbers of people, across every conceivable subject, across the entire planet, beaming straight into people's homes. While once they only existed in real time, with the advent of on-demand services they can now be accessed at times to suit the user.

From the beginning, broadcast technology was seen as teaching technology. In the UK, the BBC's original mandate was to 'inform, educate and entertain', while its first Director-General, Lord Reith, saw the purpose of the BBC as perhaps an emphasis on the first two of those words. In other countries, commercial radio and television played a similar cultural role.

Radio

Worldwide, radio remains an accessible and popular broadcast medium. Its lower production and broadcast costs together with enormous radio wave reach have always been its virtues. It is particularly powerful in places where TV and the internet are less accessible, or where distances are so vast that it has been used to deliver teaching and learning in remote places around the world, in countries such as the United States, Canada and Australia.

James Clerk Maxwell developed the ability to send radio waves through free space in 1863. In the 1890s, Guglielmo Marconi developed wireless telegraphy, and with patents and a commercial mindset, he created radio as we know it today, receiving the Nobel Prize for Physics in 1909.

Audio by radio transmission was first developed in the early 1900s for maritime communications and Marconi opened the first mass manufacturing radio factory in England in 1912. By 1920, the first sports, entertainment and news had been broadcast. Television pictures were also being transmitted by radio waves at this time, an important point as television technology had its roots in radio.

However, it was the receiver devices that made radio into a consumer phenomenon. These devices were cheap to make and, following the invention of the transistor in the 1950s, transistor radios became enormously popular, selling in the billions. Digital radio began in the 1970s and 1980s with military and commercial wireless networks, while Digital Audio Broadcasting (DAB) radio was born in 1996. Radio is now being delivered not just through free space but also on digital networks, mainly the internet. As always, it is how consumers use a medium that determines its success and, in the case of radio, it has always been through cheap and small devices.

'The new medium of the radio was to the printing press what the telephone was to the letter', said Tom Lewis (1992). What gave it this status, and made it different from print, was the power of voice. You could, for the first time, hear your president or prime minister speak, listen to your heroes and entertainers play music or act and hear authors read their own works. Music of every genre became accessible, along with drama and comedy. Through the 1920s, 1930s and 1940s, radio was all powerful, and played a key role during the Second World War.

Yet radio broadcasting in the UK had an unusual start. In June 1920, the soprano Dame Nellie Melba made the first ever live broadcast, creating a stir of enthusiasm for the new technology. However, as is often the case, the government were sceptical and tried to stop radio's expansion by refusing to authorize hundreds of requests for radio licences. US radio stations expanded in number significantly at this time, but the British government issued a single licence to a short-lived company called the British Broadcasting Company Ltd. This company was set up with shareholders from a number of companies involved in broadcasting and radio manufacture. Only radio sets supplied by these companies were licensed to receive programmes, ensuring that technology played a role not only as a medium of delivery, but in the financing of radio, as the British Broadcasting Company Ltd received a royalty on each manufactured radio. However, as people were making their own radio sets and buying unlicensed sets, it was clear this approach would not work in the long term, so a licence fee was introduced.

Restrictions on broadcasting were also put in place. For example, in order not to interfere with the newspaper business, news was only broadcast after 7 pm and had to be sourced from external providers. History then intervened, as the 1926 General Strike meant no newspapers, making radio the only source of news. In 1926, the British Broadcasting Company Ltd was dissolved and replaced by the non-commercial British Broadcasting Corporation (BBC). It was not until the 1970s that commercial radio would begin in the UK.

Radio and learning

School radio was there from the start of the BBC and by the 1970s, school radio services were used by around 90 per cent of British schools. The tradition of providing education continues to this day, with BBC Sounds offering learning for pre-school, primary, secondary, adult and language learning.

Throughout the 1930s and 1940s, the United States developed radio learning services through large commercial broadcasters such as the National Broadcasting Company (NBC) and Columbia Broadcasting System (CBS) to create an 'American School of the Air'. Australia has its own unique history, in that shortwave radio was used in remote outback areas for two-way communication with learners. This was perhaps the first example of a national blended learning approach as asynchronous written materials, sometimes dropped by plane, blended with synchronous radio-based teaching.

Radio learning has also been of huge benefit in the vast continent of Africa. It has been used to cover sparsely populated areas where schooling, resources and teachers are scarce, as well as to provide education to nomads and refugees. Girls and women have been a specific target and subjects from agriculture to healthcare have been delivered, as well as teacher training. The spread of radio learning was helped enormously by the invention of the mechanical wind-up radio in the early 1990s, which dispensed with the need for electricity or batteries.

The ability to speak to millions means that radio has had enormous power in learning. To this day, it is valued as an educational medium for informal or lifelong learning. Documentary formats, interviews and current affairs are ideal for radio, and the audio-only format means a focus on the message as opposed to the medium, since visuals such as graphics, animation and talking heads are absent. In recent years, radio has received a huge shot in the arm from the popularity of podcasting, too.

Most of us learn to speak and listen without much instruction or teaching; reading and writing, on the other hand, take many years to learn. Audio could therefore be described as a more natural form of communication than writing, with the additional advantage of leaving our working memory free of images, allowing us more space for reflection, manipulation and generation of our thoughts. On the other hand, audio on its own is a poor learning medium in that it suffers, like all narrative driven media, from the transience effect, where one tends to forget what one has just heard. It can also suffer from a lack of imagery and the fact that one can read faster than one can listen.

Radio has undoubtedly played a major role in delivering formal and informal learning globally. Cavanaugh et al (2004) and Casey (2008) see radio as being foundational for the online revolution that followed. Video has not, however, killed the radio star. Instead, podcasting and speaker devices in the car and home are its heirs. Audio, if not radio, is enjoying a resurgence on smartphones, home devices, satnavs and other devices.

James Vlahos (2019) places voice at the centre of future technology developments, humanizing technology, creating frictionless interfaces and opening up the possibility of dialogue with technology. This is starting to be used in teaching and learning, not just in accessibility, but in ways not possible before, through text-to-speech and speech-to-text as well as chatbots that use smart AI.

Even after a century of popularity, as it makes the transition to digital creation and distribution, the radio maintains its status as a medium for both informal and deep learning.

Podcasts

Podcasts have expanded rapidly as a consumer medium and the popularity of those that offer in-depth learning, across a range of topics, has surprised many. The popularity of podcasts grew with the increased availability of broadband as well as easy-to-use editing tools, computers and smartphones.

The word 'podcast' is a combination of 'iPod' and 'broadcast', first coined by journalist Ben Hammersley in 2004. Some notable podcasters include Adam Curry, often referred to as the 'Podfather', who in that same year launched Daily Source Code, and Joe Rogan, who has become arguably the world's most famous podcaster and launched the Joe Rogan Experience in 2009, featuring conversations with a wide range of comedians, sports people, academics, businesspeople and writers.

Very much a 21st-century technology, podcasts came to life as a medium for serious content. A cultural phenomenon, they caught the imagination of consumers as a way of learning about a topic in some depth. In this sense they lean heavily towards being a learning technology. Their popularity surprised the learning world, as they provide a long-form medium in a world of short-form social media, usually delivered to a prescribed schedule. Rather than deliver short bursts of content, many podcasts deliberately set out to deal with a topic or interviewee in depth.

As with radio, podcasts are carried by audio only (although some are also on video), enabling the listener to listen and reflect without being flooded with visual data. The relative informality of the format also helps, as learning is often delivered as an informal discussion, anchored by a host or hosts interviewing guests. The fact that the listener feels part of the conversation makes it more intimate. They are also easy to produce, requiring just a good microphone, some editing software and a quiet room, and can be easily accessed via a number of platforms. This new form of learning can be enjoyed while engaged in other activities – one can run, walk the dog, cook, commute or drive while listening to a podcast. The ability to listen via a smartphone has meant that this has become the most popular form of mobile learning.

A good example of learning podcasts is the series on *Great Minds on Learning*, hosted by John Helmer. These are hour-long episodes on the history of learning theory, and they provide an in-depth look at a range of theorists, including cognitivists, behaviourists and so on. These are abstract subjects that benefit from this form of learning technology, as images are not required in order to understand these theorists.

Many traditional media organizations such as television channels and newspapers have launched podcasts, widening their digital reach. The BBC has created a specific brand 'Sounds' for audio-only content, that includes the *In Our Time* series offering hundreds of episodes covering history, science, philosophy and the arts. Both the BBC and other independent production companies offer podcasts covering a huge number of topics and genres, which are available to download or stream across a range of platforms.

Some learning technologies appear suddenly, without being forecast by futurists. Podcasts are one such example, which in this case crossed over from consumer podcasts. Their role is more in line with lifelong learning than formal education and learning, although some schools, universities and organizations are also now using podcasts to educate and train.

As with radio, the limitation of broadcast audio as a learning technology is its one-way direction. However, this one-way 'monologue' is beginning to give way to audio dialogue through services such as Discord, which launched in 2016. This is a VoIP (Voice over Internet Protocol) service that was initially used mainly by gamers, to speak and listen via headphones while still paying attention to a game. Discord uses servers that have channels. In games such as *World of Warcraft*, teams of up to 40 players need to be coordinated and have the necessary skills to succeed, so many channels are required. These channels are also used to teach beginners the basics of the game as well as providing tutorials to more experienced gamers. The use of VoIP means that hundreds of gamers can play together in teams.

In 2020, the technology widened into general use and is now being used in teaching and learning. Rather than being left behind, audio is at the forefront of new developments in learning technology.

Film

Films were first shown at kinetoscope and cinema exhibitions at the end of the 19th century. Before that, devices such as the phenakistoscope, praxinoscope and zoetrope had made moving image shows popular. One of the first moving image experiences, in 1874, used a revolving cylinder which was inspired by another piece of technology, the Colt Revolver. This showed Venus passing over the sun and was one of the earliest recorded learning films. In 1878, Eadweard Muybridge made *The Horse in Motion*, famously proving that a horse does in fact have all four legs off the ground when galloping. He used a zoopraxiscope, an early projection system.

When the Lumière brothers invented movies in 1895, they were created to amuse and entertain. *The Arrival of a Train at La Ciotat Station*, directed and produced by Auguste and Louis Lumière in 1895, features a single shot of a train coming towards the audience. It is said that the audience fled in terror, although this may well be an urban myth, as there is no evidence of this actually happening.

As film became an established medium, it began to be used in learning. In 1920, a (silent) educational film was produced by the US Government to help immigrants integrate into American culture and to encourage them to learn English. *The Making of an American* is one of the earliest known instructional films. More than 112,000 people are known to have viewed the film, which showed a series of mishaps, followed by the exhortation to improve oneself by attending night classes.

A very early and more ambitious educational documentary film is *Die Grundlagen der Einsteinschen Relativitäts-Theorie* (The Fundamentals of the Einsteinian Relativity Theory), a German educational film released in 1922. Part of this silent film was used in *The Einstein Theory of Relativity* (1923), directed by Dave Fleischer. There are short and long versions of this silent film, which was designed as a companion piece to a book by US astronomer, Garrett P Serviss, who also worked with Fleischer on the film. An example of an early blended learning experience! *Feind im Blut* ('Enemy in the Blood'), a Swiss-German film made in 1931, had another moral imperative – avoiding syphilis, while in 1938, the United States produced an educational film, *The Birth of a Baby,* which was considered unsuitable for public viewing on completion. The 1940s saw a slate of propaganda films related to the Second World War, and also the rise of the public information film. There was no stopping the medium, as cinema audiences were huge, and film was seen as a way to reach large public audiences.

Film in learning institutions

Almost as soon as films began to be released to the public, scientists began to study their effects on the human mind. Hugo Münsterberg, a Harvard psychologist, set out to measure physiological responses, such as pulse, respiration rate and blood pressure, to quantify the emotional impact of films. Münsterberg (1916) went on to produce one of the earliest works on the psychological effects on film.

Moving images in schools were often shown on film projectors. These were common in schools up until the 1980s when they were replaced by VCRs (Video Cassette Recorders) and VHS (Video Home System) videotapes. From the late 1970s to early 2000s, videotapes were available for purchase and rental and VCRs became common in homes. VHS tapes were used for children and adult learning, with a wide range of learning topics available from publishers.

Around the same time, portable video cameras began to be sold as consumer devices and these could be used for personal memories and special occasions. Entire VHS tapes, the size of a book, were placed into these cameras for recording. VHS tapes competed fiercely with the better-quality Betamax system, but in the end the cheaper VHS system won. Both were used in schools, colleges, universities and the workplace to deliver learning.

Video technology took a leap forward in the early 2000s when DVDs (Digital Versatile Disc) replaced VHS tapes. The DVD offered far better picture quality and both Philips and Sony (the dominant players in the market at the time) eventually agreed to work together to create a single format. DVDs became the dominant format in the early 2000s, followed later by Blu-Ray, able to store several hours of high-definition video. What all of these formats had in common, however, was their need for a screen and in schools, this was usually a television wheeled around on a trolley. All of which, of course, was eventually eclipsed by the internet.

Film has now been an important cultural medium for over a century. As a learning technology, its range of expressions and genres make it suitable for all ages and it has been used to teach drama, literature, history, languages, science – almost any subject can be conveyed via the medium of film. We 'go to the movies' to be entertained, but film's motivational pull and high production values have always made it suitable as a tool for learning.

Television

Television became the dominant, omnipresent, consumer medium of the second half of the 20th century, building technically and culturally on radio and film but lying somewhere between. What made it dominant was its presence in almost every home, watched several hours a day, seven days a week by the vast majority of the population. Yet television is not just 'radio with pictures' or 'film on a small screen', it became a distinct medium in itself.

Television programmes that include direct or indirect learning aims have always been part of broadcasting and have played a role in educating the general population, both informally and formally. As we saw at the start of this chapter, the BBC, one of the first major broadcast companies in the world, still has the phrase 'inform, educate and entertain' in its charter and is still heavily involved in learning at all school levels, as well as providing adult education and public service education.

In 1951, the University of Chicago pioneered large-scale instructional TV teaching for higher education, delivered to over 20,000 students, enabling them to gain a degree having only studied via television courses. In 1950, Iowa State University developed its own TV channel. While the 1960s saw further initiatives, many failed as they were used to deliver overlong sessions of classroom teaching or lectures, often dominated by talking heads, and akin to early film recordings of theatre performances.

From 1971 to 2006, the BBC broadcast academic programmes for the Open University (OU), usually late at night or at times outside normal programming. It continues to retain a strong commercial relationship with the OU today, and its academic programmes can now be accessed at times to suit the learner via a dedicated website which hosts both OU and BBC learning content. This is perhaps the best example of a relationship between a national educational institution and broadcaster and has stimulated a great deal of interest in using television in learning. In addition to its OU involvement, the BBC still creates specific, formal educational content for schools.

Community Cable Television (CCTV) and Instructional Television Fixed Service (ITFS) on the microwave spectrum were also used in the 1960s to deliver education within institutions, as this relieved the pressure of teaching to increased student numbers. The 1970s and 1980s saw a continued use of television in learning, in what were sometimes called 'telecourses'.

Another example of the use of television in education was Teachers TV, funded by the UK Government from 2005–11. This was a dedicated TV channel and website aimed at everyone who worked in schools, from teachers to support staff. It stopped in 2011 when the Government withdrew funding as, by then, it had become clear that the world had shifted away from synchronous broadcasting to the asynchronous web.

Informally of course, there are several strands of TV programming that contain educational content. Documentaries are perhaps the most obvious and have been delivered for decades on topics including science, the arts, astronomy, archaeology and history, among others. Channels such as The History Channel and Discovery have proven successful in informal learning, while there are numerous current affairs programmes available, as well as 24-hour news channels offering not just news but analysis.

Potential weaknesses

Television remains primarily an entertainment medium. Despite its massive penetration and use – according to Clay Shirky, worldwide, people watch an average of 20 hours per week – it is a 'vast wasteland'. He argues in *Cognitive Surplus* (2010) that television immobilized the post-war generation into a 50-year aberration, as a passive, lean-back medium that dominated our time. In contrast, Shirky welcomed the internet with its lean-forward, interactive culture.

Television was also seen as pedagogically weak. Neil Postman in *Amusing Ourselves to Death* (2007) describes television as a destructive force in learning. He saw television as a top-down medium, where the flow prevents the learner from thinking and reflecting on the ideas presented. Postman believes that we are lulled into thinking that we are learning and remembering when we are, in fact, simply watching and forgetting. He warned us not to see broadcast media as learning, as it strips away active, cognitive effort; dialogue was being replaced by monologue. He also thought that television destroys the idea of childhood, making children behave like adults and adults like children. It also confuses entertainment and amusement with learning. When *Sesame Street* was launched in 1969 it was greeted as an educational godsend, but Postman viewed the endless promotion of learning as fun as problematic, pressuring schools to be more like television. He quotes many examples of television programmes on which millions of dollars were lavished but which had no significant educational impact. Other critiques have included *Bowling Alone: America's Declining Social Capital* (1995) by Robert Putnam, who saw the post-war social fabric destroyed, in part by television. Jib Fowles *Why Viewers Watch* (1992) took this further, seeing TV as a form of social displacement or surrogacy, where real friends are displaced by imaginary friends in sitcoms and soap operas.

The 1990s saw the introduction of video conferencing and synchronous, real-time training successfully delivered using what was called VTT (Video TeleTraining). One-way and two-way video and audio was possible using instructors at a distance. This is well documented by Tobias and Fletcher (2000).

Television has adapted, to a degree, as the broadcast model gave way to more flexible forms of television and video in learning and later, provided on-demand channels. However, with the internet came a whole range of delivery options, including YouTube and social media platforms that could deliver video, knocking television off its 50-year pedestal. Despite the impact of the internet, television as a learning technology continues, despite plummeting viewing figures for younger audiences.

Video on demand

YouTube was a seismic event for television. It not only time-shifted viewing, so that things could be watched on demand, but included features and tools that encouraged user production of videos that they could upload themselves. Whole new genres emerged and the 'how to' video, along with recorded lectures, TED talks, explainer videos and a myriad of ways to use video for learning were now available. On demand learning, especially for 'how to' videos, were useful for all sorts of everyday practical learning. Sports coaching, expert interviews and content on every possible subject was available free, at anytime, anyplace, to anyone with an internet connection. Learning had shifted from being televised to being digitized.

YouTube EDU was part of YouTube and offered high-quality educational content, largely for schools. It failed, not because of lack of demand but the flawed idea that online lectures were the way forward. In fact, the one-hour lecture simply mimicked the scheduling of the classroom lecture. Online expectations and habits were different. The TED Talk, at 15 or so minutes, became the new norm and many shorter genres evolved. Despite this, the YouTube brand remains a global brand for video, and it has branched out into a consumer channel for entertainment and streaming. YouTube is also a learning platform, as it has one of the largest repositories of content in the world, with a good search function, private channels, uploading, editing, annotations and transcription services.

Also notable is the rise of streaming channels such as HBO, Netflix, Amazon Prime and the Disney Channel, who have literally transferred traditional broadcasting to a broadband service. Most traditional mainstream broadcasters now provide their own streamed, video-on-demand services, as people have time-shifted their viewing. This has made access to video for learning easier, enabling learners to search categories to access programmes of interest.

Social media and video

Another shift in the use of video has been the delivery of video through social media, such as Facebook, Twitter, Instagram and LinkedIn. These platforms deliver video in a very different way, which is more short-form and designed to encourage likes, comments and reposts. As the internet matured and consumer bandwidth increased, smartphones became common, so video has become easier to make, distribute and access. Video is now a medium embedded within social media, not just a medium in itself. Perhaps the biggest difference in video today is in length – short on YouTube and even shorter on Facebook and Twitter. The sheer volume of video now presented on these platforms has transformed how we see and use video for informal learning. A whole ecosystem of grammar, language and conventions have grown around video in social media and YouTube.

Video began to fragment with the arrival of the first major social media platforms, becoming one among a number of media types that included text, photographs, GIFs and emojis. Then in 2016 came TikTok, first in China and then available worldwide in 2018. TikTok differs from the mainstream social media as it has a focus on 15-second videos. It uses all the power of AI and data, both individual and aggregated, to deliver video in a social context, with content that is also personalized. TikTok also delivers formal and informal learning videos that show remarkable levels of creativity. This is largely user driven, although some output is created by teachers, and TikTok also collaborates to produce campaigns such as #LearnonTikTok. There are tutorials on almost every subject, along with 'how to' hacks and tips. It is clear that TikTok is experimenting with moving the platform towards more serious learning. This may be a sign that social media could eventually move in the direction of personalized learning.

In universities and other educational institutions, lectures are increasingly recorded so that they can be used for later study, especially for those learners for whom the language of instruction is a second language, are neurodivergent, have missed lectures through illness or simply need to study, take better notes and revise. Video also became much more integrated into learning platforms, such as learning management systems (LMSs), massive open online courses (MOOCs) and learning experience platforms (LXPs). Searchability has become important as clips are searched for and retrieved from within longer videos. Video is now episodic and can be played at different speeds, thereby increasing learner control.

In terms of video for learning, informal and enthusiastic narration has been found to increase retention, as is the use of the personal 'I', 'you' and 'your'. The big lesson in learning is that video benefits hugely from additional effortful learning, where the user has to actively respond to what they have seen in the video with tools that add exercises and opportunities to expand and reflect on what they have seen. Video is also being used in nudge learning, to prompt action and in branching simulations as a form of presentation and feedback.

Conclusion

Sarnoff's Law, defined by David Sarnoff (1891–1971), defined the scalability of broadcast technology as proportional to the number of viewers. Radio, film and television had the advantage of being learning technologies that could reach consumers in their homes and educational institutions. This advantage continues today, despite competition from other mediums such as podcasts and social media.

Advances in technology have taken audio and video forward as a medium and freed them from the tyranny of format, time and space, as they freed themselves from physical projection to broadcast, to broadband. They have also been freed from the restrictions of traditional broadcasting that required content to fit into half-hour or one-hour slots. They have also splintered into many more genres within learning, and are available on almost any digital device, in any place and at any time. This enormous increase in access has meant a huge increase in their use as learning technologies, as instructional videos and podcasts.

Despite this, the broadcast media of radio, film and television remains one-directional. The problem is not that television cannot hold the attention of the learner; it is the lack of effort required by the learner to engage in this form of learning. The transience effect and lack of effortful learning mean that it is easy to give the illusion of learning, as users feel 'engaged', but most of that is just a feeling, rather than any change in their long-term memory.

Video is now moving into another phase in its use for learning. Contemporary technology has meant far more sophisticated storage and search, both for, and inside, videos. AI technology is also being used to automatically create effortful learning from video transcription. Video on its own is rarely enough to provide a meaningful learning experience, but with additional functionality it becomes a more useful medium. It has also benefited from being delivered on sophisticated platforms that store, manage and record use, as well as allowing users any time access.

References

Casey, D M (2008) A Journey to legitimacy: The historical development of distance education through technology, *TechTrends*, 52(2), 45–51

Cavanaugh, C et al (2004) *The Effects of Distance Education on K-12 Student Outcomes: A meta-analysis*, Learning Point Associates, Naperville, IL

Fowles, J (1992) *Why Viewers Watch: A reappraisal of television's effects*, Sage Publications, Thousand Oaks, CA

Great Minds on Learning: https://greatmindsonlearning.libsyn.com/ (archived at https://perma.cc/T8QM-WGV7)

Kalyuga, S (2011) Effects of information transiency in multimedia learning. *Procedia-Social and Behavioral Sciences*, 30, 307–11

Lewis, T (1992) A Godlike Presence: The impact of radio on the 1920s and 1930s, *OAH Magazine of History*, 6(4), 26–33

Münsterberg, H (1916) *The Photoplay: A psychological study*, D Appleton and Company, New York

Postman, N (2007) *Amusing Ourselves to Death: Public discourse in the age of show business*, Penguin, New York

Putnam, R D (2000) Bowling Alone: America's Declining Social Capital. In L Crothers and C Lockhart (eds) *Culture and Politics*, 223–34, Palgrave Macmillan, New York

Shirky, C (2010) *Cognitive Surplus: Creativity and generosity in a connected age*, Penguin, London

Tobias, S and Fletcher, J D (eds) (2000) *Training and Retraining: A handbook for business, industry, government, and the military*, Macmillan Library Reference, New York

Vlahos, J (2019) *Talk to Me: How voice computing will transform the way we live, work, and think*, Mariner Books, Boston, MA

06

Teaching technology

We begin this chapter with a look at the technology associated with teaching that is used in the classroom and lecture theatre, a one-to-many, closed-door space, where the teacher is the dominant force. Over the centuries, teaching has produced a set of instructional technology, from the furniture in the classroom or lecture theatre to a whole array of teaching aids that shape that teaching environment. Teaching technology has been fairly generic and is found in most learning environments, beginning with the lectern and desk, then some sort of physical one-to-many medium to enable whole-class teaching. This began with the blackboard, then evolved into the overhead projector then the whiteboard, and today includes the electronic board (e-board), also known as a smartboard.

We then consider types of learning technology that are more subject specific, which were often invented by educators to fill a gap in the available teaching aids or to improve their students' understanding of a subject.

Finally, the chapter looks at the technologies of cheating and punishment. The implements used by teachers to punish learners, over thousands of years, may not be viewed by all as learning technology, but that is exactly what they are. For learners, the rise of 'essay mills' and the ability to cut and paste in order to plagiarize text has made it much easier for them to cheat. Similarly ingenious technology is now used by teachers to detect cheating, such as plagiarism software, as well as remote proctoring to invigilate exams being delivered online.

Classroom technology

Teaching technology has had a certain uniformity across the ages, from the obvious examples of technology used to teach reading and writing, such as slates, chalkboards and later, their electronic equivalents. But there is one exceptional, educational theorist who saw technology as more than just items to aid teaching and learning. Maria Montessori (1870–1952) saw technology as a primary force in her pedagogy and also designed technology to fit that pedagogy.

After qualifying as a physician in Italy in 1896, Maria Montessori worked with children who were experiencing cognitive delay, disability or illness. She noticed the inhibitory effects of what she saw as a strict and impoverished form of teaching. In response, Montessori set up her own school, the *Casa dei Bambini*, in Rome, where she developed a thorough philosophy to teaching and learning, explained in her book, *Montessori Method* (1909). This method has remained an educational alternative to standard schools in many countries around the world, although it has never completely achieved mainstream acceptance.

Montessori eschewed whole-class instruction. For her, the classroom was not a place of direct instruction but an open environment where small groups and individuals could learn. Children following the Montessori method are taught in mixed age groups with no rows of seats and desks. Instead, they work on mats or low tables, an interesting adaptation of furniture as a form of learning technology. There are areas designated to specific subjects and tasks, with specific physical materials that are used according to a method. Working with one's hand is fundamental to Montessori's vision of individualized learning and learning by doing. The method advocates child-led education and allows the individual to make their own choices and follow their own inclinations through self-directed exploration and play. The learning is not unstructured, just structured in a different configuration. Writing is taught before reading, using a phonetic approach, and assessment is largely through teacher observation rather than tests.

Montessori's idea was to design a school environment that is a 'home from home', with furniture that feels familiar to a child. School furniture and learning objects are not always seen as learning technologies but Montessori recognized that they are indeed an important part of the learning process, so all Montessori learning environments tend to have prescribed learning furniture and physical objects used to teach and learn.

Montessori's influence on individuals such as Sergei Brin, Larry Page and Jeff Bezos, who went on to revolutionize learning technology with the advent of Google and Amazon, is well known. Sergei Brin and Larry Page attribute much of their success to their Montessori education. They claim it made them self-directed, able to think for themselves and pursue their own real interests, not the interests of others. Jeff Bezos's mother describes his single-mindedness, so absorbed in the tasks he chose at his Montessori school that they had to drag him off to give him a change of task. Perhaps an early indication of the same, self-directed drive that led to the creation of Amazon.

Lecterns

That most visible symbol of the carry-over from church to university and conferences, is the lectern, the equivalent of the pulpit. It speaks volumes about the pedagogic roots of the lecture. Used in churches of many denominations to read scripture from the Bible and preach sermons, they were promoted, especially post-Reformation, into bigger and higher entities, as churches became places where one listened, rather than taking part in purely liturgical ceremonies.

Lecterns were used in schools and universities long before the advent of printing, when books were rare and had to be laid on the lectern to be read aloud by the lecturer. To 'lecture' literally means to read out. The lectern roots the teacher to the spot and encourages the reading of a lecture from notes or worse, verbatim, from sheets of paper.

It was only in the early 20th century that the word 'lectern' was used to refer to such furniture in a public space, such as a conference hall. Just as in schools and universities, the tradition of the expert preaching from a modern pulpit is reinforced.

Interestingly, it was the computer and other technology that preserved the use of a lectern in educational establishments and conference halls. It was adapted to hold a laptop in order to deliver slides and included a microphone and even audio-visual controls. The lectern is a clear example of a learning technology that has helped shaped pedagogy, on a global scale, although it is rarely considered as such. The lectern determines the very nature of keynotes by requiring the speaker to stand behind it, helping to proffer status. The use of microphones and large-screen projectors has enabled larger audiences to attend lectures, but the format of a talk followed by a much shorter question-and-answer session has become the convention.

Their use by politicians and corporate leaders has also become more pronounced, especially in the age of television speeches, conferring seriousness and status, often with the brand or name of the organization emblazoned on the front. Speaking from a lectern also allows easy use of a teleprompter, giving the impression that the speaker can deliver without notes, straight to their audience.

In a general sense, the lectern, whether used in a church, educational establishment, conference hall, press conference or on TV, is a staged appearance, a prop that suggests status. In a pedagogic sense it does the same but promotes teaching that is didactic, requiring the novice to listen to the expert.

Blackboards

First used for teaching musical composition (Owens, 1998) , the blackboard dates back to the 16th century, with the word 'blackboard' appearing in the mid-18th century. You are unlikely to have heard of James Pillans (1788–1864) but he had a direct, lasting and profound effect on teaching and learning. Although he did not actually invent the blackboard (chalkboard in the United States), he certainly popularized its use when he used one to teach geography using coloured chalks (which he did invent). Pillans was, however, the first to put slates together to form a larger surface. At about the same time, in 1801, George Baron, at West Point in the United States, did the same for mathematics (Ambrose, 1999). Blackboards quickly became popular in schools around the world, as the teacher could write, draw diagrams, outline maps, set tasks and so on, for whole class teaching.

By 1840, the technology had evolved from a flat piece of slate and instead blackboards were being manufactured using a polished wooden surface covered with a special black paint. Green paint was adopted in the 1930s as it was found to be easier on the eye and blackboards of this type were widespread in schools by the 1950s. Stronger, longer-lasting boards were also developed using porcelain and enameled steel. Eventually, flexible materials were used that could be rolled round in a loop, providing a larger surface to write on and the ability to preserve earlier written material. Some were put on wheels to be rolled in and out of position and in higher education huge, multiple blackboards are still common today. From the outset, chalk (actually gypsum) was used as a writing medium as it was easily available, cheap and could be wiped off with a damp cloth or felt covered pad. Wood and felt erasers to clean blackboards appeared at the end of the 19th century.

Blackboards continue to have a pedagogic effect on teaching and learning that prevails today. They changed the dynamic between student and teacher.

One advantage was the ability of the teacher to write things on the board that could be seen by the whole class, although the act of writing on the blackboard involves turning away from the class, so can also lead to less interaction with students, less dialogue and less of what could be called the Socratic approach to teaching and learning. The use of the blackboard led to more presentations by 'writing' and put far more focus on straight exposition by the teacher. The blackboard is essentially a broadcast medium, written by the teacher and seen by the whole class, but with the advantage of easy erasure.

There is barely a classroom or lecture hall in the world that does not, or did not, have a blackboard, apart from progressive schools such as Montessori schools (see above) and Steiner schools, who eschew whole-class instruction. Interestingly, something designed for classroom use has now migrated to restaurants, bars and even the home as an errand pad.

The blackboard has played a key role in pedagogy as it promotes what is commonly called 'chalk and talk' teaching. Interestingly, technology has evolved to reinforce this 'chalk and talk' pedagogy, with the introduction of further learning technology such as 35 mm slide projectors, overhead projectors, flipcharts, computer projectors, PowerPoint and whiteboards.

Overhead projection

Many of us of will recall teachers, trainers and lecturers arriving with boxes of acetate sheets ready to use with an overhead projector. A trapezoid shape would appear at the front of the darkened room, be brought into focus and then images would be projected, accompanied by a somewhat disembodied voice explaining all at the front of the class.

Overhead projectors do just that: project writing and slides by way of light that illuminates the transparency, then, through a mirror and lens that sits above the acetate on an arm, forward through 90 degrees to a screen. Despite the fact that the lamps needed for this form of projection were so powerful they had to be cooled by fans, the resultant image was often quite dull. Largely developed in the United States, the overhead projector gained popularity for its use in military training during the Second World War. Sales into schools were stimulated by the Federal Aid to Education budget in 1957, and they became universally popular with teachers and ubiquitous in education and training.

The OHP was designed for live writing as it sat at a comfortable height, unlike a blackboard. And as the text was projected, one could write at normal size, as opposed to holding up one's arm for long periods to write unnaturally large text on a blackboard. A further advantage over the blackboard was it allowed the teacher, instructor or lecturer to look forward towards the class, rather than turning round to a blackboard or, later, a projected PowerPoint. The teacher had a choice of using pre-printed acetates and/or writing at will and the acetate sheets could be viewed in whatever order was required, as opposed to the tendency to stick to a fixed sequence in modern PowerPoint presentations.

The overhead projector is still the heir to the blackboard and a teaching technology that supports direct instruction. As a dominant form of teaching technology for most of the second half of the 20th century, overhead projectors had several pedagogic advantages but in the end they were too bulky, had poor projection qualities and by the 2000s were being replaced by computer projection systems and interactive whiteboards.

Whiteboards

The direct descendant of the blackboard is the physical whiteboard, a dry-erase board with a glossy, white surface for use with non-permanent marker pens. They became common in the 1990s, eventually being (partly) replaced by the electronic or interactive whiteboard.

In the UK, the government has made a considerable investment in buying and installing interactive whiteboards in schools. In 2004, whiteboards were hailed as the technology saviour in schools by the then Secretary for Education Charles Clarke, a view also put forward by the British Educational Communications and Technology Agency (BECTA), but many, including BECTA's chair Andrew Pindar, saw them as expensive blackboards (Somekh et al, 2007). So, the UK ended up with more whiteboards in schools than European or US schools.

The technology is designed to improve teaching by taking computer content and interactivity into the classroom. Teachers can take and save notes and annotations, and lessons can be recorded for future use by students who may have missed lessons through illness or absence. High-quality curriculum content specifically designed for interactive whiteboards is also available for teachers. Their use for whole-class assessment and feedback from students, polling students or gathering answers to questions can improve formative assessment, as does planning and monitoring activities. A whole ecosystem has been built around whiteboards in classrooms.

The electronic whiteboard suffered, some would argue, from high penetration and low implementation. Marketed as an interactive tool, in practice it was, at least initially, often used as a souped-up blackboard. It is an 'interactive' whiteboard but its primary use by teachers was still direct instruction. Initially teachers struggled to use the technology in a meaningful way as few knew what resources to use and fewer still how to integrate the content into their lessons. Training was often inadequate and low bandwidth into schools often meant lag and technical problems, which teachers were not equipped to deal with. Lots of whiteboards stood idle with the return on investment not realized. An early problem was also the lockdown into the whiteboard manufacturer's software, whereas demand dictated common file formats and more open source software.

Research into their use as a teaching tool was mixed and studies that focus on student achievement that are truly rigorous and comparative are rare. Glover et al (2005) found a remarkable level of conservatism in their use, as teachers clung onto existing practice and teaching methods. They found that only 10 per cent of teachers used the technology in a transformative sense. Many remain underused, with little use made of their interactive abilities. As a mere adjunct technology, the whiteboard's potential has remained largely unrealized.

Clickers

One interesting move towards active learning was clicker technology. In Chapter 3, we saw how slates were used as whole-class feedback devices, when students were asked to complete a writing task and hold the slates up in the air for observation by the teacher. A clicker performs the same function electronically. It is a profoundly learner-centric piece of technology, which also happens to be an effective device for teaching. It can be used for polling, whole-class assessment, individual assessment, answering multiple-choice questions, short answers, peer assessment and even mood measurement.

Schools suffer from one major drawback: class size. Teaching is largely a one-to-many activity and it is difficult for even experienced teachers to know what is going on in the minds of so many students. Black and Wiliam (2010) claim that this feedback failure is a major problem in poor teaching. They recommend 'hinge' questions that allow teachers to assess whether what they have taught has hit home. Clickers allow the teacher to poll students or ask key questions to get anonymous or identifiable feedback. This feedback is important as it allows the teacher to identify whether actual understanding is taking place, before moving on. Failure can be a destructive force in learning when learners are exposed to embarrassment or even ridicule. From the learners' perspective, this type of interaction is challenging and forces them to:

- pay attention
- reflect on the topic
- assess themselves
- see how the class as a whole is doing
- get some help if needed.

Eric Mazur (Crouch and Mazur, 2010), who teaches physics at Harvard, has been using clickers to improve his teaching for many years. Rather than deliver long lectures without interruption, he stops at key points and asks diagnostic questions. These questions tend to be natural language questions that really test the underlying principles of physics, rather than just the application of mathematical formulas. Students answer using a clicker and if the resultant histogram shows that many of the class have not understood the point, he arranges them into groups so that peer-to-peer learning can take place. He then asks the question again, before moving on. The data he has gathered suggests that this approach has led to significant increases in attainment and many universities have adopted this approach. Note that it is the feedback process that is important.

Web-based response systems link teachers and students across the web and allow questions to be set and the results to be viewed. Several systems now exist, usually within webinar or teaching platforms, but also for use on student mobile devices. These can be used to poll or answer questions, and SMS messages can be sent giving a more detailed level of feedback. Forums can also be added that allow peer-to-peer comments and answers to questions. With the increasing availability of Wi-Fi, these browser-based solutions are easy to access and use and obviously superior to Bluetooth, infrared or radio frequency systems.

This simple piece of technology is one of the few technologies that were designed to inject interactivity into the classroom, normally a one-to-many teaching environment. The efficacy of the clicker, proved by the likes of Eric Mazur, has meant further development across a range of technologies.

Profoundly learner-centric, it provides a feedback loop that allows the teacher/lecturer to dynamically assess the effect of their teaching. Given the low cost, ease of use and pedagogic power of this simple piece of technology, it is surprising that its use is not more widespread.

School bell

An interesting peripheral technology that speaks of the regimented nature of schools and provides a clear example of the technology of timetabling, is the handheld school bell. These were common in churches to summon people to attend worship. Later, as churches began to provide a basic education to children, so the church bell became a fixture in schools to call pupils in at the start and end of the day. A whole selection of handheld and desk bells were available from school catalogues and were used in the late 19th and 20th centuries. These were eventually replaced by electric bells that are still used today, providing an audible and interesting piece of learning technology that is instantly recognizable to those that hear it.

Subject-specific technology

In addition to the learning technology described so far, teachers have always used individual apparatus to aid their teaching, the type depending on the subject being taught. For mathematics, abaci, geometry sets, slide rules, coloured Cuisenaire rods and calculators reflect the growing sophistication of the maths being taught. They also reflect more general mathematical and technological advances in society, from the purely mechanical to electronics.

The abacus is perhaps the oldest piece of learning technology, dating back to the Babylonians, who used sand tablets and stones to perform calculations, a skill that obviously had to be taught. It was the Chinese, however, who invented the calculating abacus as we know it. This was then adapted to school use and is still widely used in some countries as a learning technology.

Galileo Galilei invented what is called the sector, a ruler and caliper device, used to calculate trigonometric formulae and various number functions. John Napier, who invented logarithms, also created Napier's Bones in 1617, rods that could be used to perform multiplications and divisions. Square roots could also be calculated. But it was William Oughtred, a 17th-century mathematician and clergyman, who used the work of James

Napier to invent the slide rule using two sliding panels to multiply and divide (Cajori, 2018). He also developed the circular slide rule. Slide rules were then designed with ever more sophisticated functions and were used as a standard piece of learning technology in schools into the 1970s, when they were made redundant by the advent of the electronic calculator. There were even teaching slide rules over a metre wide that the teacher could use in instruction. Froebel's 'Gifts' were sets of cubes, spheres and cylinders, developed in the 1840s, initially used in kindergartens in Germany. They were designed to encourage play around mathematics and science.

Georges Cuisenaire, a Belgian teacher, invented Cuisenaire Rods in 1945. They were originally different lengths of coloured cardboard strips with accompanying booklets which were used to teach mathematics. Cuisenaire Rods were widely adopted around the world as a method of teaching basic arithmetic in schools, involving attractive objects that children were drawn to through play. The mathematical educator Caleb Gattegno went on to develop a form of visible mathematics teaching using these blocks (Cuisenaire et al, 1957).

Today, primary mathematics teaching benefits from aids such as beads to provide visual representations of addition, subtraction, multiplication and division, while in secondary schools calculators are part of the curriculum, and the electronic whiteboard provides an ideal way of explaining the steps involved in mathematical concepts and calculations. Solid state calculators became available in the 1960s, with pocket versions in the 1970s. In the 1980s they accounted for an astonishing 41 per cent of the world's consumer computing capacity. This had fallen to a mere 0.05 per cent by 2007 (Hilbert and López, 2007).

Geography has been taught using maps and globes for centuries. The Ancient Greeks first established that the world was a sphere, but it was not until 1492 that Martin Behaim, a German merchant and cartographer, constructed the first globe called the Nürnberg Terrestrial Globe. Despite the exploration going on during Behaim's time, his globe was fairly inaccurate, with no inclusion of the Americas, as it pre-dates their discovery. By the 18th century globes were commonly used for teaching and various types of cartographic information were recorded on them. Today, Google Earth and Google Street View provide the ultimate map, enabling teachers to show cities and landscapes to their students with a few clicks of a mouse.

Teaching technology to promote literacy has involved alphabet blocks and spelling and grammar textbooks. John Locke (1693) recommended 'dice and play-things, with the letters on them to teach children the alphabet by playing', which eventually appeared as alphabet blocks in schools. From the mid-19th century manufactured blocks were widely used in schools. The blocks usually had letters on one face and illustrations on the other faces, such as animals and objects.

Of course, all curriculum subjects require their own technology: art has a whole range of technology for the physical production of art; music requires equipment to teach music, such as instrument stands and sheet music, as well as the instruments themselves, while physical education demands the technology of exercise and sports equipment. There is a plethora of other types of physical learning technology, used by both teachers and learners, not only in schools but also at home. We tend to forget that there is a massive market for learners and parents in simple learning technology that can be used at home. With the rise of electronic technology, those learning toys and gadgets have become a huge industry.

Technology of punishment

To be exhaustive in our history of learning technology, we must also include teaching technology used to punish learners. This is a rather odd species of learning technology, and rapidly disappearing, but was in common use for centuries.

Writing is heralded in this book as the Big Bang of learning technologies, seeing writing as a solely positive invention, but that is to ignore its role in punishing learners. Spencer Schaffner (2019) shows that writing has been used to shame and punish throughout history, from the parades of people made to wear signs round their necks, to tattooing by the Nazis.

In learning, teachers sometimes ask the miscreant to reflect on their misdemeanor in the form of an essay, while homework may be set as a punishment. More common was the practice of getting children to write out a large number of 'lines' on blackboards and in notebooks. It was thought that this would simultaneously punish the child, as well as quieten and help them practice their writing. 'Lines' often had to be written in detention, after school. Widely satirized in *Life of Brian* and *The Simpsons*, writing lines still survives as a relatively benign alternative to corporal punishment. A Chinese student even purchased a writing robot to do his lines for him!

The history of corporal punishment in learning has a long history. Scribe schools in Ancient Egypt were brutal, with hippopotamus whips used to punish mistakes. From Sparta and Ancient Rome to British public schools, punishment was seen as a necessary condition for education. Spartan education was militaristic, and punishment (flogging) was common. Stealing, meanwhile, was seen as a virtue, with only being caught considered shameful, and the ability to endure pain a mark of courage. In Ancient Rome, schools had a range of technology for beating students including the ferula (birch branches), scotia (leather whip straps) and the flagellum (hardest leather whip).

In the 19th century and early 20th century, the pointed 'dunce' hat or dunce's cap, sometimes with a 'D' on it, was put on the heads of pupils who misbehaved, and they were made to stand in the corner, sometimes with their face to the wall. The name comes from the Scottish theologian Duns Scotus, whose followers doggedly refused to adapt to the new humanities, and so 'Duns' became a byword for stubbornness and stupidity. The word dunce first appears in the middle of the 17th century and a 'dunce's cap' first appears in Dickens' *The Old Curiosity Shop*. In Europe, the equivalent was a headdress resembling a donkey's ears, to indicate 'stupidity'.

Corporal punishment involving the use of a cane was also widespread until relatively recently, in schools around the world. It was widely represented in novels and films as a key aspect of British schooling. Rattan spanking canes, used for corporal punishment, came into common use in the late 19th century, when it was found they could deliver seething pain, even through clothing. Caning was usually carried out by the headmaster or teachers but also by prefects. Whips have also been used for centuries in schools. These were used in Koranic schools, not just for bad behaviour but for failing on simple recitations, rote memorization, reading and writing tasks. Some countries have their own cultural traditions of punishment technology. In the United States, spanking on the buttocks with a foot-long wooden or fibreglass 'paddle' is still legal in some states, mostly in the Midwest and South.

Many of us know the phrase 'to wash your mouth out with soap'. This was a real punishment, used by parents and teachers, usually for discipline infringements in the United States and UK from the late 19th to mid-20th century. In the United States, it was used to stop Mexican students from speaking Spanish at school, but its toxicity was found to be dangerous to health if ingested. In a study of 211 US students, Jay, King and Duncan (2006) claimed that this form of punishment was common, with an astonishing 20 per cent of respondents reporting this punishment by parents.

The 'strap' or 'belt' was the mainstay of corporal punishment in Scottish schools and wasn't banned until 1987. It was a thick leather strap, forked at the end and applied to the outstretched hands. I can still vividly remember the pain, burst blood vessels on my wrist and injustice of being struck for being late for school (it was the bus, not me, that was late!). The Lochgelly Tawse had the largest share of the market as it had no sharp edges, didn't wrap round the hand and was lighter and easier to use. As a piece of technology it was exquisitely designed as an instrument of pain and punishment.

The argument around corporal punishment in schools, as a method to punish bad behaviour and poor performance, has been raging for over two millennia. Even in Roman times, the debate raged over the corporal punishment of children. Quintilian (35–95 AD) was

> entirely against corporal punishment in education... it is disgusting and slavish... the pupil whose mind is too coarse to be improved by censure will become as indifferent to blows. Finally, these chastisements would be entirely unnecessary if the teachers were patient and helpful... And consider how shameful, how dangerous to modesty are the effects produced by the pain or fear of the victims. This feeling of shame cripples and unmans the spirit, making it flee from and detest the light of day.
>
> Butler (1969)

Quintilian addresses the main issues of corporal punishment:

- it is degrading
- victims become indifferent
- teachers need to find better teaching methods
- it demotivates.

Other arguments against corporal punishment include the possibility of showing that hitting others is acceptable, increasing aggression in children and possible trauma. These arguments were to eventually win the day and corporal punishment is now banned in many countries.

The technology of punishment, based on the pedagogy of retribution and deterrence, has long been part of education systems around the world. It was believed to be an effective tool, especially for bad behaviour, but it has also been used to punish failure and, at its most extreme, to instil fear and push the rote learning of set texts.

The practice was banned in England and Wales in 1999, Scotland in 2000 and Northern Ireland in 2004. Although it is still common in many countries around the world, its acceptance is waning, and we seem to be moving towards its eradication. It is useful to remind ourselves that technology in schools is used for a very wide range of practices, some less palatable than others. The technology of punishment was largely mechanical. Thankfully moral boundaries and the disappearance of corporal punishment in schools happened just as the digital age started.

Technology of cheating

In the Cotsen Children's Library at Princeton University, a Chinese silk text measuring 6 x 29 inches is covered in beautiful, miniature writing. It could be folded into a tiny roll and the text, 11 essays each based on a Confucian quote, reveals that it was used to cheat in the Chinese Civil Service Exams that took place from 650 to 1905 in China. It would seem that cheating in exams is as old as exams themselves.

McCabe, Butterfield and Trevino (2012) put cheating at around two-thirds of all college students. Many learners do not see education through the same eyes as those who deliver that education. They are there to get a credential, not necessarily to wholly engage in an educational experience, and therefore likely to take the path of least resistance and even cheat to achieve that objective. Their real objective may be to get a qualification with the least effort. Subject choices can reflect that culture – easy courses, with easy exams, are often some of the most popular in universities.

Methods of cheating

Some methods of cheating are simple but ingenious, like the false arm that leaves your real arm free to use your smartphone. Professional-looking labels printed and glued around water or drink bottles or cheat notes written on the inside of a drinks bottle label, revealed when the liquid is drunk, or alternatively contained inside the cap with notes on a set of circular paper inserts. Notes can be hidden on rolls of paper, inside erasers and pens or behind the slider on slide rules. They can be placed beneath band aids, nails, transparent stockings above the knees, on internal soles of shoes and in false thumbs. This list is by no means exhaustive.

Technological methods of cheating

As institutional learning has increased globally, an arms race of cheating has arisen, accelerated by technological advances such as the computer, smartphone and earbud devices. A growing sophistication among some learners, along with commercial services enabled by the internet, have led to mass cheating via essay mills and cheat sites. Of course, getting someone else to write your assignment has been around since teaching began. What is new is the ready access to this service, enabled by the internet. Almost any form of assignment from an essay to full thesis can be bought, often from other well-qualified students and academics. Campuses are leafleted and online influencers paid to promote this form of cheating, and it has become a huge global industry. Essay mills are now outlawed in some countries, but it can be difficult to detect, as freshly written work escapes plagiarism checkers. However, the effort it takes to put a student through the process of being found guilty of such behaviour and the reputation risk for institutions if the true level of cheating is revealed means that the use of essay mills is not being clamped down on in the way that is should.

Cheat sites for homework and assessments, such as Quizlet, allow learners to copy the solutions from the flashcards. Brainly, the app used for sharing school stuff, is used mainly for cheating, as is Course Hero. Chegg, one of the most valuable online learning sites in the world, has a database of millions of answers with thousands of experts on tap in India to provide answers, including all workings and quick bibliographies. Chegg masquerades as a service for students who need help when they get stuck, but is largely used for cheating.

Teachers often reuse tests and exercises from textbooks where answers have been provided online, which has meant that answers have been easier for students to find, too. In a sense, lazy assessment results in lazy learning. Students take the path of least resistance and can find answers with ease. In this cat and mouse game, the mouse is often well ahead of the cat. When learners get stuck on a mathematics problem, looking up a textbook often doesn't help, as the worked examples are rarely close to what is needed. Instead, what is *really* needed is help for that specific problem. This is personalized learning and an app called Photomath™ does it elegantly. Simply point your mobile camera at the problem – you don't even have to click – and the app scans and comes up with the answer and a breakdown of the steps you need to take to get to the answer. It is the convenience of the mobile camera functionality that makes it special. The app is simple, but we now see technology that is, in effect, doing what a good teacher does – illustrating, step-by-step, how to solve mathematics problems. The problem is that it is also used to find answers with no effort – which is poor learning.

The ingenuity of technological cheaters is revealing as it shows how technology is always ahead of pedagogy. Technical prowess is often in the hand of the young and their ability to evade checks has become well known. Examples include students obtaining teacher email addresses and passwords to access exam papers (Mirror, 2017). Others have hacked school or university servers. One Master's student made £20,000 by hacking into the University of South Wales' computer system, then selling exam answers to students (Barradale, 2012). Finland used a crowdsourced hacking competition, with prizes, to identify vulnerabilities in their proposed online exam system (Sulopuisto, 2013). A pharmacy student used a phishing scam from a website he built to hack academic emails, then impersonated those academics and asked for exam papers to be forwarded to him (Stewart, 2012). A medical student in India was even caught with a Bluetooth device surgically implanted in his ear (Sharma, 2022). Another method to catch cheaters using technology was more straightforward: a teacher ingeniously set an impossible question and seeded an answer on the internet to catch those who were cheating.

There is a whole set of websites freely available that help computer savvy students use sophisticated techniques to hack systems such as school servers. Advice on using technology, obtained via technology, is used to teach others to hack the technology of online exam systems.

Cheating devices such as micro-earpieces, Bluetooth pens, smart glasses with Wi-Fi, bone conduction audio, invisible pens with UV to reveal text, scientific cheating calculators used to search Google, big screen calculators that display text, even video and watches that display text – there is almost nothing that cannot be bought online. During an exam, screenshots of questions can be sent or shared through screen sharing to experts or paid services. Flesh-coloured, silicone and miniature earpieces are common, along with micro-cameras for photographing questions. Cheating technology has clearly been made easier through sophisticated technology that is small, cheap and easy to hide.

Attempts to counter cheating

Given the frequency of smartphone cheating, some have resorted to blocking mobile networks with radio waves that use white noise, so that neither sender nor receiver can contact each other. The problem of cheating using the internet was so extreme in Iraq that the internet was shut down for three hours on three days while national exams were taken.

> Outside of exams, mouse jigglers – devices or apps that 'jiggle' the mouse to make the learner appear active are now available. These became especially popular during the Covid-19 pandemic when there was an increase in online learning and home working, as some schools and companies were monitoring the amount of time people spent at their computer. Physical devices can literally jiggle the mouse every five minutes, set at intervals or randomly. However, organizations can now detect such devices or activity that betrays the user's attempts to pretend that they are actively learning or working.

The technology of cheating is complicated, as the fear of failure and other contextual factors drive learners to go to extraordinary lengths to succeed in exams. This is technology at the periphery of moral behaviour. It speaks about perennial problems in the world of learning, the pressures it puts on people, both teachers and learners.

Technology and plagiarism

An old adage is, 'If you steal from one author, it's plagiarism; if you steal from many, it's research.' For most of the history of education, learners were expected to memorize, recall and recite exactly what they had learnt. Only recently, with a change in expectations, have learners expected to be original and show not only understanding but critical thought. Plagiarism in education has arisen in tandem with this expectation that the student now produces original output. At the same time, the rise in online technology has made plagiarism much easier, with huge amounts of text online.

Plagiarism checkers use similarity criteria to find external documents online or in its database(s), and look for similarity based on a selected threshold. Another technique is to use internal analysis to identify sharp changes in writing style. Matching strings or text may seem like the likely method used but it is too time-consuming and expensive. Instead, sophisticated mathematical, statistical and AI techniques are used to identify suspicious passages. This is not clear cut as similarities may still be accidental. The problem lies with the inadequacy of the essay as a common method of assessment, as opposed to other more granular methods. Paraphrasing tools are available online, to evade detection by plagiarism checkers.

Technology is therefore used as the detective to catch the technology cheats. It is an area of rapid development, as advances in natural language processing bring more sophisticated tools to bear on the problem. AI writing software is advancing rapidly and can be used to create essays and assignments from scratch. Indeed, there are already recorded cases of assignments that have been created in this way being passed by academics.

Artificial intelligence tools, called Transformers, such as GPT, can already write credible essays on demand and, as freshly written text, are likely to evade plagiarism detection. This raises some interesting questions. At what point does 'AI assistance' become cheating? Is using a writing assistant such as Grammarly cheating?

AI writing assistance will blur the line between original and aided work. AI has also been used by the University of Copenhagen (2019) to create a program that can identify cheating with nearly 90 per cent accuracy, by comparing the text to a student's previous work to see whether it was written by another person.

Remote proctoring

Remote proctoring technology, which delivers exams online, has been around for many years. As there is no human invigilation, electronic methods of monitoring are used. This form of proctoring rose to particular prominence during the Covid-19 pandemic when most students could not travel to and sit human invigilated exams.

Face recognition, digital signatures and other biometrics can be used for digital identification. A 360-degree scan of the room is often requested before the student starts the exam, their computer and/or smartphone screen can be locked, so that they cannot see or access other content. Algorithms analyse recorded video for suspicious behaviours and this is reported to the instructor. More controversially, AI can be used to monitor behaviours and look for signs of cheating. AI can be used to detect eye movements, head movements, other voices (even whispers), keystrokes and others present in the room. Automated proctoring may even detect phrases, such as 'Hey Siri'. These systems can cope with internet outages and send scripts for marking to teachers.

However, even remote proctoring software that claims to be cheat proof has technically savvy students posting workarounds, such as intercepting the video feed, using pre-recorded video fed to a webcam, projectors that deliver questions unseen by the student's webcam, virtual machines to run two separate operating systems within the same computer and even hacking multiple-choice exams to expose the right answers. The level of technical sophistication that can be utilized is formidable. Such students are wise even to the possibility that cookies or records of the same IP addresses being used need to be avoided.

Predictably, remote proctoring has been treated with caution and suspicion – which is not unusual with disruptive technology. It is also ethically controversial around student data, the stress of being continuously monitored and discrimination against some groups of learners. On the other hand, it uses smart technology to free examinations to be taken by anyone, anywhere, at any time. This provides flexibility in a system that sometimes gives learners only one single opportunity at a fixed place and time to take a final exam, with resits only available months or even a year later.

Conclusion

Teaching technology has always been present in teaching environments, from the furniture in the room to the technology that could amplify to the whole class the thoughts and instructions of the teacher. Although pedagogically similar, technology has moved from the lectern to blackboards (chalkboards), to overhead projectors, to clickers and smart whiteboards. In addition, there has always been a wide range of subject-specific learning devices and technology used by learners in formal classrooms and at home.

Punishment by teachers and cheating by learners reveal the underbelly of learning technology. Instruments of punishment and pain show a somewhat dark side to teaching through technology and, although they are being legislated out of existence, are still common in schools around the world. They are a salutary example of how previously destructive approaches to learning have been made unacceptable by cultural change, along with more sophisticated approaches to learning. It is a clear example of a learning technology intersecting with changing moral beliefs.

Cheating is more complex and a permanent feature of assessment. The increasingly sophisticated methods of cheating being employed reflect a striking mismatch between traditional assessment methods and technological advances. Some learners have more knowledge of technologically-driven cheating than teachers and invigilators. Cheating has grown into a global industry and remains an area where technology intersects directly with learning. As online assessment becomes more common it is likely to lead to a re-evaluation of current forms of assessment. In the meantime, the cat and mouse game will continue.

We next look at a fascinating interlude in learning technology, the calm before the digital storm, in the physical and mechanical teaching 'machines'.

References

Ambrose, S E (1999) *Duty, Honor, Country: A history of West Point*, Johns Hopkins University Press, Baltimore, MD

Barradale, G (2012) A guy made £20,000 by hacking into a uni and selling exam answers to students, *The Tab*, 10 September, https://thetab.com/uk/2021/09/10/a-guy-made-20000-by-hacking-into-a-uni-and-selling-exam-answers-to-students-222500 (archived at https://perma.cc/VZH4-GRPD)

Black, P and Wiliam, D (2010) Inside the Black Box: Raising standards through classroom assessment, *Phi Delta Kappan*, 92(1), 81–90

Butler, H E (1969)*The Institutio Oratoria of Quintilian: Vol 1*, Heinemann, London

Chegg www.chegg.com/ (archived at https://perma.cc/TX5Y-BD6F)

Crouch, C H and Mazur, E (2001) Peer instruction: Ten years of experience and results, *American Journal of Physics*, 69(9) 970–77

Cuisenaire, G and Gattegno, C (1957) *Numbers in Colour: A new method of teaching the processes of arithmetic to all levels of the primary school*, Heinemann, London

Dickens, C, *The Old Curiosity Shop*, published in 88 weekly parts, April 1840 to November 1841, serial as part of *Master Humphrey's Clock*, Chapman & Hall, London

Gibbs, S (2016) Iraq shuts down the internet to stop pupils cheating in exams, *The Guardian*, 18 May 2016 www.theguardian.com/technology/2016/may/18/iraq-shuts-down-internet-to-stop-pupils-cheating-in-exams#:~:text=Iraq%20has%20been%20turning%20off,the%20country's%20school%20exam%20periods (archived at https://perma.cc/M9RR-264A)

Glover, D, Miller, D, Averis, D and Door, V (2005) The interactive whiteboard: a literature survey, *Technology, Pedagogy and Education* (14)2 155–70

Hilbert, M and López, P (2011) The world's technological capacity to store, communicate, and compute information, *Science,* 332(6025), 60–5

Jay, T, King, K and Duncan, T (2006) Memories of punishment for cursing, *Sex Roles*, 55(1) 123–33

Locke, J (1970) [1693] *Some Thoughts Concerning Education*, Scolar Press, University of Michigan, Ann Arbor, MI

McCabe, D L, Butterfield, K D and Trevino, L K (2012) *Cheating in college: Why students do it and what educators can do about it*, Johns Hopkins University Press, Baltimore, MD

Mirror (2017) Students caught hacking teacher's email account for exam papers after returning 'near perfect' papers. 9 February, *Mirror* www.mirror.co.uk/news/uk-news/students-caught-hacking-teachers-email-9784055 (archived at https://perma.cc/8KQ8-YYHV)

Montessori, M (1988) [1909] *The Montessori Method*, Schocken Books, New York

Owens, J A (1998) *Composers at Work: The craft of musical composition 1450–1600*, Oxford University Press, Oxford

Photomath https://photomath.com/en/ (archived at https://perma.cc/S6MK-N4WM)

Schaffner, S (2019) *Writing as Punishment in Schools, Courts, and Everyday Life*, University of Alabama Press, Alabama

Sharma, S (2022) Medical student surgically implants Bluetooth device into own ear to cheat in final exam, 24 February 2022, *Independent*, www.independent.co.uk/asia/india/mbbs-student-bluetooth-cheating-bhopal-b2021217.html (archived at https://perma.cc/C6HS-9QSL)

Somekh, B et al (2007) *Evaluation of the Primary Schools Whiteboard Expansion Project*, Department for Education, London

Stewart, G (2012) Liverpool John Moores university student hacked e-mails to get exam papers, 18 September, *Liverpool Echo*, www.liverpoolecho.co.uk/news/liverpool-news/liverpool-john-moores-university-student-3335199 (archived at https://perma.cc/42JC-SWR6)

Sulopuisto, O (2013) We're ditching paper exams – so please get hacking our IT, asks Finnish exam board, 15 August, *Zdnet* www.zdnet.com/article/were-ditching-paper-exams-so-please-get-hacking-our-it-asks-finnish-exam-board/ (archived at https://perma.cc/25R6-B9H4)

University of Copenhagen (2019) Tempted to cheat on a written exam? Artificial intelligence is 90 percent certain to nab you, 29 May https://science.ku.dk/english/press/news/2019/tempted-to-cheat-on-a-written-exam-artificial-intelligence-is-90-percent-certain-to-nab-you/ (archived at https://perma.cc/HE7G-8HXR)

07

Teaching machines

The machine age, which began in the late 19th century, saw the invention of new technologies; in particular, communications technology. The telegraph was the first electrical telecommunications system, invented around 1837, and by the 1870s, a network of cables crossed oceans and continents, creating a whole new way of communicating (Standage 1998). The telegraph used morse code and enabled people to relay news, send money and do business deals. The telegraph shrunk the world in terms of time and space, so that a message sent from London to Bombay took just four minutes, compared to ten weeks by ship. This was quickly followed by the telephone, with half a million in use by 1890 and 10 million by 1914, followed in the second half of the 20th century by the fax machine and eventually the internet. All of these technologies changed the way the world communicates forever.

Mass production and consumption revolutionized the world and prosperity brought rising levels of literacy and schooling, and yet learning technology, in terms of teaching machines, never really developed. Although innovative mechanical machines revolutionized how we worked, communicated, did business, travelled, waged war and entertained ourselves, mechanical innovation had a limited effect as a form of learning technology. There is a mismatch because mechanical technology cannot cope well with the demands of teaching and learning, which are essentially cognitive.

What is clear, however, is that the scientific and industrial revolutions that lay behind the ages of mechanical innovation were only possible because of writing, reading, books, maps, mathematics and technical drawing. Machines were not fashioned like clay pots. It was educated minds that imagined and designed mechanical innovations. They recorded their theories and sketched their designs in notebooks – a form of learning technology – before moving on to construct their designs. Inventors known to have used notebooks include Leonardo da Vinci, Galileo Galilei, Alessandro Volta, Thomas A. Edison, Albert Einstein, Nikola Tesla and many others. They had learnt how to use the technology of learning to come up with their ideas.

Teaching and learning machines

Mechanical teaching and learning machines arose in the late 19th century, but it was in the early 20th century that they started to be built according to pedagogical principles. Early attempts produced clumsy, mechanical devices without display screens, whose limitations were obvious. As the science of electronics advanced they became more sophisticated until, of course, the personal computer became the dominant driver of learning technology in the 1970s and 1980s.

Nevertheless, these early machines are fascinating, as they highlighted the need for the technology to reflect good pedagogy. The 19th century was also a period when the psychology of learning was flourishing as an academic discipline and some psychologists tried to embody their different pedagogic principles into the emerging technology, opening up debates on the relationship between learning and technology that are still relevant today.

Mechanical precursors

For over 2,000 years, from the Greeks and Egyptians in Alexandria to the Byzantines in Constantinople and subsequent Arab dynasties, craftsmen created highly imaginative, mechanical devices that performed fixed choreographed movements and tasks. These were usually created for political and religious rulers, to impress their people as well as visitors.

In the 18th century automata appeared, which really did seem to execute complex mental abilities beyond that of articulation and movement. Vaucanson's 1738 flute player really did play the flute, a complex skill that involved not only difficult finger movements, but variations in tongue position, lip movements and pressure of blowing. It could even go up an octave! Jaquet-Droz moved automata even further towards the emulation of the mind when he produced a draughtsman that could write (one of three automata built between 1768 and 1774). The creation of illusory, mental activity is still a dominant feature of humanoid robotics today.

Another important innovation was the introduction of 'cams', a mechanical device that converts the rotation of a shaft into linear motion. The mechanical Turk that played humans at chess was in fact a magical trick, but others produced amusing, even amazing creations. These mechanical wonders inspired pioneers like Edmund Cartwright, who went on to develop a mechanized loom for weaving in 1786, improved and made programmable by Jaquard in 1804. This prefigures two future developments in robotics – automated human labour and programmable intelligence.

We have already seen how the typewriter became a mechanical bridge between writing and the computer keyboard. The modern version of the typewriter is recognized as having been invented in the 1860s, with the first commercially successful machine being sold in 1868. Its QWERTY keyboard is still a feature of most mechanical and screen keyboards.

But it wasn't until the 19th century that mechanical devices were patented for teaching and learning. Mellan (1936) uncovered hundreds of patents for such devices, going back to 1809, although most were hand-cranked devices that offered little in the way of feedback. In 1866 Halcyon Skinner patented an automated spelling educational machine (Buck, 1990). A scroll, with pictures, was turned using a hand crank, so that one picture at a time was presented. The learner had eight keys, each one displaying the 26 letters of the alphabet and a blank. The learner turned the crank in an attempt to spell the word shown in the picture. George Altman also invented a scrolling device for teaching arithmetic, patented in 1897 (Benjamin, 1988). However, there were no feedback mechanisms in these devices, so they fell short of being 'teaching' devices.

The late Victorian era was a period when industrial solutions to make mass schooling more efficient were being sought. However, none of the devices described here were actually manufactured and sold in mass, so the slate, pencil, pen, chalkboard and books still held sway.

In 1912, US psychologist Edward Lee Thorndike sought to eliminate the distraction of wrong answers through trial and error (Benjamin, 1988). His box used cards that were inserted to find the answers to spelling or arithmetic questions, although he claimed it could be applied also to foreign languages, history, geography or any other subject. Serrated edges on the correct answer cards meant that only the right answer cards would fit to get the correct answer. Again, there was no feedback mechanism.

In 1913, another US psychologist Herbert Austin Aikins obtained a patent for a spelling machine that required the user to match letters to a shown object. He referred to Thorndike's theory as a justification for its efficacy, with the idea that wrong stimuli may lead to wrong learning (Benjamin, 1988).

We see here, for the first time, learning technology developed on the basis of a claim from the science of learning. Within a few years one academic psychologist was to patent the first credible teaching and learning machine – Sidney Pressey.

First teaching machines

There were many Victorian precedents, but one man stands out as the first inventor of teaching machines, Sidney Pressey (1888–1979). While at Ohio State University in 1915, he came up with his idea for a teaching machine, only to have to shelve the idea because of the start of the First World War. He eventually filed a patent for his machine in 1926. Pressey's vision was one where technology would revolutionize learning, with some tasks automated to reduce the burden on teachers. His was the first known machine to genuinely deliver content, as well as receive input and output feedback – the three necessary conditions for a teaching machine.

Pressey saw himself as an early cognitivist psychologist, decades before it replaced behaviourism as the dominant school in psychology, and saw learning not in terms of simple reinforcement but a more complex process involving internal cognitive features of the brain.

Refusing to accept the reductionist behaviourism of Pavlov and other animal psychologists and behaviourists such as Watson or Skinner, he had little time for behaviourism as it deliberately excluded consciousness, language and mental phenomena (Pressey, Robinson and Horrocks, 1959). The suggestion, therefore, that these early teaching machines were based on crude behaviourism is false; Pressey's teaching machines reflected his cognitive-based learning theory.

Old typewriter parts were used to build his first machine, which presented four-option multiple-choice questions. The user pressed a key for the right answer and the results were stored and displayed on a counter.

His second machine looked more like a small box-shaped typewriter with five keys. Using this machine was easier, as the learner simply pressed keys numbered 1 to 5. A small window showed the numbers of questions asked and a window on the side showed the number of questions answered correctly. The user had to keep trying until the correct answer was chosen before the next question appeared. The machine could be preset using a lever, so it would only move on if the learner got the right answer, or it could be set to assess their performance by recording all of their answers, both right and wrong. This was important as the machines could then be used for both teaching and testing. Pressey continued to refine the machine until the late 1950s.

Pressey's argument was that his machine was quick to use and gave immediate results – the learner did not have to ask the teacher to mark their work and provide feedback. This also saved the teacher time as it eliminated marking mistakes and freed them from the drudgery of marking, allowing teachers time to teach in a more inspirational manner. The learner could independently repeat the learning experience until they attained full mastery. Resetting the machine for the next student could be done in seconds and it coped with up to 100 questions. These arguments are pedagogically sound. An enticing attachment to the machine delivered a sweet once the learner passed a threshold number of correct answers, with the threshold alterable via a dial. All at a price of less than $15. Unfortunately, the Great Depression put an end to Pressey's dream of manufacturing a machine to provide individualized learning.

It is important to remember that Pressey had very specific views on learning theory, in line with cognitive psychology, and this was reflected in his design. He saw errors and the correction of misconceptions were fundamental to learning, hence his use of multiple-choice questions, with their wrong answers. Learning, for Pressey, was a complex process where cognitive structures had to be created through the analysis of errors, along with individualization, diagnosis and feedback. He believed learning was not a form of behavioural reinforcement, as with animals, but was a deeply cognitive process involving uniquely human mediation through speaking, listening, reading and writing.

Remarkably, Pressey was the first to define an early theory of blended learning, which he rather clumsily called 'adjunct auto-instruction' (Pressey, 1951). This involved learning thorough a combination of programmed learning using technology and human teaching. He never saw his teaching machines as replacing teachers, but rather as a way of extending teaching and testing and freeing them from the more mundane tasks of teaching.

Skinner's teaching machine

Joseph Ray of Tennessee had worked on a combination of instruments in the 1930s, using strips of tape and a binary correct–incorrect system with lights, but it was B F Skinner who, nearly 40 years after Pressey, grabbed attention with his own teaching machine, the GLIDER, in 1954.

Skinner had published an article on his idea for a teaching machine in 1953, which Pressey read. This sparked correspondence between the two and Skinner later acknowledged Pressey as the originator of the teaching machine, although there were theoretical and physical differences. Skinner claimed that his was a 'teaching' machine, while Pressey's was a 'testing' machine.

Skinner's radical behaviourism

As a psychologist, Skinner promoted a pure or, as he termed it, radical, form of behaviourism. Only observable phenomena, stimuli and their behavioural responses were allowed as evidence. Mental events were considered inadmissible, being subjective, unobservable and less verifiable. Learning, therefore, was the ability of an organism to learn to operate within an environment, using what Skinner called operant conditioning, where a behaviour, if reinforced through repeated stimuli, was more likely to be repeated. An important feature of this theory is that carrots are better than sticks – positive reinforcement is more powerful than negative reinforcement. Withdrawing a reinforced behaviour also leads to the extinction of the behaviour. One problem is that if one relies just on observable behaviour, then what is taken as evidence of reinforcement is the repeated behaviour itself and therefore the evidence is self-fulfilling.

A practical output of Skinner's behaviourist theories were his 'teaching machines'. Like Pressey's before him, they were a product of their time – mechanical but quite ingenious, even accepting open input by the learner, which is rare even today in online learning.

Disappointed when he witnessed poor teaching in his daughter's mathematics class, Skinner thought the teacher was ignoring almost everything known about learning. The children were being forced as a group, all at the same time, to complete sheets of problems with no immediate feedback on each problem, so there was no adaptation to the ability of the individual child. Skinner felt they clearly needed help and reinforcement as the teacher was not shaping the behaviour of any of the children in the class. He also observed that the learner often had to wait several days before receiving the results of their tests.

Skinner immediately started to build his teaching machine and within three years had developed his method, which broke down material to be delivered in small steps – what we now call chunking – and as performance improved, less and less support was provided. He called this programmed instruction. The end product was his famous, yellow, wooden box that contained a spindle for various rotating, paper discs. The questions were written along the radii of the discs and shown one by one in a window.

In the first version of the machine, the learner physically moves figures or letters to respond to a question and the machine recognizes whether the response corresponds with the correct answer. If correct, the next question is presented while an incorrect answer requires the learner to have another try. The learner cannot proceed until they get it right.

Skinner's second, more advanced machine, had a roll of paper in an aperture for the learner to write the answers to questions shown in another aperture. On pulling the lever, a model answer was seen, allowing the student to compare what they had written with the correct answer, without being able to change their answer. The machine punched a hole in the question, marking it as correct, so that it did not appear again as the presentation disc rotated. The learner continued until all the steps were correctly answered and when the disc rotated freely, the learner had finished that sequence of programmed instruction.

As the learning was structured in a series of small steps, hints and prompts could be used to maximize success, always with progress towards more complex knowledge. Pedagogically Skinner, like Pressey, saw his machine as providing quick feedback, free from error, with active learning. That the learner moved at their own pace was seen by him as an important benefit, allowing the machine to be personalized for each student. Skinner claimed that his machine-based learning doubled the rate of learning, compared to traditional teaching. He even went as far as installing a batch of these machines to teach science to his own students at Harvard.

As this was before the age of computers, most of this programmed instruction was delivered as books. However, Skinner's article *Teaching Machines* (Skinner, 1958) is still relevant today, as is his book *The Technology of Teaching* (Skinner, 1968), a collection of writings on technology and education. It was Skinner's analysis of the sequencing and feedback required that was so far ahead of his time.

Learning theories

Although the 19th and early 20th centuries were a period of mass manufacturing, the educational system and manufacturers remained stubbornly immune to the psychologists' arguments and commercial propositions. So nothing happened at scale, and few who work in technology for learning today know much about these early machines; they had no real influence on the work on technology-based, adaptive and personalized learning that came much later.

As serious psychologists, with deeply held beliefs about learning theory, Skinner and Pressey based their machines on very different assumptions. Skinner, the antithesis of Pressey, designed his teaching machine around positive reinforcement, so avoided the inclusion of multiple-choice questions where the number of wrong answers outnumbered the right answer (negative stimuli). Skinner saw this as weak learning and felt the study of wrong answers was a distraction and, more seriously, might seed confusion in the learner.

There is also a difference in their approach to interaction and feedback, with Pressey sticking to multiple-choice questions and their variants, while Skinner favoured open input. Today, AI is being used to automatically create Skinner-type open input content, but this is still rarely applied in online learning. It can be interpreted using semantic analysis of the open text answers and requires more cognitive effort than multiple-choice questions, where the answer is already given, as the learner has to think deeply and recall the correct answer. In fact, both turned out to be correct, with Pressey seeing error correction with feedback as a powerful force in learning (Metcalfe, 2017) and Skinner seeing effortful learning through retrieval as an important driver in learning (Brown, 2014).

Both Pressey and Skinner were convinced that education needed to be reformed, and Pressey called for an 'industrial revolution' in learning, based on the use of technology (Pressey, 1932). Sadly, he suffered a breakdown when his devices failed to sell and was deeply disappointed in witnessing the education system become closed to innovation. Skinner experienced similar disappointments and by the 1960s both Pressey and Skinner's mechanical teaching machines were largely forgotten. They were both right in their view that technology could significantly revolutionize learning, but neither lived to see the true impact of computers and the internet.

Importantly, the advantages which automated, computer-based learning now offer are much the same as they were 100 years ago, when Pressey built his first teaching machine. Indeed, there is renewed interest in spaced, deliberate and retrieval practice, learning in small steps (chunking), as these techniques have all shown significant gains in learning. Advanced, adaptive learning systems match the individual student's progress by resequencing the learning experience, optimizing the path the student takes, based on a mix of individualized and aggregated data. This keeps the student on course, at the right level of competence, neither pushing too far ahead nor making it too easy, either of which can reduce motivation and learning. Although there is no real direct link between these technologies and the early teaching machines, as some claim (Watters, 2021).

Mechanical to electrical

Skinner-like machines continued in small batch production in the years after the Second World War. Their content was carefully programmed to build, step by step, towards synthesis and complex ideas, and they began to include more complex branching together with audio and screen presentations. This was the post-war era of mass manufacturing and labour-saving consumer devices, where machines were replacing humans everywhere, from the kitchen to the factory. Mail order and door-to-door salespeople also led to teaching machines being sold directly to consumers.

TMI-Grolier's 1962 Min-Max Teaching Machine was a sleeker version of Skinner's machine. It had a moulded plastic pad and cylinder with inserted paper worksheets that taught spelling, maths, science, foreign languages and skills such as shorthand. The spelling course had around 3,000 questions and answers, with spaces to write in the correct answer, which were then turned to compare to the correct answer. With a minimum of 15 hours of learning, it included the use of prefixes, suffixes, contractions and homonyms, as well as proofreading techniques. It was marketed with the same benefits of learning technology today, that learners go at their own pace, get immediate feedback and can progress in the absence of a teacher. The manufacturer's bold claim was learn 'in half the time, with half the effort' and they sold hundreds of thousands of machines.

Although an array of teaching machines were designed, manufactured and sold to the public, they proved too simple, mechanical and difficult to use in classrooms. Some were specialist machines used to teach specific knowledge and skills. There were also corporate machines and the military developed and used their own specific devices. However, cultural resistance proved too strong and the teacher in the classroom, using old learning technology of writing and chalkboards, remained the dominant model. Teachers found teaching machines difficult to integrate into their traditional practice and often mistakenly thought they could do more than they promised. By the 1960s, these mechanical teaching machines had had their day.

Assistive technology

Assistive technology is an important but often ignored part of the history of learning technologies. It is a topic that would merit a book in itself, and has for many decades been providing access to millions of learners with visible and invisible learning issues. In addition to technologies that increase mobility and therefore access to places of learning, and general communications technology that opens up access to learning assets, there has been a long history of assistive 'learning' technologies. Those with sight problems (which eventually is almost all of us) benefit from technologies such as glasses and contact lenses. Yet although we see better with them, we often don't 'see' them as learning technologies, despite them having been around for two millennia.

Assistive technologies through history

Emperor Nero is reputed, by Pliny the Elder, to have used an emerald to read text (Jones, 1971). Rock crystal and glass 'reading stones' were used to magnify text in the 11th and 12th centuries (Rubin, 1986). Then, in the 13th century, reading glasses emerged in Italy. For centuries, reading glasses have helped improve failing sight, enabling people to read and engage in learning. Another landmark in the history of assistive technology, Braille, was based on a code called 'night writing' invented by Charles Barbier in the 19th century, who wanted a form of communication for silent, military communications by Napoleonic soldiers that did not require light. He met Louis Braille in 1821, who significantly improved the system for use more generally by the blind.

Assistive technology for those with reduced hearing first appeared in the 17th century, with the first ear trumpet, while the electronic, amplifying, hearing aid was invented in 1898 by Miller Reese Hutchison. Miniaturization through transistors and processors made the hearing aid small and more wearable in the second half of the 20th century.

Assistive learning technology

The history of assistive learning technology is neither one of steady, smooth progress, nor techno-utopianism. It is a story of technology used to help those most in need of education but who often find themselves furthest from it.

At the turn of the 19th century, French psychologists Alfred Binet and Theodore Simon wanted to identify children who needed extra help with learning. In response to a French Government Commission for ideas, they created the first IQ test in 1905. This was to have profound effects, both good and bad, on the education of young people. Binet wanted to measure the mental age of children, so that they could receive help to improve the rate at which they could learn (Binet and Heisler, 1975). The idea was not to focus on their problems but improve their learning to catch up with others. Binet and Simon claimed to achieve a full year of improvement using their methods.

The Binon-Simon scale was based on 30 tasks such as naming body parts, counting coins, recalling numbers, defining words and identifying missing words in sentences. The tasks were designed to identify understanding, rather than recall of facts, to give a mental age based on the results. In 1911, William Stern, a German psychologist, took this mental age and divided it by real age to produce a 'Mental Quotient'. In the United States, Louis Terman then multiplied this quotient by 100 to create an Intelligence Quotient (IQ). It is important to remember that Binet and Simon were evidence-based scientists who did not believe that intelligence was wholly inherited and fixed – we see here a genuine attempt to level up those who faced difficulties in learning.

Cyril Burt, an English educational psychologist, took the opposite view and convinced the government of the day not to use levelling up measures (Joynson, 1989). He wanted to implement the 11+ exam, which determined admission to grammar and other secondary schools and is still in use in some parts of England and Northern Ireland. At age 10 or 11, children take an IQ test that separates them out into two groups, with one group going to a selective school. IQ was therefore used in a more instrumental manner, not to help but hinder the education of the majority.

In the face of this tendency for schooling systems to stream, select and focus attention on brighter students, assistive learning technology has taken us back to Binet and Simon's goal of supporting learners who need additional help. This covers a huge number of learners who are now referred to as neurodiverse, encompassing those with dyslexia, autism and other delayed development issues, as well as learners who are deaf or blind and others with physical learning difficulties.

Telephone as assistive technology

Alexander Graham Bell's wife and mother were both deaf, and his work on hearing devices inspired him to invent the telephone. Of course, the telephone as an instrument for teaching and learning is not much practical use for people who are deaf. Bell himself refused to have one in his study and never really saw it as a device for simply talking to each other. Oddly, he was far more interested in its cultural potential to broadcast orchestral music and sermons. In 1876, the year Bell obtained his patent, *The New York Times* reported that the new telephone:

> cannot fail to prove of great interest to musicians, and, indeed, to the general public... it can be used to transmit either the uproar of a Wagnerian orchestra or the gentle cooing of a female lecturer... By means of this remarkable instrument... many persons will prefer to hear lectures and sermons in the comfort and privacy of their own rooms, rather than to go to the church or the lecture-room.
>
> *The New York Times* (1876)

Of course, people immediately took to the telephone as a device for talking to each other. That is what drove the dramatic rise in the number of telephones, from 230 in 1877 to 10 million by 1914, and it was in 1919 that the first real application of the telephone for teaching and learning occurred (Fischer, 1994). Just as the Covid-19 pandemic led to the mass use of video conferencing such as Zoom, the 1918 Spanish Flu pandemic led to the first use of the 'teaching telephone' in Long Beach California, although the phone system was unable to keep up with the demand so it didn't result in any large-scale adoption at that time (McCracken, 2020). One niche audience, however, did use the telephone to learn. In 1939, Iowa's Department of Education began using a teach-a-phone system to link teachers with infectious or seriously ill pupils, not only to be taught but also to enable them to listen to their fellow students' sports games and concerts. By 1953, 43 states were subsidizing telephone teaching systems, often supported by charities. One user of the system, Frank Huettner Jr of Bloomer, Wisconsin, had been paralyzed in a road accident involving his school bus, but became the first person to both graduate from high school and law school by telephone (McCracken, 2020).

By 1962, the Bell Telephone Company had a School-to-Home Telephone System with a specific home device with a speaker and switch for speaking back. It was fed directly into the classroom. By 1964, there were 15 tele-teaching centres in Los Angeles using dedicated phone lines on automatic dialers, each supporting 15 to 20 students, over dedicated one-way phone lines and rented speakerphones. In New York City, the authorities provided blended learning, with students listening to lessons on the radio, then discussing the lesson on the telephone. It was called the 'High School of the Air'. These systems persisted into the early 1980s (McCracken, 2020).

The Open University in the UK used the telephone for tutorials and teacher student interaction from 1973 and there were brief flirtations with audio conferencing systems, but in the end telephony ended up being the stepping stone to the internet and all of the video conferencing tools we use today. As the Covid-19 pandemic brought the world to a virtual standstill, these tools, once again, became a saviour for teachers and students alike.

Assistive computer technology

It was in the 1970s, with the rise of the microprocessor and computer, that assistive technology, both general and specific to learning, began to have a direct and hugely beneficial impact on people with disabilities. By 1976, Ray Kurzweil had assembled his Kurzweil Reading Machine for the blind that could scan text then produce text-to-speech. Cochlear implants, which were first developed in the 1950s and 1960s, were made practically possible with the modern multi-channel implants appearing in the late 1980s.

ASSISTIVE TECHNOLOGY FOR BLIND AND VISUALLY IMPAIRED PEOPLE

At its simplest, learning technology for people who are blind may simply connect them to volunteers who can provide help to deal with say, computer viruses. Be My Eyes is one such service, which employs hundreds of volunteers. Other assistive technologies for those who are blind include personal assistants such as Siri, Google Assistant and Alexa, which provide access to knowledge and services via smart speakers.

Screen magnifiers are available that allow the user to pan from side to side or zoom in and out to enlarge items on the screen. Subtitling and customization of text is also possible. Gesture control, which recognizes and interprets the user's movements in order to interact with the computer system, is available. There are even adjustments on the preferred speaking rates of voice assistants. Requests such as to-do lists can be set up, and a blind person can even show commonly packaged food in cans and wrapping, which are difficult to tell apart with just touch, to their webcam to identify their contents. Voice activated calls can be made and a vast number of audio books are now available online. Learning worlds, once only available to some, are now available to those who are blind or who have visual impairments.

The smartphone also brought a wide range of assistive learning technologies, usually free, together into one mobile device, and apps have also been a boon, as websites in themselves often fail in terms of their accessibility. Of course, other additional technologies are needed, such as refreshable Braille displays, touch free control and so on, but it is clear that huge advances have been made in terms of the sophistication, cost and availability of assistive learning technologies for people who are blind or visually impaired.

ASSISTIVE TECHNOLOGY FOR NEURODIVERSE PEOPLE

It is not just people with visual and hearing impairments that have benefitted. People with dyslexia, attention deficit hyperactivity disorder (ADHD) and those with autism spectrum disorder (ASD) have also seen an increase in the range of learning technologies available to support their specific needs.

Dyslexia creates problems for learners as it disrupts fluent reading, spelling and writing, as well as planning and organization of work, such as essays and assignments. It is more common than many realize, with some estimates suggesting it affects as many as 1 in 10 of the population, and it is a trait that is often identified in successful entrepreneurs. Tools to assist those with dyslexia have become widely available, along with the supportive use of emojis, voice chat and multimedia messaging. Speech-to-text and text-to-speech software is now on computers. Programs such as Microsoft Word or Google Docs allow the user to set different background colours on documents. The most commonly used web browsers also have screen tinting, 'reading mode' options or free extensions that allow the screen to be tinted. Physical monitor overlays can also be used to alter the screen appearance. Text and icons can be made larger, and voice control reduces the need for dependence on physical input devices. Head pointers have also been developed.

Technology cannot cure dyslexia, but can help overcome the difficulties it creates. Text-to-speech software reduces the need to read text, so is invaluable. When it is necessary to read something, it can be helpful to change the font style, font size and colour and background colours, as well as the size of spaces between rows. Optical character recognition (OCR) is a technology that can scan text into a device for text-to-speech software. Reading pens have been developed that scan printed documents and read them aloud, and many have in-built dictionaries that provide spoken definitions of words. To assist with writing, word processing programs provide spellcheckers, predictive text and grammar checkers. Voice assistants are also useful.

For many years, the solution for learners in schools, colleges and universities who experienced difficulties in making notes was to provide peer note takers. This took away agency from the learner, increasing their dependency on others. Software such as Glean has reduced that dependency, enabling those with dyslexia, ASD, ADHD, anxiety, depression or physical disabilities to record, capture and subsequently organize, refine and integrate their notes into their learning.

ASD, which may include sensitivity around sensory overload or cognitive rigidity, has also benefited from learning technology, which provides a window into learning that is personal but without the exposure to the issues found in busy classrooms. Augmentative and alternative communication (AAC) is used to increase communication, social skills and interactions. Tablet technology with images and speech are used to encourage and teach children to talk. Tablets and smartphones can also help with a range of other communication and behavioural activities. Many of these learners acquire skills and find employment in IT as they become focused and skilled systematic thinkers. In the workplace those with ASD often find that assistive technology helps them find communications methods they feel comfortable with.

ASSISTIVE TECHNOLOGY FOR COGNITIVE ISSUES

Loneliness and cognitive issues such as dementia and Alzheimer's are starting to be addressed by assistive technology. Digital Voice works with people who are often excluded from digital media. They run a project called LifeBook for older people, particularly those with dementia, to create a digital book that contains their memories and old family photos, providing a digital story of their life that they can then share with others. Dementia is a cognitive problem that benefits from technology, with tools now available on tablets to help those with memory loss to recall important information and links related to their schedule, health, family and support groups. Prompts, buttons and tools that make interfaces and communications easier have led to improvements for those with cognitive issues and their families and carers. Similar, specific tools are available for most neurological disorders.

Web accessibility guidelines

In addition to hardware and software advances, web content accessibility has received international attention, with guidelines and laws emerging over the last 20 years. Web accessibility guidelines were first put forward by Gregg Vanderhofen in 1995, prompted by Mike Paciello and Tim Berners-Lee at a conference in 1994. These evolved into the Unified Web Site Accessibility Guidelines from the University of Wisconsin-Madison. Its eighth version in 1998 formed the basis of the World Wide Web Consortium's (W3C) Web Content Accessibility Guidelines (WCAG).

WCAG 1.0 was published in 1999 and has now developed into WCAG 2.0, with mobile phones and other devices also being covered. In many countries, these recommendations have been enshrined in law. Most of the large technology companies including IBM, Apple, Microsoft, Google and Amazon are active in supporting accessibility.

Simulators

Returning now to teaching machines, the flight simulator is another example of a mechanical training machine, developed after the first flight in 1903. The first flight simulator was the French Antoinette Barrel (literally a barrel cut in half!), which appeared in 1910, while the First World War provided an urgent need for such training, as firing from an aircraft was tricky.

A flight simulator called the Link Trainer first appeared in 1929, powered by pneumatic bellows and vacuum motors and designed to teach pilots to fly by instruments. However, sales didn't take off until 1934, when the US Postal Service purchased a number of the simulators as a result of losing pilots flying in bad weather. The Second World War led to 10,000 Link Trainers being purchased to train 500,000 new pilots, with almost all US pilots being trained in a Link Trainer.

The first commercial flight simulators were purchased in 1954 by United Airlines, and it has now developed into a vast global industry and an integrated part of pilot training. Computer game flight simulators have also been developed and used in training.

Aviation has led the way in simulation, but simulators are also used in areas such as medicine. Wax models have been used for centuries in medical education as wax is malleable and realistic. Guillaume Desnoues, a French surgeon, created and sold anatomical models at the start of the 18th century, but they came of age in the 19th century when anatomy teaching was widespread and a shortage of cadavers meant models were needed to simulate anatomy. Models incorporated detachable organs or realistic wounds, and as well as being used to teach anatomy, they were used for diagnosis and to teach amputation. Many medical teaching institutions now have entire medical simulation departments, with realistic mannequins and sophisticated functionality, and the use of VR and AR is becoming widespread.

Conclusion

There are several lessons we can learn from the history of learning technology. First, that the cultural inertia against the use of technology in education is as strong today as it was in the 19th and 20th centuries. Second, that learning technology, if it is to teach effectively, should provide the presentation of material, cognitive interaction *and* feedback. Third, that marking is an area suitable for automation, freeing up teacher time to do more and better teaching. One area where learning technology has proved particularly successful is in its application as assistive technology and in the field of simulation.

The next chapter looks at the rise of the personal computer and the internet, which have their origins in the original calculating machines. Algorithms are the workhorses of calculating machines, developed by Pascal (1641), then Leibniz (1671) and much later Babbage (1812). The phrase 'calculating machine' may give the wrong impression, as what even early calculators could do is implement lengthy operations and approximations to a solution. But it was Babbage's calculating machine in 1882 that was the real breakthrough, paving the way for computers and computer-based learning.

While these mechanical devices were being designed and built another technological revolution was taking place in parallel, one that was to have a profound impact on teaching and learning. From the 1930s onwards, the rapidly developing field of electronics began to enable computation. It was computers that were to provide the hardware and, more importantly, the flexibility of software, logic and media presentation abilities that form the real evolutionary path for technology-based learning.

As we shall see next, the 1970s saw the rise of the personal computer that would eventually lead to actual teaching machines in the form of desktop computers, laptops, tablets and smartphones. A confluence of hardware and software that would be manufactured and bought by billions of consumers on a global scale using that global network – the internet. We see here the start of machines and computation to solve learning's largest problem – how to scale teaching.

References

Benjamin, L T (1988) A history of teaching machines, *American Psychologist,* 43(9) 703–12

Binet, A and Heisler, S (trans) (1975) *Modern Ideas About Children*, Suzanne Heisler, Menlo Park, CA

Brown, P C (2014) *Make it Stick,* Harvard University Press, Cambridge MA

Buck, G H (1990) A History of Teaching Machines, *American Psychologist,* 45(4), 551–2

Digital Voice www.digitalvoice.org.uk/ (archived at https://perma.cc/F9T8-KYMC)

Fischer, C S (1994) *America Calling: A social history of the telephone to 1940*, University of California Press, Oakland, CA

Joynson, R B (1989) *The Burt Affair*, Routledge, New York

McCracken, H (2020) Before Zoom and Coronavirus, How the Telephone Became the 20th Century's Most Successful Remote-Learning Technology for Homebound Students, 21 July, *The 74,* www.the74million.org/article/how-the-telephone-became-the-20th-centurys-most-successful-remote-learning-technology-for-homebound-students/ (archived at https://perma.cc/V9K7-CDHD)

Mellan, I (1936) Teaching and educational inventions, *The Journal of Experimental Education*, 4(3), 291–300

Metcalfe, J (2017) Learning from errors, *Annual Review of Psychology*, 68, 465–89

New York Times (1876), The Telephone, 22 March, *The New York Times*

Pliny and Jones, W H S (trans) (1971) *Natural History Volume VII*, Loeb Classical Library, Harvard University Press, Cambridge MA

Pressey S L (1932) A third and fourth contribution toward the coming 'industrial revolution' in education, *School and Society*, 36(934), 668–72

Pressey S L (1951) Teaching machines (and learning theory) crisis, *Journal of Applied Psychology* 47, 1–6

Pressey, S L, Robinson, F P and Horrocks, J E (1959) *Psychology in Education*, Harper, New York

Rubin, M L (1986) Spectacles: Past, present, and future, *Survey of Ophthalmology*, 30(5), 321–7

Skinner, B F (1958) Teaching machines, *Science*, 128(3330) 969–77

Skinner, B F (1968) *The Technology of Teaching*, Appleton-Crofts, New York

Standage, T (1998) *The Victorian Internet: The remarkable story of the telegraph and the nineteenth century's online pioneers*, Phoenix, London

Watters, A (2021) *Teaching Machines: The history of personalized learning*, MIT Press, Cambridge, MA

08

Computers and the internet

Personal computing devices and global connectivity across the internet have transformed the world's economy. They have also rapidly and irreversibly altered the learning landscape. Since its inception, 50 years ago, the personal computer is now used by half the population of the world, and that reach is growing exponentially. It is an extraordinary story of innovation and scale that touches all areas of human endeavour, not least learning. This technology is intrinsically learning technology, and ranges from low levels of communication and connection to the full delivery of formal learning. However, learning should not be seen only as the result of formal teaching, teaching technology or teaching machines, as explored in the last two chapters, because teaching is not a necessary condition for learning.

Informal learning

Most learning, acquired across a lifetime, is done by people themselves through informal learning. Learning theorists view learning as continuous – a personal and informal process – not only obtained through formal teaching. Incidental and informal learning was first described in the 1930s (Tolman and Honzik, 1930), with further research by Marsick and Watkins (1990) and Gery (1991) on incidental and unintentional learning. Cross (2006) describes the impact of the computer, internet and social media, media sharing through YouTube and knowledge bases such as Wikipedia, as well as fast, cheap and ubiquitous connectivity, as essential to informal learning and the acquisition of knowledge and skills.

This instant access to knowledge and skills has changed the learning landscape away from formal teaching and experts and towards learner-driven experiences, even though users may not see it as learning. Search engines, social media, Amazon, YouTube and other content services deliver personalized, tiled services, mediated by smart AI. This is happening in learning, from smart learning platforms to services such as Duolingo, and in almost all services delivered online.

The personal computer brings together several of the technologies we have examined so far – the television screen, the QWERTY keyboard and the storage of information previously found only in books. With peripherals like storage devices and printers, the computer is its own potential library and printing press. As a learning device, it has brought together personal agency in the form of creation, communication and interaction by the learner, with scalable smart content and resources. It is an example of a combination of technologies that were decades in the making, and its impact can be compared to the transition from writing to printing.

The advent of the internet means the planet suddenly now has one central nervous system that links billions of people via technology. It has taken all that has gone before and made it possible to access all media abundantly on one network. As discussed in Chapter 1, the internet's use as a learning platform was also fueled by some laws defining rates of change:

- Moore's Law – which showed that computer chips became cheaper as they became more powerful, helped to drive the computer industry.
- Metcalfe's Law – which stated that the power of a network increases rapidly as its nodes increase drove the internet.
- Reed's Law – which stated that the power of a network increases in relation to the human groups using it.

The internet has transformed the learning landscape in ways we are only just beginning to comprehend. Almost all formal learners are also online learners, and almost everyone who is online has used the internet to learn. It is an unstoppable and irreversible transformation that determines *what* we learn, *where* we learn and *how* we learn.

Personal computer visionaries

Vannevar Bush (1890–1974)

Vannevar Bush was a US inventor and engineer who claimed his leadership qualities came from his family, who were sea captains and whalers. He was a practical man with many inventions and dozens of patents to his name. In addition to his Differential Analyzer, he was an administrator and visionary who not only created the environment for much of US technological development during and after the Second World War (which would eventually lead to the creation of the internet), but also gave us a powerful and influential vision for what eventually became the world wide web.

Bush built his analogue Differential Analyzer, arguably the first computer, in 1931. It was an analogue electrical-mechanical device the size of a small room, able to solve equations with up to 18 variables. A more digital mindset had begun in the late 1930s and further developments in technology began to emerge when the English engineer, Tommy Flowers, used vacuum tubes together with on-off electrical switches to create Colossus. A century after Babbage, the concept of the modern computer was born.

At the same time, Alan Turing (1936) saw computing in terms of a 'mechanical process' with his concept of a *logical computing machine*. That same year, Claude Shannon (1938) at Bell Labs brought binary and Boolean mathematics and electronic circuits together. He realized that on-off switches, binary states, could execute Boolean operations. In other words, mathematics could be executed electronically through switches as logic gates, and with his now famous line 'It is possible to perform complex mechanical operations by means of relay circuits', the digital age was born.

Subsequent pioneers such as George Stibitz, Howard Aiken, Konrad Zuse and John Vincent Atanasoff melded a sound knowledge of mathematics with the practical knowledge of the engineer to make advances in prototype computers (as we now know them) that had processing and memory capabilities. This led to the development of the personal computer in the 1970s and was the foundation of the vast industry it is today.

Bush saw basic science, especially physics, as the bedrock of innovation. It was technological innovation, he thought, that led to better work conditions: 'Advances in science when put to practical use mean more jobs, higher wages, shorter hours, more abundant crops, more leisure for study, for learning how to live without the deadening drudgery which has been the burden for the common man for ages past.' (Bush, 1945). His post-war report saw the founding of the National Science Foundation, and Bush's triad model of government, private sector and universities became the powerhouse for America's post-war technological success. Research centres such as Bell labs, RAND Corporation, SRI and Xerox PARC were bountiful in their innovation, and all contributed to that huge invention called the internet.

Bush was also fascinated with the concept of augmented memory, and in his wonderful essay *As We May Think* (1945) he described the idea of a 'Memex'. It was a vision he came back to time and time again: the storage of books, records and communications, an immense augmentation of human memory that could be accessed quickly and flexibly – basically what is now the internet and world wide web. Fundamental to Bush's vision was the associative trail – the creation of new trails of content by linking them together in chained sequences of events, with personal contributions as side trails. Here we see the concept of hyperlinking and personal communications, which Bush saw as mimicking the associate nature of the human brain. Users would call up this indexed motherlode of augmenting knowledge with just a few keystrokes – a process that would accelerate progress in research and science.

Bush realized that users should be able to personally create and add knowledge and resources to the system, such as text, comments and photos, linked to main trails or in personal side trails – thus predicting concepts such as social media. He was quite precise about creating, say, a personal article, sharing it and linking it to other articles, anticipating blogging. The idea of creating, connecting, annotating and sharing knowledge, on an encyclopedic scale, anticipated Wikipedia and other knowledge bases. Lawyers, doctors, historians and other professionals, Bush thought, would have access to the knowledge they needed to do their jobs more effectively.

In a book published 22 years later, *Science Is Not Enough* (1967), Bush relished the idea that recent technological advances in electronics, such as photocells, transistors, magnetic tape, solid-state circuits and cathode ray tubes, had brought his vision closer to reality. He saw in erasable, magnetic tape the possibility of erasure and correction, namely editing, as an important feature of his system of augmentation. Even more remarkable was his prophetic ideas around voice control and user-generated content, anticipating the personal assistants so familiar to us today. He even anticipated the automatic creation of trails, anticipating that AI and machine learning may also play a part in our interaction with such knowledge bases.

Ted Nelson, who invented hypertext, also acknowledged his deep debt to Vannervar Bush, as did Tim Berners-Lee, who specifically mentioned Bush, Engelbart (see below) and *As We May Think* as inspiration for his development of the world wide web.

What is astonishing is the range and depth of Bush's vision, of both the personal computer which he built, but also the internet and its combined research forces. His was a realistic vision of how technology could be combined with knowledge to accelerate progress, all in the service of the creative brain. It was an astounding thought experiment.

Douglas Engelbart (1925–2013)

Douglas Engelbart was another visionary of the modern computer, who was profoundly influenced by Bush's man–machine ideas and often quoted him as the inspiration for his ideas and practical inventions. Engelbart's far-sighted, practical work established human-computer interaction as an area of technical and psychological research. He had an instrumental role in the invention of the computer mouse, joystick and tracker-ball, as well as bitmapped screens and hypertext. All of these we now take for granted in computer technology, but they were first shown in 'The Mother of all Demos', his famous computer demonstration in San Francisco in 1968. This was the demonstration of a complete hardware and software system that featured many elements that would become essential in the modern personal computer.

More than this, Engelbart also had a vision of collective intelligence and the idea of collective IQ, defined long before the advent of the internet. Like Bush, he foresaw the importance of networks as shared knowledge across networked organizations. His vision was not just technological; it continued Bush's idea of the augmentation of human capabilities for the common good, something Engelbart was to call 'collective intelligence'.

Engelbart also read Bush's *As We May Think* and saw the possibility of a shared network that was more than the sum of its parts. He defined his goal as getting better at getting better by augmenting our individual intellects with techniques that leverage collective knowledge. As a solution for solving complex problems, he called this process 'bootstrapping'. Engelbart placed his dynamic knowledge repository (DKR) at the heart of the bootstrapping paradigm, which enabled a process called the concurrent development, integration and application of knowledge (CoDIAK) (Engelbart, 1995). This DKR is also subject to the CoDIAK process. However, it suffered somewhat from being too acronym-driven, ambitious and proprietary.

Unhappy with just a qualitative description of the network as a place where collective intelligence could flourish, in 1994 Engelbart proposed a measure for such shared intelligence, a collective IQ, in other words. It was goal-driven and measured effectiveness or how well groups work together to anticipate and respond to problems and situations. The goal, whether a product, service or research goal, would use collective IQ to determine the effectiveness of the response. Along with development and deployment, speed and quality of response were key measures. Rather than an abstract measure of reason, as a practical man as well as theorist, Engelbart wanted a measure of getting things done and completed to meet the goal.

Inventing the mouse, and his initial work in imagining the internet, is reason enough to see Engelbart as a groundbreaking and influential pioneer. He went much further with his work on collective intelligence, producing one of the first pieces of serious analysis of networks and the internet in terms of collective effort and intelligence. Both he and Bush set the scene for the personal computer and internet that was yet to come.

Personal computer

The mass production of the microprocessor in 1971 led to an explosion of activity around personal computers in the 1980s, with the release of the IBM PC in 1981, an important landmark in the history of computers. Other machines such as the Commodore 64 (my own first computer) and BBC Micro in the early 1980s in the UK, were immediately seen as having applications in education and training.

The storage and distribution of computer learning programs needed storage devices. The home computer industry dabbled with cassette tapes, but it was the invention by IBM of a floppy disc, a magnetic storage media that held digital data available in three sizes (the huge 8", 5½" and 3½") that became hugely popular in the 1980s and 1990s. They were so popular that the save icon was a tiny floppy disc shape, and still is! The floppy disc gave learning designers the extra storage and the ability to save learning data for analytics.

Interactive learning programmes were produced, and peripheral devices began to appear for this purpose. Interactive video tape players, for both audio and videotapes, used controller cards to scroll to time coded points and retrieve the audio and video segments relevant to the learner at that moment.

Laserdiscs allowed the storage of large amounts of video, still images and two audio tracks, although the video was analogue. Although launched as a consumer product and a rival to VHS and Betamax videotapes, they couldn't record and so never became dominant. However, in the late 1980s and 1990s laserdiscs did lead to a thriving industry in interactive learning programs containing full video that were synchronized with computer overlay. The Domesday Project and hundreds of very creative education and training programs were produced, often branching simulations, using video clips.

The compact disc, later changed to CD-ROM, was launched in 1982 by Philips and Sony and a range of CD formats followed, some of which were writable. These were also used for interactive learning programs. CDi, developed by Philips as a consumer product to bring interactivity to television, was also used for education and training, although it was hampered by low resolution imagery and limited memory.

A significant e-learning industry then developed which designed programs for all of these formats, leading to a burst of creative activity in learning design. In the UK, the British Interactive Video Association (BIVA) and the Interactive Designers Association (IDA) were formed. In some ways, the availability of media such as audio and video were better than when the internet first arrived, as initially there was very limited local storage on computers and low bandwidth. It wasn't until broadband arrived that similar levels of media diversity were again possible.

More visionaries

Another two visionaries appeared on the back of the fledgling personal computer business, Bill Gates and Steve Jobs. One had a focus on the core software and tools that would turn the computer into a usable learning tool. The other had a vision to create an integrated set of hardware and software that would move well beyond the personal PC.

BILL GATES (1955–)

Bill Gates is the college drop-out who became the richest man in the world. His role in the world of learning is twofold; first, he built Microsoft, the world's leading provider of software tools such as Word, PowerPoint and Excel, that have come to dominate how we write, present and, to a degree, teach and learn; second, his later personal and philanthropic interest in education. As one of the most significant technological creators and innovators, Gates' interest and active participation in the learning game has grown.

Microsoft Office has had a huge impact on teaching and learning. As the *de facto* word processor, Microsoft Word is the tool used to produce most educational content. PowerPoint is arguably the most popular and influential teaching presentation tool that technology has ever produced. It fits the dominant pedagogy of most universities and colleges (lecturing) and also the structure of conferences and company presentations. Its effect has been profound, if not always attractive. 'Death by PowerPoint' is a not uncommon criticism, but one that is not the problem of the tool rather the traditional teaching methods that encourage too much text and too little thought on pedagogy, design and communication. OneNote for note taking and Outlook for personal communications may also be said to have influenced the world of learning. Although not a Microsoft-developed product, Microsoft owns Skype, which proved to be a popular communications tool for collaboration, tutoring and so on. More recently Microsoft Teams has been used extensively for teaching and collaboration, especially during the Covid-19 pandemic. It is easy to underestimate the role of these tools in teaching and learning, but their direct influence has been global and long-lasting.

When Gates gave up his position as CEO of Microsoft in 2000, he switched his attention to the Bill & Melinda Gates Foundation. He believes that technology, both hardware and software, will literally revolutionize learning, especially in developing countries. Gates' funding reflects his research interests, such as personalized/adaptive learning across the educational system, aggregation of good ideas for teachers and world-class content. Among the many major organizations he has continued to support is the Khan Academy, a nonprofit organization that provides free education around the world.

Gates has taken a keen interest in higher education too, with a focus on using technology to lessen failure. He sees the problem as not that too few people are going to college, but that too many go and fail. Enrolment in post-secondary programmes has grown enormously but not enough people are finishing. In 2015, more than 36 million people in the United States, one fifth of the working age population, left college without achieving their degree. Given the fiscal constraints in education, he sees technological innovation as the way in which education will solve its current problems and continue to scale. Part of his solution to dropping out from college is his support for the common core, a set of standards that aim to bring students up to a common standard for college entry. But Gates also supports more personalized, adaptive learning and support systems, using AI, that are responsive to failing students' needs.

Gates has had a long-standing interest in education, way beyond the interest taken by other significant technological leaders at companies such as Google, Apple, Facebook or Amazon. It is a deep and personal interest that has a very practical approach – smart funding and support of ideas, institutions and real initiatives that will scale to improve learning. Microsoft continues to provide tools that shape the learning landscape.

STEVE JOBS (1955–2011)

Steve Jobs was adopted and raised by working class parents who didn't go to college. However, he had a significant advantage for his future role, as his father, Paul Jobs, was a machinist and mechanic. His father had a workshop and instilled an engineering outlook in Jobs when he was around five or six years of age, by giving him his own bit of the workbench where he was encouraged to take things apart, build things and fix them. Being poor meant making do and making things work.

Never fond of school, Jobs soon dropped out of Reed College in Portland, as he explained in an interview in 1995: 'I encountered authority of a different kind than I had ever encountered before, and I did not like it. And they really almost got me. They came close to really beating any curiosity out of me'. Neither was his college experience particularly formative: 'I dropped out of Reed College... I couldn't see the value in it' (Computer World, 2011).

Jobs' impact on education has been indirect but significant through his innovative Apple hardware and software. This book was written on a Mac, a computer known for its slick design, as is the software it runs. Microsoft and Apple have been the two underlying software systems that have dominated the computer world at the level of the operating system, and although they have diverged, one with focus on the organizational, corporate world, the other the consumer world, they have both become giants in the modern world of computer technology. As well as computers and laptops, some unique devices, notably the iPod, iPad and iPhone, have all had uses in learning. Podcasts were literally named after the Apple iPod and have popularized audio-only learning. The tablet, boosted through the iPad, has also become common in schools, due to its easy interface, ergonomics and apps. Bearing an uncanny resemblance to the Victorian school slate, many claim it has become a valuable tool, especially in early years and primary school learning. There has been some criticism, however, of its large-scale deployment in schools, when procurement, planning and training for teachers has been poor.

M-learning (mobile learning) received a boost from iPhone smartphones. It is said that if you put the 2.8 billion iPhones sold to date, end-to-end, they'd go all the way to the moon and a third of the way back! Their superb design and great interface have made them the smartphone of choice for millions. Learning experiences such as search, Wikipedia, YouTube and other specific, online resources, such as Khan Academy and Open Educational Resources, are increasingly accessed through mobile devices.

Learning content also received a boost with the App Store, a distribution service that includes educational apps, so that teachers and learners have thousands of general and subject-specific apps available. Schoolwork, assignments, alerts and tracking are all available from Apple educational products. Jobs' major contribution was a stream of innovative technology that changed hearts and minds. It was this integration of devices and services that made Apple so attractive to both consumers and learners. Above all it has been their attention to design detail, good interfaces and integration that has made them one of the most successful companies on the planet.

Tablets

Tablets resemble their precursor, writing slates, as they have the same shape, aspect ratio and are of a similar weight. With erasable content, tablets are easy to use in either portrait or landscape. More importantly, the tablet shifted learning away from the giant tablet that is the whiteboard, just as the writing slate shifted learning from the blackboard, into the hands of the learner. The tablet as a flat, mobile, touchscreen device had innumerable early versions. Utilizing the technology of the computer with a touchscreen and the portable technology of the smartphone, the tablet emerged as a combined technology with its own identity, although the creation of hybrid tablet/laptops, mini-tablets and 'phablets' (a portmanteau of phone and tablet) suggest that there are blurred lines.

The GridPad, released in 1989, was the first commercially successful tablet, and a whole slew then appeared in the 1990s, including the IBM ThinkPAD, Apple's Newton and Palm. It was thought that 'palm technology' was the key to success but that proved to be just a distraction. The event that created the mass market for tablets, along with huge interest from educators, was Apple's launch of the iPad in 2010. Android tablets have also always been in the market, from the Samsung Galaxy Tab onwards, and still have significant market share.

The large-scale sale of tablets into schools has been criticized for encouraging device-fetish in learning. Poor procurement, high costs, little attention to pedagogy and lack of teacher training has led to a number of failed projects. Huge budgets were allocated to tablet devices, while bandwidth and software services took second place. Major schemes, such as those in California, were scrapped as the cost and implementation proved disastrous. Pedagogic problems were also unanticipated, as the design of tablets make them poor for long-form writing and more advanced skills, such as coding, that require keyboards. Indeed, touchscreen keyboards can actually inhibit writing skills. Price is also a divisive issue for poorer students. Education often succumbed to 'device fetish' as iPads were designed to be consumer, not producer, devices.

Ebooks

Another species of tablet with significant impact on learning is the ebook reader. These flat devices have similar technology to the tablet, with electronic paper (or electronic ink) rather than LCD screens, but they have a specific purpose, which is the storage and display of written text for reading. They can store thousands of books and have additional functions, such as adjustable fonts and spacing, inbuilt dictionaries, underlining and links to sources for free books and public libraries for book borrowing. Sony released the first commercial electronic paper devices, but it was the Amazon Kindle in 2007 that, like the iPad, popularized the idea of reading books on a portable tablet. Apple then fought back with e-reader software in the iPad.

Ebooks are mostly a consumer reading device, with reading seen by many as an activity that is usually an informal learning experience. As assistive technology they also have page zoom and brightness adjustment, and some have a read-aloud function. Updates can also be made on the cloud, a problem that plagues paper textbooks, but it is the sheer volume of books (especially, old and more obscure texts as well as those out of print) available to download for free, borrow or buy that has changed the book landscape.

Smartphones

The first mobile phone (cellphone) was demonstrated by John F Mitchell and Martin Cooper of Motorola in 1973, using a huge handset weighing an astonishing 2 kilograms (4.4 lbs). The prototype offered a talk time of just 30 minutes and took 10 hours to recharge. In 1979, Nippon Telegraph and Telephone (NTT) launched the world's first cellular network in Japan. This was followed by the DynaTAC 8000X in 1983, the first commercially available handheld mobile phone.

Since the beginning, voice telephony involved a device tethered to a wall, at home or in a public booth. Mobile phones not only became wireless, freeing themselves from location, they began to contain the same powerful technology as computers. The mobile phone has become the smartphone, a personally-owned device that now provides navigation, the communications functionality of a computer, social media, all media types from text to VR and a personal voice assistant. It was inevitable that they would eventually play a role in largely informal but also formal learning.

Text messaging

Text messaging was the first major mobile medium. The first text message was sent in 1992, and within 10 years billions were being sent every month. Nokia, the Finnish telephone maker, was instrumental here, as Finland was the first to adopt GSM (Global System for Mobile Communications) and to build a GSM network. Built into this standard was the capability to send a short 140-character SMS (Short Message Service). It was packet switched, not circuit switched, and spread like wildfire.

The role of culture in text messaging

Countries like Japan were early adopters of texting, as teenagers lived in small houses where privacy was difficult and so the technology provided an escape from this restriction. Texting was also very popular in Middle Eastern countries, where many generations of a family live together, enabling young people to communicate with each other. Texting took much longer to become popular in the United States, as GSM was a European standard and there was no free flow of messages across all networks in the United States, as well as fewer restrictions on teenagers.

The mobile phone market was, for a long time, a fragmented market and lack of bandwidth, limited screen size and methods of display, along with awkward input and the absence of any universal standards, were serious design and technical limitations. There was an abundance of options, including iOS, Android, BlackBerry, Windows Phone, Symbian and Palm, but no standardization. Developers had to use tools that created core code then cross-compiled to create native apps across a range of platforms. This was not easy. A solution was to use a virtual machine (VM), which was slower but gave control and flexibility, or to use web applications such as browsers to cope with worldwide standards, for example, HTML, Javascript and

CSS. One additional barrier was integration with the LMS or VLE, as mobile learning (M-learning) isolated from either of these could be orphaned and was difficult to justify.

Mobile learning

M-learning, and its failures, showed that different devices have different learning attributes. The mobile phone is a small device for short, episodic activity, not long, deep, reflective learning experiences. Large e-learning courses delivered on mobiles have been shown to be largely ineffective. However, it was inevitable, given the advantages of having something in your pocket that is personal, powerful and portable, that it would increasingly be promoted as a tool for learning.

Just as tablets have been pushed in schools, despite their limitations in complex learning tasks such as long-form writing, coding, tools etc, mobiles were also pushed in formal learning. Yet different devices have different learning affordances, and few people read entire ebooks or perform long pieces of linear learning on their smartphones. Indeed, research by Reeves and Nass (1996) showed that knowledge retention falls with a decrease in screen size. This naturally pushes mobile learning towards more episodic learning, such as access to knowledge, recording performance and collaborative learning, rather than studying a whole course. Its main use is, of course, for learning through search and reference, asking others for help and episodic language learning through apps such as Duolingo, or listening to podcasts while engaged in other tasks such as travel to work or exercise.

Leapfrogging in Africa

The spread of mobile phone use in Africa has benefited from the continent's gaps in infrastructure such as roads, fixed line telephone networks and transport options, and has made technological leapfrogging possible. Fixed line networks barely reached remote rural areas, such as those in Sub-Saharan Africa, meaning a large percentage of the population was cut off from the outside world. As there is less competitive pressure from incumbent technology and infrastructure, investment in leapfrog technology makes sense. Many countries in Africa have kiosks that offer phone charging, airtime, money transfer, recycling and repair, and so leapfrogged the landline infrastructure. Countries such as Kenya, Malawi, South Africa and Uganda have over 90 per cent GSM coverage and, with over a billion mobile subscriptions, at first on simple phones, often with FM radio and torches, then more sophisticated smartphones, Africa is a fast-growing market for mobile telephony. Internet access was a natural consequence of mobile access.

Innovation in these environments, with their absence of precedents and incumbents, is easier than in wealthier or more technologically advanced countries. The relative absence of a retail banking infrastructure and the fact that many people did not have a bank account, created an environment ripe for the introduction of cheap mobile devices. This allowed Africa to pioneer the concept of mobile banking – something that richer countries did much later. In its wake came other significant advantages in communications, including the ability to look for work, pay bills, search for agricultural information and markets and so on. In 2007, M-Pesa, the mobile money transfer service launched by Kenya's largest mobile operator Safaricom and Vodafone, became a huge success. It allowed millions to pay bills, buy goods, receive remittances from abroad and even access learning. In Africa, a mobile phone provides a lifeline to work, money transfer, running a small business, communications with family, medical advice, veterinary advice, market prices and increasingly, knowledge and education.

There was, and still is, huge amounts of innovation in mobile learning in Africa, with Dr Maths through Mxit, Wikipedia Zero, even SMS requests for SMS delivery of Wikipedia in Kenya. Basic literacy was also enhanced, as children want to read and write so they can text and read texts. We now know that this constant text writing leads to better literacy, a fuller phonetic understanding of the language and more social skills.

The internet

In 1957, the Soviet Union surprized the United States when it launched Sputnik. In response, the US Department of Defense formed ARPA (Advanced Research Projects Agency) and within 12 years ARPANET was born, a decentralized computer network, used for research. Borne from the need to develop a communications network that would survive during a nuclear attack, the US government developed a decentralized network that, if one part was destroyed, would survive by rerouting.

US universities such as Harvard, Stanford, MIT and UCLA, along with research agencies, found the shared network useful and, in 1973, it crossed the Atlantic to University College London and the Norwegian Royal Radar Establishment. Usenet newsgroups emerged, along with email and FTP (File Transfer Protocol) in the 1970s.

The Homebrew Computer Club

Around this time another significant group, the hobbyists, was emerging. The Homebrew Computer Club was a group of hobbyists interested in personal computers who began meeting in 1975. The Altair, the first personal computer kit, appeared in 1974, and in 1976, the Club received a letter from a 21 year-old programmer who had written the operating system for the Altair, saying that they had to pay for it. His name was Bill Gates.

The development of the internet continued with the invention of TCP.IP, domain names and network news transfer in the 1980s, while UNIX remained the internet's operating system. Meanwhile international organizations such as Mintel in France, EUnet (European UNIX Network) and JANET (Joint Academic Network) joined the internet. In 1986, the National Science Foundation Network (NSFNET) in the United States networked five university mainframes, which attracted a frenzy of interest from other educational establishments interested in sharing processing power. Within a few years countries all around the globe were part of this network – the internet had been born.

Internet relay chat (IRC), an instant messaging service for one-to-one and group communication, took off, as did file sharing. The infant internet had started to speak and communicate. ARPANET withdrew and NSFNET took over, turning the internet into a public, rather than defense, entity. In 1991, the network invited interest from the private sector but continued to prohibit for-profit use. This was the point at which the choice of network providers exploded. The internet at this time was still part of a geek world where a user needed a knowledge of UNIX to use it. It was a magnificent achievement intended for the public good but, to make it accessible to the wider public, the network needed to become user friendly.

Howard Rheingold in *Smart Mobs* (2003) gives a full account of how the early coders on the fledgling internet had a culture of sharing and learning as a group. Sharing and learning became the impetus behind the design of the early internet and in creating a network, it became a platform for learning and accelerating innovation. First came connectivity, then primitive text messaging and file sharing. This created a critical mass of like-minded people, eager to share and grow the network. Reed's Law was at work. By 1994 the internet had become a global network of educational institutions, mainly universities. At this point in the 1990s, in stepped our next set of visionaries, who made the internet possible, not in terms of networking and hardware but software. The first, Tim Berners-Lee, allowed us access to the internet through the world wide web, while Larry Page and Sergei Brin allowed us to search that web. These are the two foundational technologies that created the possibility of online learning.

Tim Berners-Lee invented the world wide web. His 1989 proposal was redistributed and accepted at CERN in 1990, and by 1991 the first website was up and running. Fiendishly simple, with just three standards: HTML (write your letter), HTTP (delivery of your letter) and URLs (postal address), it was an easy way to use the internet to publish, distribute, send and receive information (Berners-Lee, 1999). This was an invention that gave scale and reach, on a par with writing and the printing press, and was ideal for learning. It meant that the internet could step out into the real world and engage with everyone.

Berners-Lee approached a friend of mine, Ian Ritchie, who had by then developed a hypertext product called Guide, which Berners-Lee could see was how the web should be. He asked Ian if he could create a front end for the internet, what we now call a browser. Ian made a fateful decision and said he was too busy! Nonetheless, in 1993, Marc Andreessen released Mosaic, the first browser, at the US National Centre of Supercomputing Applications (NCSA). The web was open for business.

Berners-Lee's gift to the world of learning was the creation of a virtual world in which teachers and learners could have unlimited access to knowledge using a network – the internet – to do things that were scarcely thought possible. It is one of the greatest of all inventions and of unimaginable importance for the future of education and learning.

From the very start, the web was used to share academic knowledge and collaborate on learning and research, making it, in effect, a knowledge-sharing network. Berners-Lee understood that he was creating a web of people by connecting them and was therefore creating a social effect. Without the world wide web there would be no search function, web content such as

Wikipedia, open educational resources, online learning, online book stores or social media. The humble hyperlink changed forever the way content is written, read and navigated. It enables us to move through content, drill down into that content, get help and learn in a way that was difficult with flat, linear media. Of course, media other than just text was shared as images, audio, animation and video, and now 3D worlds.

An important principle for Berners-Lee is open educational resources. He favours 'net neutrality' and defends the position that the web should not be controlled by companies or governments. Open educational initiatives such as Wikipedia, Khan Academy, YouTube and MOOCs have become major forces, with hundreds of millions of learners using their services. The promise of free at the point of delivery learning has already emerged with new business models, new forms of delivery and new forms of pedagogy.

Beyond this, Berners-Lee's vision encompasses the intelligent analysis of the data that the web creates and he looks forward to this leading to the emergence of a truly semantic web. In 2012, Berners-Lee co-founded the Open Data Institute (ODI), which pushes for open data in both the UK and globally, and he has advised a number of governments and corporations on ongoing digital strategies.

Cloud

The cloud symbol appeared as the representation of a network of computers as early as 1977. Decades later, in the 21st century, smart cloud computing is fact and the use of computing and data resources, on-demand, outside of organizations, is becoming ubiquitous. Amazon launched AWS (Amazon Web Services) in 2002 and continues to be a major global player. Google and Microsoft came into the market in 2010, followed by Rackspace and IBM in 2011 and Oracle in 2016.

The cloud's impact on professional learning services has been considerable, due to its flexibility, lower costs, lower capital expenditure, ability to deliver to any device, ease of maintenance, security and better performance and productivity. It also allows organizations to cope with the unpredictability of demand by users and learners, gives access to services across broad networks and multi-tenanted services and differentiated services. Demand has become scalable and can be increased, decreased, metered and measured, giving a more transparent view of services. This is of huge benefit to large educational institutions and organizations who want to get the best out of their platforms without having to invest in physical hardware. Cloud-based solutions rapidly became the norm, especially as organizations moved towards having more data-centric solutions, i.e. data that needed to be stored and used.

Search

Search is arguably the greatest single pedagogic change in the last half century. It massively reduces time to access learning research and resources. Search is, in essence, people who are looking for answers to questions, both personal and professional, and it is this need to know something that drives search.

The mathematical laws relating to the growth of broadcast, processing power and nodes is one thing, but what gives networks real power is Reed's Law, where the number of people and social groups determines actual value. Replace the word 'people' with 'learners and teachers' and there is perhaps another law that can define value. This second order effect arises as people learn from the network and pass that on to others, either through word of mouse or word of mouth. It is not the physical connectivity that matters but the connecting of minds. These minds learn and pass that learning on to others. Bush and Engelbart understood this, with their early ideas on collective intelligence. Whether it is to find something or someone, it is the inquiring mind that searches.

Google

Larry Page and Sergei Brin met at Stanford in 1995 and their business, Google (now Alphabet), has become one of the most significant global businesses ever. Their search engine has transformed the way we search for information and has changed our very relationship with knowledge, making it a significant contribution to learning. As the world's most successful search engine Google has become an indispensable tool for learning and research.

Page and Brin's mathematical approach to search problems led to a search engine, that ranked sites by popularity. Their scalable model looked at links, so the larger the web became, the better their engine became. Famously based on a spelling error (Google should have been Googol), Google's mission is to 'organize the world's information and make it universally accessible and useful' (Google). Specialist searching of text, images, video, books, academic papers, news, maps and prices have given the ordinary user unparalleled access to knowledge stored in different media. It is the speed and efficiency of this search that has accelerated our ability as learners to identify relevant knowledge. Learners of all ages and abilities now see the web as a useful source of knowledge.

Google Scholar is a free search service for scholarly literature. It contains most academic journals, books and other academic literature. Search is weighted towards citations and its ability to choose a citation format is a strong feature. Other search services for images, news and so on have also been useful in education.

Google Workspace (formerly known as G Suite) is a cloud-based set of educational tools, launched in 2006. It includes Gmail (email), Meet (comms and collaboration), Calendar, Drive (storage), Docs, Sheets, Forms and other tools for shared resources and collaboration. As a cloud-based solution, data is stored securely and backed up effortlessly. Tens of millions use the service in education. Blogger provides free blogging software to tens of millions of bloggers, and has a large community of education and training bloggers, which has proved useful in continuous professional development. Google Books, Google Earth, Google Translate and Google Assistant are just some of the free services that have also contributed to education.

Google's mission to digitize the content of some of the world's great libraries is also contributing to the storage and dissemination of knowledge. Its aim is to make the contents of books (text and images) searchable and available, while remaining sensitive to copyright and public domain restrictions. Google is looking to make millions of books available over and above the existing Google Books program it has with publishers. This takes Google beyond searching to the creation of online resources for searching.

Page and Brin have created a toolset that has already revolutionized access to knowledge. Their organization continues to revolutionize learning.

Conclusion

Computers, in terms of their hardware and, just as importantly, their software and logic and media presentation capabilities, laid the foundations for modern technology-based learning. These contemporary teaching machines were beautifully designed as consumer products, manufactured to a high quality and sold at consumer-friendly prices. Desktops, laptops, tablets and smartphones are bought by billions of consumers on a global scale, and all use that global network, the internet.

When seen as learning technologies, personal computer devices and the internet are huge drivers of human teaching and learning. Yet adoption and pedagogic progress in institutions has been slow. 'Chalk and talk' in schools and lectures in tertiary education remain dominant, but new digital learning devices are now found not only in the schoolroom, but in the workplace, homes and pockets of learners. Their very presence, power and portability make them learning technologies by default. A learner who does not regularly use online services to learn, directly and indirectly, is rare.

We have also seen the rapid appearance of many different species of service on the web, from content to cheat sites. The explosion of searchable services and content, in all media formats on the world wide web, has demanded attention and use. As a Darwinian environment, the web is ruthlessly eliminative of pedagogic ideas that are difficult to use, unfriendly, not useful or expensive. Some applications have transcended these barriers to become almost ubiquitous, namely Google, Wikipedia, YouTube, Messenger, social media and video conferencing services. The technology side of the equation has come to the fore, while the tech giants have moved in different directions from their original starting points. Most notably Apple, which began as a device company but now delivers services, Microsoft, which began with PC software and now develops games consoles, Amazon as an online retailer that now provides cloud services and a voice-activated personal assistant, and Facebook, that has developed Oculus while looking ahead to the Metaverse.

We are beginning to see a battle between learning technology and institutional inertia. Ultimately, it is between the past and the future. Learning technology, pedagogically, pushes the pendulum towards more learner-centric models that fit with what we know about the science and psychology of learning. This tension between learning technology and human delivery is a battle between avoiding the expensive duplication of human effort and replacing it with what is possible using technology One of the ways this technology has managed to become a standard fixture in institutions is through learning platforms. We shall examine these next.

References

Berners-Lee, T (1999) *Weaving the Web: The original design and ultimate destiny of the world wide web by its inventor,* Harper, San Francisco

Bush, V (1945) *Science, the Endless Frontier*, Princeton University Press, Princeton, NJ

Bush, V (1945) As We May Think, *The Atlantic Monthly*, 176(1), 101–08

Bush, V (1967) *Science is Not Enough*, William Morrow, New York

Computer World (2011) Steve Jobs interview: One-on-one in 1995, 6 October, *Computer World*, www.idginsiderpro.com/article/2498543/steve-jobs-interview-one-on-one-in-1995.html (archived at https://perma.cc/K5FW-RAQG)

Cross, J (2006) *Informal learning: Rediscovering the natural pathways that inspire innovation and performance*, John Wiley & Sons, Hoboken, NJ

Engelbart, D C (1995) Toward augmenting the human intellect and boosting our collective IQ, *Communications of the ACM*, 38(8), 30–32

Gery, G J (1991) *Electronic Performance Support Systems: How and why to remake the workplace through the strategic application of technology*, Weingarten Publications, Inc, Boston MA

Google www.google.com/intl/en_uk/search/howsearchworks/our-approach/ (archived at https://perma.cc/WFS4-QKSV)

Marsick, V J and Watkins, K (1990) *Informal and Incidental Learning in the Workplace*, Routledge, London

Reeves, B and Nass, C (1996) *The Media Equation: How people treat computers, television, and new media like real people*, CSLI Publications, Stanford, CA

Rheingold, H (2003) Smart Mobs, *Société*, (1), 75–87

Shannon, C E (1938) A symbolic analysis of relay and switching circuits, *Electrical Engineering*, 57(12), 713–23

Tolman, E C and Honzik, C H (1930) Introduction and removal of reward, and maze performance in rats, *University of California Publications in Psychology* 4, 257–75

Turing, A M (1936) On computable numbers, with an application to the Entscheidungsproblem, *Journal of Math*, 58(345–63), 5

09

Platforms

Learning technology gains momentum and power when it can scale, and scale needs a particular type of technology if it is to move beyond the individual or classroom. Platforms provide that scale across large organizations and globally via the internet. They have become the controlled, owned and used institutional software for teaching and learning in schools, universities and the workplace.

We have enveloped our planet with the single greatest platform our species has ever created – the internet. This is the mega-platform that supports a plethora of smaller global platforms for learning, and beneath this are an untold number of micro-platforms that deliver teaching and learning. All are growing in size, fueled by expanding technological access, greater available bandwidth, smarter software, a recent pandemic and an insatiable demand for education and learning.

Wikipedia can be seen as a learning platform as it is a huge repository of knowledge, but we will deal here with platforms deliberately designed for teaching and learning. Several species of platform have taken teaching and learning to millions, even billions of learners, and almost all are now internet or cloud based. These include virtual learning environments (VLE), learning management systems (LMS), learning experience platforms (LXP), webinars, MOOCs, adaptive, social and practice.

Learning platforms

Turning to formal learning, learning platforms deliver the bulk of structured learning within educational institutions such as schools, colleges and universities. Learning platforms are also widely used in larger public and private organizations. It is rare to find a large organization, private or public, that

FIGURE 9.1   Learning platforms

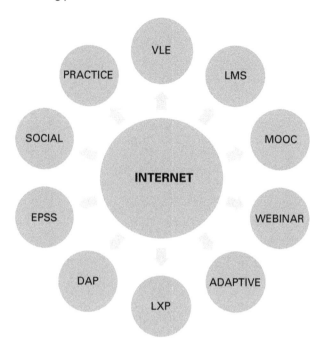

does not use a learning platform, often a VLE (the term applied to educational platforms) or a learning management system (LMS). Open source approaches like Moodle, along with its forked corporate versions, have also changed the landscape, offering a lower-cost approach to the management and delivery of learning.

A separate and parallel MOOC movement has also developed, some of which have a corporate arm. These are full course delivery platforms that began in education but have since gained traction in adult and corporate learning.

Webinar platforms are another separate category, whose use accelerated as a result of the Covid-19 pandemic. Their primary focus is on live, synchronous learning experiences but with added functionality. In addition there are social platforms that focus on communication, collaboration and sharing. Beyond all of these, other types of platforms have emerged to challenge the dominance of the course delivery platforms – smart platforms.

Smart platforms

Smart adaptive learning platforms personalize and sequence content so that each learner receives a unique learning experience. They use aggregated and personal data to allow different learners to vector through a course using different routes, depending on the individual's performance.

Smart LXPs focus on delivering workflow dynamically, with more focus on supporting learners in context than on delivering courses. This has been a move towards bridging the informal and formal learning gap with platforms that are less concerned with the management of learning and more focused on the delivery. This is a move towards using smart technology to deliver adaptive and personalized learning when it is most needed by the learner or in the workplace. Practice platforms have more focus on retrieval, deliberate and spaced practice, tackling the issues of forgetting and knowledge retention.

Given this widening of options, organizations are faced with more choice and ecosystems of learning technologies, sometimes described as technology suites, are also on offer. Some vendors offer a single platform with LXP/LMS functionality, while others offer both separately with interoperability. LMS vendors are moving towards adopting LXP functionality, and LXP vendors are moving backwards to include LMS functionality. The suites may also include bespoke content production, catalogues of courses and authoring capabilities.

At the heart of all this, data has emerged as a critical function. The learning record store (LRS) or alternative data management approach has become critical in terms of description, analysis and more sophisticated prescription and automation of learning. This is less of a platform and more of a database.

Digital adoption platforms (DAP) focus on supporting new digital or IT roll outs, while electronic performance support systems (EPSS) deliver performance support. In the past their focus was on supporting new software training, but a new breed of performance support platforms applies to learning in general.

Platforms change as technology and organizational needs change. There is a recognition that the older centralized LMS model is giving way to a more sophisticated model that uses smart software and can respond to what learners want in their workflow. Smart statistical techniques, AI and data-enabled search, notifications, nudge learning, curation and workflow tools are used to better target learners and learning.

History of learning management systems

From Nazi punch cards in the 1930s to the LMS in the early 2000s, and now the development of smart platforms, it is important to understand the rise of enterprise learning and educational platforms. The LMS and now

LXP are best viewed historically as growing from several roots – hardware, software, business software, connectivity and pedagogy. Much maligned, they have endured and prospered as large organizations need their learners and learning managed and tracked. There is no avoiding the fact that this requires enterprise-level software.

The punch-card system was an early hardware development. It was first used in 1804 in Jacquard's loom to automate the production of complex patterns in weaving. Babbage also wanted to incorporate punch cards into his Analytical Engine, but the idea was eventually carried forward by Herman Hollerith, who worked for the US Census. He patented a punch card system in 1884 that could record human characteristics for the 1890 census. This was the first use of electronics for data storage. Hollerith's machine could calculate totals but also combine traits. In 1890, the time taken to complete the US census went down from eight years to a single year. Hollerith's company became IBM in 1924.

In 1933, Hitler was also keen to do a national census, to identify specific races and traits. Tom Watson, the first CEO of IBM, flew to meet Hitler in 1933 and made a sizable investment in the company's German subsidiary. As Hitler began to occupy neighbouring countries, the Hollerith system stored data on their population's skills, race and sexual orientation and was used to identify those selected for labour camps and concentration camps (Black, 2012). The LMS did not start well.

Early experimentation is summarized by Atkinson and Wilson (1969) in 21 papers looking at the then trends in computer-assisted learning (CAI). Experimentation in CAI was especially strong in the military, as explained by Fletcher and Rockway (1986). Among the earliest management systems were PLATO and its rival TICCIT, which were largely confined to academic experimentation, although there were some corporate examples.

Home computers, made possible by mass production of the microprocessor in 1971, led to an explosion of activity in the 1980s. However, it was the release of the IBM personal computer in 1981 that gave real impetus to computer-based training (CBT) and helped to create a huge hobbyist community. This in turn led to an embryonic computer-based training industry. I first used a program to learn Russian in the early 1980s on a Commodore 64. Other machines, such as the BBC Micro in the early 1980s, were immediately seen as having educational uses.

As discussed in Chapter 8, many learning programs were produced and distributed on storage devices, beginning with the original floppy disc all the way up to the CD-ROM. There was a burst of creative activity at this time, because video, audio and images could be included and the computer could combine these and control the whole learning experience.

Then came networked enterprise systems with client-server structures, which networked and distributed software to the clients. For example, IBM, which was originally a hardware company, then also became a software company, competing directly with Microsoft with its Lotus SmartSuite, Lotus 1-2-3 and Lotus Notes. These were intended to rival Microsoft Office, with the last release in 2014. SAP was an early 1975 spin-off from IBM that built enterprise business software. Microsoft was also on the rise, creating its Office software in 1988. Cisco, a networking company, arrived in 1984, having originated at Stanford University in California. Enterprise and organizational software then became the norm across large organizations, as it did in learning. All of these hardware and software developments set the scene for learning platforms that operated at the enterprise or organizational level.

Virtual learning environments

From the outset, a distinction emerged between the VLE and LMS. The VLE is a web-based platform used in educational institutions such as schools, colleges and universities. They are designed to deliver teacher and faculty resources, activities and communications, rather than self-paced e-learning courses, although they have this facility. They also support teacher and faculty authoring around the curriculum and course syllabus, along with all the pre-course information students need.

A social communication facility is usually available, along with some collaborative functions such as access rights, whiteboards, chat rooms, discussions and email, with teachers as moderators. Such platforms also have learning analytics. They are a universal presence in large educational institutions, but are now under pressure from newer LXP systems.

Yet there is a feeling that the dominant platforms – Blackboard, Brightspace, Canvas and Moodle – are there because of institutional inertia. Platform companies that were early to the market (in the 1990s) and who acquired competitors to add functionality and eliminate competition did well. Their platforms also integrated well into other administration systems, so that migration to a newer platform was difficult.

Learning management

The LMS is enterprise software aimed at the corporate and large organization markets and many were built and launched, especially in the period from 1999 to 2005, as companies took an interest in Human Resources. SAP, Peoplesoft and Oracle all entered the LMS market. The LMS is very much the product of its time, having come to the fore in the 1990s in the years before the internet. In the early 2000s it offered a database management solution to problems. It was clear that this type of solution would emerge at this point, as this was how enterprise software was constructed at the time – a way of storing, managing and delivering courses.

Then a split emerged between the LMS (corporate) and VLE (education market), with the latter opting for platforms such as e-college, Blackboard and WebCT. There were eventually two main groups: those that developed out of client-server, training systems and those that were born on the web. Saba, Click2Learn, Pathlore, Learnframe and Thinq were originally client-server and had to be rewritten for the web. They often used Java applets, client-end software and plug-ins, with a client-server back-end for administration. The born-on-the-web group included Docent, KnowledgePlanet and Teamscape, which had web browser interfaces. These platforms had the advantage of being more scalable, easier to roll-out and maintain, with fewer technical changes.

Later, open source learning management systems emerged, the most successful being Moodle. This in turn was forked and corporate versions created. In late 2001 the market was made more complicated by the introduction of the learning content management system (LCMS). These vendors claimed to offer additional functionality around authoring, learning object repositories and dynamic delivery. The distinction was soon blurred as LMS vendors adopted these features, and so the LCMS faded from view.

At the same time advanced distributed learning (ADL) and others came up with *de facto* (rather than *de jure*) standards. It is important to note that there are few real standards in e-learning. Instead, there is a collection of specifications, guidelines and reference models. Across the range of LMSs on offer were varying degrees of adoption of AICC, IMS and SCORM, but there was an increasing demand for accessibility standards, especially from the public sector. The Brandon Hall Group (a research and analyst firm) issued a specification list of accessibility standards that led to organizations opting to purchase based upon this list, and so their complexity grew. The Brandon Hall Group reported there were 27 LMSs in 1998, 50 in 2000, 70 in 2002 and by 2003 there were 200 (Itmazi et al, 2005). Since then there have been lots of failures, mergers and acquisitions, but today the market is worth billions, having shifted to a cloud-based, SaaS (software as a service) model over the last decade.

For the last 20 years the LMS has been the dominant model, but there has always been dissatisfaction around its integration, lack of data and shortfalls on functionality and delivery; for example, it had poor interfaces, required multiple sign-ons and had clumsy menu and course delivery systems. In a sense, LMSs did and still do mimic the classroom course model, essentially managing courses after they have been converted to online. The LMS fell short of providing the flexibility needed on both push and pull, during moments of need and more sophisticated pedagogy, especially around motivation. As a repository for content, the LMS is more about management than learning.

So, the LMS is dead, long live the LMS! Some love them, some hate them, some love to hate them. It is easy to criticize LMS platforms, and critics have been predicting their death since their inception. In truth, large organizations need large solutions. No one in an organization with tens of thousands of employees knows everyone. A database is needed to handle HR issues and payroll. Similarly with learning, especially in an age where legal and regulatory pressure is intense and growing, it is impossible to track and manage learners without an enterprise-wide piece of software.

The LMS was no different from other enterprise software markets. It started small, then when the market created a thirst, lots of RFIs (requests for information) and RFPs (requests for proposals) came out. As stated above, analysts like those at The Brandon Hall Group then compiled checklists of features, and buyers used those checklists to select systems. It didn't matter that many of the functions would never be used, a mini arms race was created to tick all the boxes on the checklist, leading to scope creep. This scope creep meant that developers had to build features that were better handled outside of the LMS. A good example is social learning, where LMSs extended their reach into all sorts of areas where they didn't belong. Suddenly LMS vendors had a 'chat' offer, which was often primitive – but part of the 'complete LMS solution'. For a few extra bucks they promised to solve all a purchaser's problems related to performance support, corporate comms, HR and talent management, locking them in, bit by bit, into the space they built for their learners.

Course delivery

The LMS on its own encourages an obsession with courses. Maslow (1966) came up with a great line: 'If you only walk around with a hammer, you tend to see every problem as a nail.' That is precisely the problem with the LMS – give an organization an LMS and every problem is seen as solvable by a 'course'. This has led to a culture of over-engineered, expensive and long-winded course production that is often aligned with the use of the LMS and not with organizational or business needs.

One consequence of the spread of LMSs has been a tsunami of compliance training. Learning and development exaggerated the argument that the law and regulators demand vast numbers of long courses. In fact, no law and very few regulators demand overlong, poorly designed, overengineered, largely dull courses, with no proven efficacy. Too often such courses are counterproductive, creating a dismissive reaction among learners. Yet the LMS model of course delivery encouraged this area of glib solutionism. Organizations can get locked into LMS contracts that limit their ability and agility to adopt innovations and adapt to new environments.

> Many an LMS lies like an old fossil, buried in the enterprise software stack, churning away like an old heating system – slow, inefficient and in constant need of repair. Long-term licences, inertia and the cost of change mean an organization may be locked into a barely functional world of half-dead software and courses.

On the positive side, it is often forgotten that the LMS was, in the early days, the prime mover for shifting people away from pure classroom delivery. This is still an issue in many organizations, but at least LMSs effected a move away from often lacklustre and expensive classroom courses. In fact, with blended learning, it is now possible to manage a pantheon of delivery channels, including classroom delivery, through an LMS (classroom planning is often included).

Scale

Scale is another advantage of the LMS. Organizations often want 24/7, on-demand, self-paced, secure, location-flexible, responsive, multi-language, global and local, affordable, value-added learning. Without technology this is undoable. An LMS not only gives scalability, but it also makes an organization think about using scalable solutions to solve problems. Organizations with national and global structures, multiple sites and multiple languages need to manage this complexity. Later, this was made even easier by metered, cloud delivery.

Need for re-enterprise solutions

An LMS is a centralized system and there are arguments for letting a thousand flowers bloom, but this can turn into a nightmare if everyone starts to do their own thing. Amateurism can turn learning into a cottage industry with lots of duplication of content, poor quality resources, unnecessary licence costs and an unmanageable mess across an organization. In the early days, large organizations did, in fact, end up having several different LMSs. This is rarer now. A single LMS can bring order to potential chaos.

Large organizations, especially global organizations, need to have some level of consistency in terms of strategy, brand and messaging as this affects learning, and an LMS can help deliver this. If managed properly, consistent rules about design, development and delivery can lead to an increase in relevance and quality, as well as strategic intent.

An organization will also have a lot of systems that need integration. However it identifies its people, stores and delivers information and manages data, there will be integration issues. An LMS is a single integrated piece of software. Even organizations that try to do without one will end up integrating things they use – and that will become a sort of LMS.

Big organizations need to manage large numbers of people, especially where staff turnover is high, so linking HR data to the LMS can ensure that people receive the right training and learning. The LMS also allows organizations to provide essential, even legally required training, as well as options for induction, management training, personal development, compliance, product knowledge, management needs, technical needs, sales skills, practical skills and so on. To operate in a complex environment a business has to be as good as, if not smarter than, the competition. This level of complexity needs management. An LMS will manage, not only learners but what has to be learnt. Enterprise software may seem expensive but at the 'cost-per-user' or 'cost-per-learner' level, an LMS often makes sense.

Organizations also need some level of management data. Let us not forget that in the supposedly good old days, the only data obtained from classroom trainers were feedback sheets. Data, with analysis, provides insights. Insights are what managers need to make decisions and innovate. A good LMS spits out data, albeit limited in scope, and that is useful.

Finally, the IT department plays a vital role in today's organization, dealing with problems around bandwidth, loading, legals and security that most people don't fully understand. In this age of DoS (denial-of-service) attacks, phishing, hacking, malware and ransomware, we should be grateful that these people are looking after our interests.

The LMS market has now moved on with new players, open source options, xAPI and more data sensitive delivery. It is a multi-billion-pound market that grows every year, as there will always be a need for single enterprise solutions. It is, however, changing, as smarter and more sophisticated forms of learning technology have emerged that meet identified organizational and pedagogic needs.

Open source LMSs - Moodle

Martin Dougiamas is an Australian who gave the world Moodle, an open source learning management system. His early education at a school 1,000 km from his home was via distance learning (every two weeks a plane dropped materials) and he worked at home in the desert, using a short-wave radio. This experience was a formative one. Dougiamas found himself one year ahead of his peers in high school and learnt how to get the best out of 'limited bandwidth'. The transition to receiving education on the internet was a natural extension of his experience.

Seeing the gulf between the early internet experts and academics and administrators, Dougiamas set out, in the early 1990s, to use WebCT (Course Tools). Tired of the licence restrictions of the commercial LMS at Curtin University in Perth, Australia, he developed Moodle – Modular Object-Oriented Dynamic Learning Environment. The beta version appeared in 2001, with 1.0 released in August 2002. It now has thousands of implementations and is used by millions of teachers and learners. Moodle is now the most widely implemented LMS in the world, and is especially popular in higher education.

Open source is not, as some imagine, a loose community of developers; it has a hierarchy, processes and central organization, and so Moodle has a team of core developers. This is paid for by Moodle partners, who pay royalties that come back to the trust. Partners provide services, often add-ons, to Moodle, as well as hosting and providing content. One of Moodle's strengths was the directory of shared plug-ins – extensions to the core product – which are available for free to the Moodle community. The Moodle mobile app, along with many other features, has also extended its functionality.

Dougiamas is more than a developer. He has a PhD in educational theory, on the use of open source software to support a social constructivist epistemology of teaching and learning. This has led to Moodle development that adheres to these constructivist principles. Moodle's course structures and features have emerged from his belief in some firm principles.

Dougiamas had to be tough at times, as this is a large, diffuse and diverse community of administrators, developers and users. Initially there were problems with security, the interface and integration, but this is not unusual in open source projects that deliver usable tools with real user interfaces, as opposed to back-end open source software. Dougiamas drives for consensus but describes himself as a 'benevolent dictator', as he has to make difficult decisions between different streams of development. He also successfully fought and won a patent battle with Blackboard in 2003, over what many saw as standard LMS functionality. Many admired him for this strong action against what some saw as an overly aggressive commercial vendor.

Some argue that Moodle's focus on social tools is at the expense of more relevant management, teacher and learner functionality; others that the 'social constructivism' angle is a myth, as most use it as a repository for fixed resources, used in didactic teaching. Like many open source products, Moodle can also suffer from poor user interface design. Customization has always been a problem. Although used in organizations outside of education, it lacked some of the functionality one finds in that type of LMS, although Totara, based on Moodle, is an open source corporate LMS that has had some success.

There are other open source LMSs, but Dougiamas has built the largest and most successful of these communities. He gave education an open source tool that is used on scale all around the world, and which really set the tone for this type of open source development in education. It has been a balancing act between core and non-core functionality, central and partner needs, as well as harnessing the effort of the many people who work and maintain the product, but his influence is through direct development of a globally popular online learning tool.

Learning experience platforms

The LMS is largely about managing learners and learning (the clue is in the word 'management') rather than engagement. However, around 2020 there was a breakthrough with the arrival of the learning experience platform (LXP). It is not that the functionality of an LMS is flawed, but its user interface design/user experience design (UI/UX) is most certainly flawed. As a repository, the LMS is insensitive to performance support, especially learning embedded in the workflow, and makes people do a lot of work to find what they need. The LMS puts obstacles in the way of learning and fails the most basic demands for data, as it is trapped in the inadequate SCORM standard. It was important to get rid of the multiple sign-ons, nested menus, lists of courses and general noise, too. Training needed to see learning as a process not just events, and it had to become more flexible. All of this has been achieved with the new type of smart platform, the LXP.

An early mention of learning experience design is by McLellan (2002) who, prophetically, mentions Harvard Case Studies, simulations, virtual reality, artificial intelligence and recommends the rehabilitation of the emotional side of learning. She also mentions Pine and Gilmore (1999), who talk of the 'Experience Economy', transformative experiences that change us in some way. This line of thought was heavily influenced by the type of attention and experiences that people were receiving in games, TV, film and social media.

There was also a growing interest in UI and UX, which began with Norman (1988) in the late 1980s, then Nielsen (1999) in the 1990s, who both recommended more focus on simplicity, consistency and usability. Then the web started to deliver a UI experience that was slick, personalized and used recommendation engines, from the simple but effective Google Letterbox for search, through to vertical scrolling in social media, to the tiled interfaces of video services such as YouTube, Netflix and Prime.

Performance support

The move from LMS to LXP also came from a line of thought that had been around for 30 years – namely a focus on performance support, as opposed to platform delivered courses. Gilbert and Rummler (1970) published a paper that expressed real scepticism about the direction towards training delivered in classroom courses, and pushed instead the idea of a system that could provide job support and improve performance. Thirty years ago, Gloria Gery (1991) defined this as 'EPSS – electronic performance support systems'. To shift from a training mindset towards performance, and therefore performance support, required going back to viewing learning as more of an apprenticeship. Training delivered through classroom courses had become the dominant paradigm during and after the two World Wars, when large numbers of people had to be trained quickly. Gery recommended a shift in mindset away from traditional training courses to performance support. Learning should not be separate from work but integrated into work. This, she thought, reduced mistakes, reduced the time needed to become competent and increased productivity.

These EPSS were designed from the user's point of view, to deliver fast, online access to help, support and tools whenever they were needed, usually via an IT system. They are not traditional help systems, which are limited in scope and not personalized to the user or task at hand. Barker and Banerji (1995) refined the EPSS and suggested they had four levels:

1 user interface shell (interface) and database

2 tools (help system, documentation, text retrieval system, intelligent agents, tutoring facility, simulation tools and communication resources)

3 application-specific support tools

4 target domain (schools, particular business settings, military, etc)

Written before the introduction of the internet, Gery's vision was pushed forward by performance experts such as Jay Cross, Bob Mosher, Conrad Gottfredson, Alfred Remmits and many others to become part of modern performance support systems. Rossett and Schafer (2012) put flesh on the bones in their 'Job Aids' work. Charles Jennings (2013) also pushed for this as a solution to the great need for on-the-job support. Beyond this, the LXP movement that delivered push and pull support in the workflow follows in Gery's footsteps. It has taken nearly 30 years for the technology to catch up with Gery's foresight.

Use in informal learning

Jay Cross (2006) was a theorist who invented the term 'e-learning' and worked tirelessly to get learning and development to think seriously about informal learning, workflow learning and working smarter. He urged us to focus more attention and budget into this form of workflow learning by putting more control into the hands of learners – 'more like driving a car than taking the bus', was one of his favourite mantras.

Cross realized that organizations spent almost all of their budgets on formal learning, when the empirical evidence showed that most of us learn informally. Cross wanted training to be honest about this 'spending paradox' – the fact that most learning is informal, yet almost all the spend is on formal courses. He invited us to think about learning in a more naturalistic way, seeing learners as real people in real organizations, who use real tools in real networks, both offline and online. Informal learning is driven by conversations, communities of practice, context, reinforcement through practice and now social media to optimize organizational performance. Blogs, podcasts, peer-to-peer sharing, aggregators, social media and personal knowledge management were all emergent phenomena across the 2000s and were very different from the top-down tools and content that traditional online learning has provided. When we look at the internet we see powerful tools and techniques emerging through genuine use. It is these, Cross believed, that point us towards success in learning. It is not that formal learning does not matter or should be abandoned, only that there was a need for a wider mix of solutions to learning needs. This model, of rebalancing learning towards the informal, without entirely abandoning the formal, he saw as a more naturalistic form of learning, based on real human needs and behaviours. It also moved technology away from the course delivered by LMS.

Learning in the workflow

The 70:20:10 movement, spearheaded by Charles Jennings (2013), also helped highlight the need for real traction in the workplace with more of a mixture of formal content and informal techniques to remove the 'conspiracy of convenience', where courses are ordered and delivered without proper alignment to business or learner needs.

Conrad Gottfredson and Bob Mosher (2011) took this idea of learning in the workflow further and have focused on 'moments of need' and innovative forms of curation and performance support. Their '5 Moments of Need®' idea helps learning professionals design, develop, maintain and measure effective learning and performance support. They build on the fact that most learning takes place on the job and not on training courses. In *Innovative Performance Support* (2011) they recommended a whole raft of techniques, tools and tech which can be used to implement performance support. Their arguments are that it reduces costs of formal training, while simultaneously improving performance and productivity, along with managing cognitive load and transfer. A positive side effect is that expensive internal IT support and helpdesks can also be reduced.

A training mindset is about building an 'instructional' system, mainly courses, while being an instructional 'order taker' determines what turns up on your menu – time-based courses. The shift Mosher and Gottfredson recommend is to move away from this service mentality, to being a partner in learning and development and helping to solve problems.

Learning should meet these needs and deliver to the right people, at the right time, in the right context. In organizations this means in the workflow, at the point-of-need. Gottfredson and Mosher's famous 5 Moments of (learner) Need (2021) are:

1 new – learning for first time

2 more – wanting to learn more

3 apply – trying to remember and apply

4 solve – something goes wrong

5 change – something changes.

Although 'new' and 'more' might be considered most important, 'apply', 'solve' and 'change' tend to be more common actual needs. This is where delivery must be orchestrated, as it also needs to be a combination of pull and push.

Failure really matters in work, for both the individual and the organization. Learning in the flow of work means learning from those hesitancies, failures and mistakes. A digital coach or EPSS allows the learner to take the relevant steps to overcome failure, as they continue their work. A workflow map unpacks context, and the digital coach supplies the resources.

Of course, as all resources are not created equal, there is a hierarchy of support available, from the simple to complex. One must always look towards delivering the minimal amount of support to reach a desired goal. At its simplest there is the 2-click, 10-second access to 'support' in response to the 5 Moments of Need. Then there is 'steps support' (quick and detailed). This is followed by supporting knowledge, documents, policies, procedures, job aids, FAQs, articles and so on. Only if these resources have been exhausted does the user move to real-time learning, such as e-learning. And if all else has been tried, they go to people, email, chats, social networks and communities of practice.

Gottfredson and Mosher's 5 Moments of Need have been used to underpin the development of performance support technology, the sort of technology that Gery envisioned. More than that, their precise identification of the needs of real learners in the workflow have been fundamental in helping shape LXPs that push and pull learning in the workflow. Above all, they have pushed learning and development to wake up to the idea that learning is a process that for most, takes place in the context of work, by doing.

All of these theorists' recommendations are consistent with Tolman's idea of 'latent' learning (Tolman and Honzik, 1930), Marsick and Watkin's (2002) work on 'incidental' learning and Cross's 'informal' learning (2006). It is also consistent with the work done on transfer at the start of the 20th century by Thorndike and Woodworth (1901) and others, where the transfer of knowledge and skills really does determine performance and is a real challenge as learning is rarely close to the point of use.

This is a case of technology catching up with learning theory. Performance technologies, such as learning experience platforms and performance support systems, need smart technology to identify, enable and deliver into the workflow. It is only now that such systems have been possible.

Personalized push and pull

It had been difficult to deliver personalized push and pull techniques, along with deep search within documents and other assets held by an organization, from an LMS. A more AI- and data-centric approach was needed, along with more powerful 'pull' through search and 'push' through notifications, nudges and curated content. This, as we shall see, has led to a wider definition of 'smart content', which now includes checklists, job aids, FAQs and simple responses to moments of need. As the technology has got smarter, content has become more variable, targeted and relevant.

Organizational needs change, workforce needs change, and there is a recognition that learning is a process and that learner needs are much more dynamic that the LMS-course model allows. People largely learn by doing, in the workflow. As Degreed and other companies entered the corporate market, LMS vendors busily transformed their LMS into an LXP or built an LXP from scratch. LMS vendors are moving towards being LXPs, while LXP vendors are having to become LMSs. There has already been consolidation in the LMS market, and these two will, in the end, converge into single platforms that are more dynamic and responsive.

These new platforms use AI and data to signpost, recommend and automate workflow processes. xAPI will replace SCORM and data-driven approaches will push the old static forms of delivery aside. We live in the age of algorithms, and just as everything we do online is mediated by AI and personalized by using personal and aggregated data, so it will be with learning, as explained in *AI for Learning* (Clark, 2020).

Webinar platforms

The online webinar has been a staple teaching and learning technique for decades, used by individuals and small groups of individuals and, at the conference level, it mimics the traditional talk or lecture, so is familiar to most of us.

Webinar software has its roots in real-time text messaging, such as IRC. These developed rapidly in the 1990s as web chat and instant messaging. Screensharing with file sharing and messaging appeared in 1995 with LiveSharePlus, and in 1996 Microsoft launched NetMeeting within its Internet Explorer browser. In 1997, Placeware appeared out of Xerox PARC with a full range of webinar features. It was acquired in 2003 by Microsoft, who renamed it Microsoft Office Live Meeting.

It wasn't until 1998 that the word 'webinar' was first trademarked, and in 1998 Cisco developed WebEx for webinars that could deal with up to 1,000 participants. A whole number of products then appeared from 2000 onwards, as broadband became more ubiquitous in companies and homes. More recently, the Covid-19 pandemic led to enormous growth in webinars as a result of the need for home education and training, as well as home working.

There were also proposals to stream video for learning in the 1990s, with Hayes and Harvel (1999) synchronizing audio with PowerPoint images. This evolved into the lecturer becoming visible alongside their lecture. The first streamed lectures were uploaded to YouTube by the University of California in 2008. Note that a webinar is different from a webcast. A webinar is a seminar on the web, while a webcast is a talk that includes limited audience chat and participation.

Standard meeting software is often used for webinars, such as Zoom, Microsoft Teams and Google Meet. Zoom became a *de facto* standard during the Covid-19 pandemic, while Microsoft Teams also gained traction as an organization-wide communications and collaboration platform. The pandemic brought an abrupt halt to most educational classes and lectures in early 2020. Most organizations were ill prepared for this shock and turned to the piece of technology that most approximated classroom teaching, a person talking via Zoom. Some used well established asynchronous techniques, but it was all quite crudely executed, with some describing it as emergency remote learning.

There are also specialist webinar platforms for larger gatherings that include additional functionality, such as polls, handouts, Q&As, live chat, transcription, translation, feedback forms, analytics reporting and end-to-end encryption. These webinar products can handle thousands of students simultaneously and can be recorded for future access and distribution. They are used in class teaching, lectures and adult and workplace learning. They free learning from having to be in a fixed location and are designed to include features that encourage learner participation. These webinar platforms and features are often included inside other learning platforms but remain a species apart, especially when used for conferences.

MOOCs

MOOCs are massive open online courses. 'Massive' in that the number of students on a course can be way bigger than traditional college courses, usually in the thousands but some with hundreds of thousands. 'Open' in that they rarely require pre-qualifications and are open to all who sign on. 'Online' means precisely that and they are structured as formal 'courses', often copying the 6–10-week semester structure.

History of MOOCs

MOOCs have several sources. Distance learning has been around since the 20th century, delivered by post, radio, TV, CDs and so on. Open access universities, such as the Open University in the UK that began in 1969, were often a source of MOOCs. We owe these organizations a debt in creating an environment where access and entry were open and costs free or low, in the spirit of open licensing. The Open Education Resource (OER) movement also contributed. David Wiley played an important role here, involved not only in open content but also the definition and evangelising of OER, and encouragement of open learning communities. MIT OpenCourseware was a landmark development in 2002, but there are plenty of other sizable examples.

The first MOOC is acknowledged to be the Connectivism and Connective Knowledge course (CCK08) delivered in 2008 by Canadians Stephen Downes and George Siemens. They deserve to be seen as the origins of one particular type of MOOC, what they called a 'connectivist' MOOC. There was then a hiatus before the MOOC phenomenon was amplified by Salman (Sal) Khan and his Khan Academy, with its millions of video views and free courses. This was significant, as it created short, faceless videos of mathematics, screen-capture style that hugely influenced subsequent MOOC development. Sebastian Thrun, Research Professor of Computer Science at Stanford University, publicly acknowledged his debt to Khan, and along with Peter Norvig, Director of Research at Google, delivered a landmark AI course, Introduction to Artificial Intelligence, in the fall of 2011 (Udacity, 2011). This got huge attention and boosted the phenomenon even further, with impressive participant numbers.

Stanford University has played an important role in the history of MOOCs as it produced a number of courses and entrepreneurs, including two courses delivered by Andrew Ng, an AI specialist in machine learning, and Jennifer Widom, Chair of the Computer Science Department, shortly after the Thrun and Norvig course. Ng and Daphne Koller, another Stanford academic, then left to set up the MOOC Coursera in 2012. They claimed that Coursera could never have happened within Stanford. This was followed by MIT who produced their first course, EdX, in March 2012, an event which was unlikely to have happened without MIT OpenCourseware.

MOOCs today

All these courses and entrepreneurs have contributed to the growth of MOOCs up to the present day, with their multiple investment streams and models, and they continue to evolve quickly. We have moved well beyond the early cMOOC versus xMOOC binary, connectivist, social MOOCs and other more content oriented MOOCs, once a useful distinction but no longer relevant now there are a wide range of MOOC types – lecture-based, resource-based, adaptive, connectivist, gamified, lab-based, vocational, synchronous, asynchronous, mini-MOOCs – on a wide range of subjects from educational, public, not-for-profit, government and corporate organizations, delivered to a wide range of audiences of all ages, including school children, students, employees, adults, professionals, people in the developing world and retirees.

The predominant delivery model that underpinned MOOCs was that they were either free or very low cost, and enrolled large volumes of users. This low-cost delivery dictated that the service costs had to be in the order of cents or pence per learner per hour, and be capable or scaling up as well as down. It was unsurprising to see that MOOCs became cloud hosted, typically constructed in infrastructure that can 'elastically scale' to meet demand.

EDX

Other platforms then came along. EdX, one of the early big players in the market, also had academic status (because it was funded by Harvard and MIT). It established a firm position with its 'open source' offer, backed by solid funding and with global reach. When there was a 'land grab' by MOOCs, EdX was already out there in the Americas, Europe, Asia and China. There was lots of noise about them being the sole French MOOC platform, until École normale Supérieure (ENC) and HEC Paris signed up Coursera. Even Stanford, the MOOC platform generator, had gone for EdX. EdX were eventually bought by higher education company 2U for $800 million in 2021.

COURSERA

Coursera started with deep pockets, as it received an initial $85 million of funding, enabling it to enjoy massive global growth and a solid management team. Quite simply, Coursera delivered. Deals with US state universities and dozens of others around the globe including in Europe, China, Korea, Russia and Mexico gave Coursera the ability to get their Signature Track revenues going. The company floated on the New York stock exchange in 2021.

FUTURELEARN

FutureLearn, a private company, was set up by the UK's Open University (with government support) as a bulwark against US domination. Although it has done deals with a large number of UK universities, it has failed to expand abroad. FutureLearn built their own platform, even though the OU has tried this before, with less than stellar results. With a traditional CEO from BBC Radio at the helm, FutureLearn lacked the commercial edge of the US players. Despite a $50 million investment by Seek Group, and a new CEO, they have failed to maintain momentum.

UDACITY

Much has been made of Udacity's initial offering – Thrun and Norvig's famous AI course from 2011 (see above). At the time, Thrun was teaching 200 Stanford students. Suddenly he had 160,000 students who were paying nothing! The fact that his own Stanford students then opted for the online course, 26,000 students eventually finished the course and that the top 400 students were all external and working online was astonishing. Udacity then branched out with The Open Education Alliance, as well as their online master's degree in computer science with AT&T at Georgia Tech.

UDEMY INC
Udemy is another MOOC provider, headquartered in San Francisco. It began in 2010 and offered a wide variety of business and IT-oriented courses as well as lifestyle, music and English courses to name just a few, with fees that vary from free to around $500. Users can also create their own courses. Like Udacity, Udemy Inc were aiming for the corporate market and set their sights on increasing revenues from the start.

OTHER MOOCS
There are many other MOOCs with less US focus:

- iversity, a Berlin-based MOOC set up in 2013, offered a range of courses – some in English, others in German – but lacked the reach of the larger players.

- OpenupEd is a pan-European initiative, launched in 2013 and supported by the European Commission, with 12 partners in Europe (also Russia, Turkey and Israel) and an emphasis on Open Universities.

- A rather vague consortium exists in India, consisting of Infosys, Cognizant, TCS and Nasscom, along with seven Indian Institutes of Technology (IIT) that claim to offer MOOCs. However, the Bombay IIT has announced a partnership with EdX, so it is possible some of these were more aggregators than platforms.

After an initial period of intense hype and publicity, followed by a more sober analysis, MOOCs are no longer seen as a serious threat to higher education, although they have had a significant effect on universities and adult and corporate learning. As one of the most fascinating developments in higher education learning technology, MOOCs are, in many ways, a pioneer of a more 'open' spirit in learning. For all their promises and faults, they have been at their most effective in forcing a *rethink* in higher education.

Demand for MOOCs

MOOCs uncovered huge demand for education beyond what was offered by the traditional university system. They were a solution to a demand problem, which continues to grow even today. For example, in 2021, there were over

4,550 MOOCs available globally, with around 200 added each month and getting on for 40 million enrolments. MOOCs have now moved well beyond the early adopter phase, where only those in the know knew about them. Their graduate profile includes a much wider and diverse audience than is found in universities, and includes school students and those in work as well as those that have retired.

The evidence over the last decade also suggests that there is greater demand for courses at the vocational rather than academic end of the spectrum. This is not to say that humanities and other forms of liberal arts courses are not in demand, just that MOOCs have shone a spotlight on real demand, which is more practical than most predicted. We have seen a huge demand for courses that satisfy not only educational but career demand, especially in business, IT and healthcare.

MOOC course models

MOOC courses initially followed the existing semester model of up to 10 weeks, drip-feeding content, with a largely linear curricular structure. Universities find it difficult to deal with shorter courses, more asynchronous learning and less linear course delivery, but MOOCs moved strongly in this direction. There are also courses with looser, more collaborative and open structures. The very concept of a course is, in a sense, being redefined by the variety of MOOCs that have emerged.

MOOCs eschewed long-form lectures for shorter episodes and a more mixed selection presentation. MOOCs most likely pushed many institutions to rethink their lectures in terms of their length and whether they should be recorded. There were many other pedagogic issues that were rethought of in regard to types of resources, media mix, active learning and collaboration. MOOCs also forced a rethink on assessment techniques. A range of assessments have been tried, including statements of completion or attainment, through to fully proctored, online examinations.

Of course, online learning is not just about MOOCs. There is now an increased focus on digital strategy. Even at faculty level, few academics can afford to ignore the simple fact that every student, researcher and teacher uses the internet as a fundamental tool. This has reshaped the very nature of course delivery.

The MOOC phenomenon has uncovered another uncomfortable truth: that higher education is no longer the sole provider of adult education. As

MOOCs moved out of their traditional curriculum and pedagogic struc-tures, they began to be produced by other types of organizations, for audiences beyond the 18-year-old undergraduate demographic. In fact, the main opposition to MOOCs comes not from learners or the public, but from those within current institutions, who see MOOCs not as progress but as a threat to the status quo. Higher education will not suffer greatly from their presence, but the provision for higher education will be greatly widened.

COMPARISON WITH TRADITIONAL UNIVERSITY COURSES

A common charge made against MOOCs is their high dropout rates. However, it is inappropriate to take the word 'dropout' from one context and stamp it upon another. This is a category mistake, when a word is used to mean one thing (pejoratively) in the context of a long college or university course, then applied with the same pejorative force to a very different type of learning experience. Stopping during a MOOC is very different from drop-ping out of an expensive three- (or four-) year degree. With open courses, the commitment of the learner need be no more than signing up to have a look or just a browse to see if it is right for them. The decision to take or drop out of a MOOC is not a life-changing decision in terms of money, time or commitment. It is important to look at uptake, not dropout. MOOCs should be viewed as widely available opportunities, not compulsory attendance schooling.

It is clear that MOOCs have led to a rethink when it comes to the use of technology in terms of learning, teaching, demand, pedagogy, curricula, assessment, accreditation, culture, cost and role, and their impact as a learn-ing technology cannot be ignored

Social platforms

Organizations are being changed by this external and internal connectivity. External social platforms like Twitter, YouTube, Instagram, Facebook and TikTok clearly fuel informal learning, as people have open access to learning and learning support through social connections. It is easy to forget that social platforms include social media platforms with their billions of users. These are undoubtedly used for learning, with Twitter and LinkedIn often used in continuous professional development. Tools such as the messenger service within these platforms can be used to contact people and share infor-mation, while others such as TikTok allow us to share content.

Another platform development is the rise of corporate social platforms. Many learning platforms also had their own internal social systems, but these competed with other systems, such as email, and those social systems already in place, such as Yammer and Slack. (Yammer was bought by Microsoft in 2012 and eventually folded into Microsoft Teams. Slack appeared in 2013, went public in 2019 and was bought by SalesForce in 2021.) There was also a move by Microsoft, SalesForce, SAP and large enterprise software companies to focus more on products which brought them into the workflow learning and meeting/webinar space. Microsoft Teams is a good example. It replaced Microsoft Classroom in 2017 and offered a free version of Teams in 2018, Skype for Business was phased out, and now Microsoft is focused wholly on Teams, with Chat, Channels, Meetings and some educational services.

There are dozens of other social and social media channels supporting communications, blogging and media sharing, along with those that have a sector or subject-specific focus. These still play a significant role in learning, especially blogging platforms such as Blogger.

Adaptive platforms

Adaptive learning takes several forms. Learners' routes through a learning experience or course can be determined by pre-testing, or continuously adapted through real-time resequencing. These platforms take personal and aggregated data to decide personalized learning routes through a network of learning objects. Like the GPS or satnav in your car, these platforms know where the learner needs to get to and if they go off course, smart technology is used to get them back on course, helping to reduce the risk of them getting stuck or failing. Different learners take different vectors through the course depending on their prior competences and their performance as they proceed.

Adaptive platforms require a high degree of preparation, as content has to be chunked and put into a structure with relationships established in terms of dependencies. Good examples include CogBooks and Area9 Lyceum for general courses and Duolingo for language learning, with their sophisticated, personalized delivery of content based on advanced data and statistical and AI techniques.

Digital adoption platforms

A digital adoption platform (DAP) does exactly what it says, that is help organizations adopt new pieces of enterprise software. Software rollouts that replace previous systems and processes can be tricky in terms of training employees in advance of their deployment. Typically a DAP would accompany the roll-out of large business process software, such as changes to financial or sales systems and provide detailed training and support on the software's detailed functions. Increasingly, the systems providers themselves are providing training and support, however.

Practice platforms

Practice platforms focus on retrieval, spaced practice and revision, as well as known and well-researched techniques for increasing retention. The algorithms vary from simple sequenced spacing, through variations of the Leitner flashcard system, to Half-life models. They increasingly use AI as a form of analysis and delivery.

Flashcard systems, with learning objects or test items together with feedback, also help structure the learning process. The focus of this post-learning experience is the identification of weak items, reinforcement, revision and recall. Note that practice platforms such as Glean use AI on students' notes in order to generate better note taking and learning experiences, to increase their learning and retention.

Smart platforms

Smart platforms that use data to personalize, improve and provide more efficient, flexible and targeted learning are already here. They require a shift towards smart analysis and smart content. Their focus is on measurable delivery, rather than storage and management of courses, which means more alignment with personal and organizational goals.

There has always been a tension in learning between what Neal Ferguson called *The Square and the Tower* (2019) – between the horizontal and the vertical. In learning, this manifests itself as formal versus informal learning, with the majority of learning taking place informally and horizontally, and formal learning in the form of courses imposed vertically and top-down by education and training departments. This has been reflected in the evolution of platforms.

Platforms such as LMSs and MOOC platforms are almost always towers of control within organizations that impose management control, consistency and structure, as do adaptive and practice platforms. They seek to define, manage and deliver formal learning courses. There is always, therefore, a tension between this and the wish among organizations and learners for learning to be more flexible, looser and smarter. The LXP model loosens things up into the workflow, but it is still a tower, albeit shorter, more open and accessible. Beyond this lie smart platforms that use data, AI and performance support platforms and services to deliver the right thing, at the right time, to the right person, in line with an organization's needs.

Platforms have become more accessible, dynamic, invisible, personalized and aligned with organizational needs. Organizations almost always have ecosystems of technology for learning, but they also need enterprise-wide solutions that provide control and consistency – and this is being provided by smart platforms.

Databases

Finally, a word or two about the unsung hero of almost all platforms – the humble database. It underpins almost every online service and learning platform. At first, data was accessed sequentially on magnetic tape, then on discs in the mid-1960s, and now today via the cloud. The types of access and structures have also changed. A lot of learning technology sits on top of these mighty workhorses.

From simple spreadsheets to blockchain, there is a myriad of database forms that differ in the way they store data and the way that data is accessed. They have existed for many decades, long before the arrival of the internet, and now, with their move to the cloud, have immense capacity as online learning solutions. Almost all scalable solutions in online learning require databases to function. They store not just the learning content but details of learners and their achievements. Increasingly, the data gathered and held in such databases is used to personalize and increase the flexibility, adaptability and efficacy of learning.

Conclusion

Learning platforms vary in scope, sector and purpose, and they are evolving fast. They overlap in functionality and, although new types emerge, such as LXPs, there has been an overall and accelerating trend for them to merge and converge. There is also convergence across sectors, so for example, platforms such as Microsoft Teams are now common across both education and large corporate organizations, despite their fundamental differences. MOOCs are becoming more like traditional platforms and now operate in both the education and corporate sectors. LMSs and LXPs are also likely to converge into smart platforms.

We must also remember the large number of other, specific platforms, such as Wikipedia, Duolingo, VR, AR and even the coming Metaverse, which will be explored in Chapter 12. Online large-scale learning services are almost invariably built upon platforms of one kind or another.

Platforms store, manage and deliver learning content in various forms to learners, and no platform is complete without deliverable content and services. To understand their true efficacy we must now unpack the nature of that content and services. The platform space has become more dynamic, with platforms changing, converging and merging. Smart platforms are emerging, with intelligence that focuses on needs and personalization. These smart platforms, alongside smart content, are moving technology towards a much neater fit between learners, learning and organizational needs. In the next chapter, we look at the evolution of learning content, as it too has used technology to develop into smart content.

References

Atkinson, R C and Wilson, H A (1969) *Computer-Assisted Instruction: A book of readings*, Academic Press, New York

Barker, P and Banerji, A (1995) Designing electronic performance support systems, *Innovations in Education and Training International*, 32(1), 4–12

Black, E (2012) *IBM and the Holocaust: The strategic alliance between Nazi Germany and America's most powerful corporation* (Expanded Edition), Dialog Press, USA

Clark, D (2020) *Artificial Intelligence for Learning: How to use AI to support employee development*, Kogan Page Publishers, London

Cross, J (2006) *Informal Learning: Rediscovering the natural pathways that inspire innovation and performance*, John Wiley & Sons, Hoboken, NJ

Ferguson, N (2019) *The Square and the Tower: Networks and power, from the Freemasons to Facebook*, Penguin, London

Fletcher, J D and Rockway, M R (1986) Computer-based training in the military. In J A Ellis (ed), *Military contributions to instructional technology*, 171–222, Praeger Publishers, New York

Gery, G J (1991) *Electronic Performance Support Systems: How and why to remake the workplace through the strategic application of technology*, Weingarten Publications, Inc

Gilbert, T F and Rummler, G (1970) *Praxis Reports*, Praxis Corporation, New York

Gottfredson, C and Mosher, B (2011) *Innovative Performance Support: Strategies and practices for learning in the workflow,* McGraw Hill Professional, New York

Gottfredson, C and Mosher, B (2021) The 5 Moments of Need: A Performance-First Approach, www.5momentsofneed.com/ebook.htm (archived at https://perma.cc/ZDW8-SMCE)

Hayes, M H and Harvel, L D (1999) Distance learning into the 21st century, *1999 Annual Conference,* 4–203

Itmazi, J A et al (2005) A comparison and evaluation of open source learning management systems, *Proceedings of the IADIS Conference on Applied Computing*, 1(11), 1–11

Jennings, C (2013) *The 70:20:10 Framework Explained*, FastPencil, Inc

Marsick, V J and Watkins, K E (2002) Informal and incidental learning, *New Directions for Adult and Continuing Education*, 2001(89), 25–34

Maslow, A H (1966) *The Psychology of Science: A reconnaissance*, Harper & Row, New York

Norman, D (1988) *The Psychology of Everyday Things*, Basic Books, New York

Nielsen J (1999) *Designing Web Usability: The practice of simplicity*, New Riders Publishing, Hoboken, NJ

Rossett, A and Schafer, L (2012) *Job Aids and Performance Support: Moving from knowledge in the classroom to knowledge everywhere*, John Wiley & Sons, Hoboken, NJ

Tolman, E C and Honzik, C H (1930) Introduction and removal of reward, and maze performance in rats, *University of California Publications in Psychology*, 4, 257–75

Thorndike, E L and Woodworth, R S (1901) The influence of improvement in one mental function upon the efficiency of other functions, II. The estimation of magnitudes, *Psychological Review*, 8(4), 384

Udacity (2011) Introduction to Artificial Intelligence https://sites.google.com/site/aiclass2011archive/ (archived at https://perma.cc/K858-W85D)

10

Content

When people use the word 'content', as in learning content, they often view it narrowly, homogeneously, even pejoratively. Content is best seen in terms of who uses it and how it is used, not solely as types of content or as a thing in itself. It is a deep, wide and complex set of resources, used in many different ways by many types of learners, in lots of different contexts.

We have seen in earlier chapters how learning content has deep origins in prehistory. Content has existed longer than our species. From the first drawn geometric marks on shells by *Homo erectus* and symbolic cave art with undoubtedly instructional intentions, then writing and later printing, followed by computers and their networking on the internet. All of this has enabled the global creation and distribution of content up to the present day, where artificial intelligence now has the ability to create content. Across this vast span of time, content has been captured as knowledge outside of our minds and has been the driver and primary form of transmission for our history, culture and progress.

Our culture has literally been shaped by learning technologies. From the invention of writing, where we first began to store and manage large amounts of knowledge outside of our brains, content has increased in scale. It has been created on clay, wood, papyrus, vellum and codexes, while printing brought the mass replication of pamphlets and books. The internet provided massive scalability of not only print but audio, video, interactive media and an explosion of professional and user-generated online content. Whether in books, images, podcasts, videos, social media, courses, curricula, created in libraries, custom-built, crowdsourced, user-generated and now created by AI, content has always been used in learning. Never have we had so much easy access to knowledge and content in so many forms and media types, from so many sources, produced by so many different types of organizations and people.

So let us take a look at how a wide variety of content forms have been *used*, as this is the first and most important lens through which content can be viewed.

Where does content come from?

The meanings of words, as an example of simple content, do not come from definitions in a dictionary. The definitions come from how words are *used* in the real world, before they are captured in the dictionary. So it is with learning content. As a learning technology, content is not an isolated thing in itself because it is always used by people, so it needs to be seen in terms of who, where and how it is used, usually, but not always, as a means to some end.

Learning can be described as a lasting change in long-term memory. We all learn every day from simply being in the world, doing things and interacting with others, and that is how it has been throughout our history. As soon as we started to create tools, these external artifacts became objects with the potential for teaching and learning. With the first marks, we started to externalize and fix our thoughts so that others could see and understand them. The cognitive revolution brought this to a level of pictorial genius in cave painting, which was deliberately created content, made by people who needed to teach others. Pre-literate societies used imagery in rock art, sculpture and other forms to represent what they wanted others to see and learn from. Images are still a fundamental teaching technology. It's worth noting that near universal literacy is relatively recent in our history, and that in earlier times most people learnt from images, hence the ubiquity of religious art, for example.

Writing emerges from these oral and pictorial traditions to capture thoughts that can then be used to teach many others beyond the immediate limits and range of speech. It too was strongly pictorial before phonetic forms of representation were invented. Writing itself had to be taught and learnt but, more importantly, the products of writing became the content that could be stored and used by others to teach and learn. Print was the amplification of writing and images through replication, which gave content greater reach numerically, temporally and geographically. It gave it permanence, so that it could be used by many.

Other more recently invented media such as photography, moving images, audio, VR and AR have added further useful dimensions to teaching and learning. Computers and the internet then gave almost free replication, manipulation and delivery of content, across the entire globe, with AI and data providing new, fledgling methods for creating and dealing with content.

Most learning does not need mediating content. Instead it comes through doing and from others, and is often incidental and informal.

How is content used?

When we see content in terms of use, by whom and in what context, we can examine the many *types* of content that meet those uses. Content is not so much a spectrum, from simple learning resources to courses, it is a set of related constellations. These constellations are diffuse, have variation within them and sometimes overlap, yet they are defined enough to be seen as types of content.

One can categorize these content types in terms of their media types and function, each with different sets of affordances, as text, graphics, audio, video, animation, engagement and feedback, scenarios, simulations, VR, AR, games, gamification, social learning, practice, curation, performance support, AI and data-driven (Clark, 2021). Within each of these are many different types of learning experience, from basic knowledge to complex learning through simulations. The sheer range and variety of online learning has been widening and deepening as the technology used to create and deliver content has become more powerful, but we can also select a few examples to illustrate how learning content has evolved.

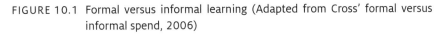

FIGURE 10.1 Formal versus informal learning (Adapted from Cross' formal versus informal spend, 2006)

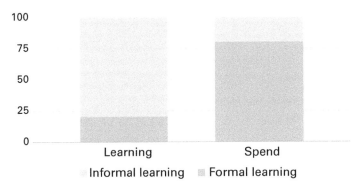

It is the context that often determines what content is used, how it is used, by whom and to what ends. There are vast differences in what content is and how it is used, depending on *context*. The big distinction is between *informal* and *formal* learning.

As Cross (2006) claimed, the spending paradox was that although 80 per cent of learning is informal, 80 per cent of the spend is on formal learning. This contradiction is starting to be resolved, but let us begin with informal learning.

Informal learning

Learners are increasingly finding immediate answers online through search via Google, Wikipedia and YouTube, all of which have a consistent interface and layout. These monolithic systems are familiar and reliable, and are often supplemented by additional online systems chosen by learners.

Take just one medium, text, which for 5,000 years as content has been a medium for both informal and formal learning. Text is an easy to produce, replicable and searchable medium and is the mainstay of email, texting, messaging, online forums, social platforms in the workplace and many social media platforms. It is what teachers write on blackboards and whiteboards. We also forget that written feedback is a key driver in teaching and learning, perhaps better described as 'feedforward'. Once a learner has had feedback that they have completed good work, that feeling of success transforms them.

Technology has freed text from the physical technology of paper. Writing and printing may have been the two Big Bangs of learning technology in the physical realm, but learning is a cognitive act and the means of delivery matters less than access, speed and relevance. It was computers and the internet that freed learning from the tyranny of time and space by delivering any searchable content to anyone, anytime, anyplace.

Internet content

Tim Berners-Lee gave us a technological leap that may yet prove to be more significant than the arrival of the printing press in the 15th century. This quickly allowed massive open pedagogies to emerge that were to change the learning landscape forever. We saw in Chapter 8 how Page and Brin gave us Google, a major pedagogic shift that provided instant access to knowledge, images, maps, translations and other tools and services. Wikipedia surprised everyone with its success as the biggest, open, free, crowdsourced knowledge base ever seen. Short, instructive video is another massive open online pedagogy, and YouTube's short video clips provide a huge contribution to learning. Khan Academy, Duolingo and MOOCs, along with many other learning service and content providers, have irreversibly changed the learning landscape.

These are innovations in learning technology which understand the use of media and pedagogy in learning and have adapted it to their audiences' needs. Jeff Bezos not only turned the book industry on its head, making it easier to both buy and sell the 'long-tail' of more obscure and second-hand books, but also ebooks. Gates and Jobs led Microsoft and Apple to dominant positions, not only on devices used for learning but also software such as Microsoft Office and iTunes, putting enormous power in the hands of teachers and learners in terms of the production and consumption of learning tools, services and content. None of these entrepreneurial figures were learning theorists but their learning technology creations had a massive and direct impact upon teaching and learning. As well as increasing efficacy through search (Google Scholar is an obvious example), these technological advances aid the delivery of learning content, communications and collaboration.

From Gutenberg to Zuckerberg, technologists have scaled up access to learning, as well as providing tools that accelerate learning. Online learning is more than just courses on the web, it is computer-mediated learning. In practice, Amazon for books, Wikipedia for knowledge and YouTube for video have contributed hugely to learners' access to knowledge, albeit in very different ways, with millions now routinely using these to advance their knowledge and learning.

Books arguably still drive learning in many contexts, both formal and informal. They remain a mainstay for teaching and learning in schools, colleges and universities, and we have convenient access to more books than ever before. Technology has played a huge role here, with online access allowing readers to search, browse and buy a larger range of books than was ever possible in traditional bookshops.

Yet we are faced with a problem regarding the 'worth' of media for learning. The media for learning that some (often older) tribes like, such as books, are a conviction, whereas media that these tribes don't like, such as social media, are dismissed as an addiction. This happens with most forms of new technology, but more especially with learning technology because education is the domain of the young. Reading may not be in decline but reading long-form books may well be in decline.

WIKIPEDIA – KNOWLEDGE AS CONTENT

Wikipedia has become a dominant force and has grown into the largest and most used wiki on the web, a vast encyclopedia built, edited and policed by its users. It is a huge knowledge base that is created by its users, who can publish and amend without having to download special software. Other users who correct errors oversee the accuracy of the content. In addition, Wikipedia allows users to see edit histories and discuss these issues. Realistically, it recognizes that knowledge is sometimes not absolutely certain and will be subject to debate and discussion. Since its inception in 2001, Wikipedia has grown into one of the largest and most used knowledge sources in the world. With millions of articles in over 200 languages, and thousands of new articles added every day, it is one of the most visited sites on the web.

Its remarkable achievement was not only to produce the world's largest and most popular knowledge base, but to do it through a model that was truly innovative. Previous paper and CD-ROM encyclopedias, like the *Encyclopedia Britannica* and Microsoft's Encarta, were produced at great cost and sold to customers to recoup that cost. Wikipedia came along and relied on volunteers who did this for free, relying not on a corporate business model but the peer reputation of its writers and editors. This low-cost model allowed founder Jimmy Wales to offer this wonderful online service for free. It showed that people were willing to create and share for the public good.

There has been some debate about the reliability of Wikipedia, but a blind-trial research project published in *Nature* (Giles, 2005) found little significant difference between it and the *Encyclopedia Britannica*. There is little comparison between a fixed, linear paper encyclopedia and a dynamic, open, free resource, with edit trails and search, constantly growing in multiple languages. Its crosslinks, links to external resources, transparency on edits and discussions also make it different from print repositories of knowledge.

Although derided by many academics and teachers for being inaccurate, Wikipedia has remarkable levels of use by teachers and learners. On top of this it has been used for assignments, such as editing articles. In practice, however, it is mostly used as a reference tool. It has a consistent layout featuring a general introductory paragraph, a linked index and headings, making it appealing to those who want to find things quickly. The fact that it is searchable, cross-linked and provides bibliographies and citations is also academically useful.

The web now has a plethora of wiki applications including Wiktionary (wiki dictionary), Wikinews, Wikibooks, Wikilaw and so on. In addition, wiki technology is being used to revolutionize the way in which we capture, create, publish and update knowledge within organizations. Wikis are becoming common within corporations as a method of knowledge management. Their bottom-up ethos appeals to those who see knowledge emerging from expertise within an organization, as opposed to being handed down from single authorities.

Wikipedia, as a source of knowledge and learning, is one of the world's most successful websites. Google even scrapes from Wikipedia biographies to feature as sidebar profiles. It has, in effect, become the world's *de facto* standard for knowledge searches. This is a radical shift in learning technology and in the way knowledge is made available on the web. As a learning resource, it is truly one of the modern wonders of the web.

VIDEO CONTENT – YOUTUBE

In 2005, Chad Hurley and Steven Chen founded YouTube, one of the most successful and remarkable websites ever created. It is the largest audio-visual channel in history and the second largest search engine after Google. In 2006, it was sold to Google for £1.65 billion.

Teachers and especially learners make enormous use of YouTube. It is used both as a complementary method for teaching and on a massive scale by learners, on almost every imaginable subject. In one study, 86 per cent of users reported using YouTube to learn new things and in another, both Millennials and Gen Z stated that YouTube was their preferred learning method (Pearson, 2018).

YouTube's staggering success came on the back of word-of-mouth recommendations, starting with *Saturday Night Live's* 'Lazy Sunday' clip. Although set up to share entertainment that was often funny and surreal, it now has thousands of education and training videos. It has become the go-to video website for many learners.

Like Wikipedia, YouTube is growing exponentially and as more serious content appears, teachers, trainers, lecturers and learners can use this content as a free resource. It has also influenced the way video appears and is shown on the web. Most of the clips are short, avoiding overlong instructional content and cognitive overload. YouTube has uncovered new ways of watching, patterns of attention and ways of interacting with an audience. In short, it is a new learning platform that breaks many of the old rules around learning. If you can video it, it is somewhere on YouTube. Features such as captioning, automatic generation of transcripts and editing features have increased its usefulness for educators.

Learning by doing has always suffered in the unreal world of the school classroom, so an important advance in vocational and practical learning has been made through YouTube, where real tasks are shown on video. These often involve the manipulation of real objects and the demonstration of processes, all of which can be seen full screen on portable tablets and mobile devices. Musical education has been revolutionized by the demonstration of fingers on chords and other techniques. Sports coaching in almost every imaginable sport is also commonplace.

Although easily denigrated, the talking head is still popular on YouTube. The video blog, expert talk and many other examples of someone giving their all, is still there. TED Talks are perhaps the most interesting example of this, a respected brand that focuses on the expert speaker to deliver punchy sessions that eschew traditional lecturing in favour of short, passionate and informative talks. TED Talks gives strict instructions to its speakers and believes that its video and lectures are not about the transfer of knowledge but the passion of the expert and a vision. Lectures, interviews, drama and other learning formats can also be found.

YouTube has the advantage of being a powerful global brand. The fact that video cameras are now relatively cheap and are embedded in mobile phones has meant the massive creation of popular content. It is shaping the way video is created, distributed and watched on the web and has the potential to act as a vast education and training resource of free content, lowering costs for learning. More than this, YouTube has introduced pedagogic changes around the use of video in terms of its length, quality, format and breadth of uses. As a learning technology, it is clearly useful in both formal and informal learning. It is an enduring pedagogy that pushes the creation of video for learning as bandwidth increases and more devices become able to handle the delivery of video.

Social media

Increased bandwidth and lower storage costs have also led to an explosion of video content on social media such as Twitter, Facebook, LinkedIn, Instagram and TikTok, among others. Some social media platforms, such as Facebook and Instagram, remain largely social and offer relatively little learning activity. Twitter has proved to be a useful and enduring source of content for continuous professional development as large numbers of learning professionals share opinions and links to relevant content. LinkedIn has become a more professional social space, with a business focus around services and recruitment.

> Social media can be described as mobile (anywhere, anytime), engagement, feedback, chunked, reinforcement, practice, personalized, social, data-driven, AI-driven. These are the things learning theory points us towards, yet they are so rarely used in teaching and learning.

Learning is now often driven by data and AI, and services like those described above, as well as more subject-specific services like Duolingo, point the way towards newer, more personalized approaches to education and organizational learning. However, while looking at globally popular social media services doesn't suggest that this is how education and training will be delivered in the future, they do give some very important pointers towards what is *possible* in delivery. It is worth dwelling on this functionality as it has important lessons about the future of learning technology.

TIKTOK

Another platform that has become a source of content is TikTok. Its name is catchy and suggests time (tik... tok... – the sound of mechanical clocks), a key feature of the platform, which delivers snappy, short videos. Like YouTube, Facebook, Twitter and Instagram, it is insanely popular.

TikTok videos can be up to 15 seconds long, but it is possible to connect multiple video clips together for up to 60 seconds of total recording. The discipline of producing super-short videos for learning is an art form.

> TikTok videos are often wonderfully concise and point the way towards the sort of learning support that an LXP may want to deliver for push or pull learning events in the workplace or practice and reinforcement in education. Longer videos, recorded separately outside of TikTok, can also be uploaded unto the platform.

TikTok is different to YouTube because of the way it supports smartphone technology, making it so easy to make videos: the user just selects 15 or 60 secs, points the camera and taps. Tap is used to start and stop, in order to include a range of different shots. There is also a Timer button to allow a few seconds before recording starts. The Checkmark button is used to preview the video and to add sounds, effects, text and stickers. Then the user taps Next and the video is done. All the user needs to do after that is add a description and hashtags, tag their friends and choose who they want to view their post. TikTok has a Bookmark icon to see videos that have been favourited or saved to watch later. It is even possible to search by sounds and effects! Hashtags, however, are more popular and relevant for learning. It is possible to like, comment, save or download videos for offline viewing (if the creator allows), and even be allowed to 'duet' or react to their TikToks. Then there are options to create a live photo or GIF from the video and share.

The speed adjustments are also fascinating, allowing the user to record at 0.3x, 0.5x, 1x, 2x, or 3x speed. The ability to speed up or slow down videos in learning allows the learner to see the process in slow motion or faster for a quick overview. It is possible, for example, to create flashcard apps and revision tests at different speeds.

Another feature is the ability to film your reactions to a video, in picture. Think of the possibilities here, for teacher, lecturer and trainer commentary, user-generated assignments and feedback. The 'duet', or sharing two video feeds on one screen, is also popular.

TikToks can be set to be viewed publicly, shared with friends or shared privately, and there is a 'live' feature if the user has a large number of followers. Analytics are also available. What TikTok shows is that there is an insatiable appetite, especially among the young, to create, edit, add music and effects to video online.

TikTok captured something that was hinted at in the move towards massive YouTube and Instagram use – video. Reflecting on what this tells us about how technology can be used in learning, it seems clear that it has to be data and AI driven. Chunking matters, along with layers of social interaction. The switch towards AI-driven learning is here (tick... tock...).

There is, of course, a wide and deep reservoir of content available through search, which has become much more sophisticated, giving the learner access to knowledge steps in processes, as well as access to learning tools and services. Never have so many had access to so much at so little cost.

Formal learning

Most formal learning takes place in an institutional context, for example, in pre-school, primary school, secondary school, tertiary education and then workplaces or bodies that provide professional development and certification. In education, learning is often credentials based, whereas in the workplace it is more to do with performance and organizational goals. Formal learning can also be adult learning, public education and sometimes just for the joy of it, as part of a curious mindset.

In formal learning, we tend to think of content as *courses*. These courses can include seminars and modules as part of a degree, catalogues of long-form classroom or online courses in the workplace that take days or weeks to complete, as well as courses that take only hours to complete and even micro-courses. VLEs and LMSs typically deliver such courses. As we saw in Chapter 9, MOOCs similarly deliver long-form courses from MOOC platforms. Adaptive platforms (also discussed in Chapter 9) can deliver long-form, personalized, adaptive courses. These formal courses have a designed structure and specifically created content. Credentials, curricula and courses are the primary currency of educational institutions. They rarely deliver anything beyond formally, defined, time-bound courses.

Workplace learning

In the workplace, generic courses are used to cover the basics of business-related learning, and this has turned into an enormous global business. Several companies deliver generic catalogues or specific catalogues on, say, health and safety, ethics, compliance or equality and diversity. This type of content has come in for criticism for being too generic, dull and predictable, but it serves a need at an affordable price. However, buying the same generic content from catalogues does not give an organization any competitive advantage or edge. Choosing custom-designed or bespoke content that covers an organization's particular needs will, however, give freshly designed content with a particular spin that can provide a competitive advantage.

One problem has been the confusion of schooling with training. Organizational learning, especially online, often defaults back to theory-heavy content that lacks the necessary push in terms of application and transfer. Bloom's taxonomy (1976) is used as a baseline, but usually only the cognitive component. In fact, Bloom recommended three components – cognitive, affective and psychomotor. This can lead to over-engineered, theory-heavy courses that try to push maximum content to learners, rather than recognizing that much of it need not be memorized and that workplace learning is largely about performance, not memory.

Returning to actual use and delivery, there are some notable landmarks in the provision of large amounts of free learning content on the web, that are *intentionally* designed to teach, as opposed to say, Wikipedia and YouTube, which are resources that *could* be used to teach, among many other things.

Open educational resources

One species of formal content that is defined by its use is open educational resources (OER). David Wiley was an early and influential figure in the OER movement. He was involved not only in open content, but also the definition and evangelizing of OER and the encouragement of open learning communities. He started the Open Content project, which gave Open Content Licenses and was superseded by Creative Commons in 2003, where he became the Director of Educational Licenses. Creative Commons is a not-for-profit organization and has licensed over 2 billion works, including Wikipedia and Flickr.

OER was a development that encouraged the open license of educational content, in all forms of media, for teaching, learning and assessment and also research. 'Open' is not a simple concept, in opposition to closed; it is a matter of degree in terms of the nature of the content as resources, courses, books and so on, as well as the degree to which they are in the public domain. Hilton III et al (2010) identified four things that Open Educational Resources allow from a license:

1 *Reuse* – The most basic level of openness. People are allowed to use all or part of the work for their own purposes (e.g. download an educational video to watch at a later time).

2 *Redistribute* – People can share the work with others (e.g. email a digital article to a colleague).

3 *Revise* – People can adapt, modify, translate or change the form of the work (e.g. take a book written in English and turn it into a Spanish audio book).

4 *Remix* – People can take two or more existing resources and combine them to create a new resource (e.g. take audio lectures from one course and combine them with slides from another course to create a new derivative work).

OER has been somewhat confused by the availability of free resources, such as MOOCs. Free is different from open. There is also the 'not invented here' view that often prevents such resources from being used by a research-oriented faculty who have a natural disposition towards using only content they have created, even content that is to be taught.

The OER movement has been growing steadily due to the efforts of theorists and contributors. In practice, reusability, redistribution, revision and remixing have not turned out to be relevant. OER targeted directly at learners rather than teachers has had far more success and on a greater scale thanks to resources such as YouTube, MOOCs, Khan Academy and Duolingo, almost in spite of the institutional OER movement. In fact, there seems to have been a bifurcation in OER between the flood of publicly funded projects that tended to atrophy and even die, and a successful crop of global successes.

Opposition

Rather than promote the use of OER, some teachers and academics have taken a distant, sniping and even hostile stance against their use. Yet the use of OER could widen the experience and pedagogic sophistication of most teachers. It is OER that allows more blended learning and flipped learning. In practice, it is rather disappointing that the success of OER has been due to learners, in their hundreds of millions, by-passing teachers and using these resources without their knowledge, sometimes defying their prohibition.

OER, in its early days, got bogged down in an obsession with reusable learning objects (this led to the largely hopeless SCORM standards) and a far too 'teacher-oriented' view of reusability. In some circles the obsession with the reuse of content by teachers, rather than straight use by learners, has led to an inward-looking attitude and poorer quality resources. Teaching is a means to an end and the most valuable OER resources are those used directly by learners. Reuse by educators remains a tiny part of OER overall use. Tkacz (2014) shows that so-called 'open' resources often contain overly hierarchical structures. This is certainly true with the reusability argument, where old ideas about quality and reusability are really epistemological arguments about control and certainty.

OER initiatives often lack the marketing skills to promote their resources. Poor marketing results in repositories of unknown and unloved resources. The failure to see 'sustainability' in terms of a business model and funding has also been a real Achilles' heel. The successful examples, such as Wikipedia, YouTube, Khan Academy, Duolingo and MOOCs transcended the traditional 'keep it in the institution' model, to provide hundreds of millions with valuable resources.

Empirically, we have seen Wikipedia, YouTube, MOOCs and other resources on the web emerge as truly wonderful examples of how pragmatic and sustainable openness can be achieved. These are the open resources that point towards the decentralization, democratization and disintermediation of learning. These examples have grown because they started and exist outside of educational institutions.

The web also has more structured and subject-specific content that is used by tens of millions of learners. Khan Academy and Duolingo both illustrate the type of open and largely free learning technologies that have emerged to teach both children and adults. These specialist learning services satisfy every desire in terms of subjects and approaches and are increasingly sophisticated in terms of pedagogy, AI and personalization.

Video resources

KHAN ACADEMY

Khan Academy was set up by Sal Khan, and the company's ambitious mission statement is 'to provide a free, world-class education for anyone, anywhere.' As an outsider in education, in that he comes from business, Khan has attributed his success to not being part of the educational establishment. It is this that allowed him to get on and do what he did, which was create a large set of YouTube videos and learning management software, used by millions around the world.

Khan's work started by accident when his cousin failed a mathematics test and he began tutoring her (Khan, 2012). Her brothers joined the tutoring sessions and word spread. Khan tried Skype but it was too unwieldy for four or more students, so he recorded sessions and uploaded the videos to YouTube, which proved to be immensely popular. This is a good example of how synergistic online services can mutually support each other. Innovation begets innovation.

Khan decided, boldly and deliberately, to keep the background of his videos black, like a chalkboard, and eliminate the talking head. This was to make students feel as though he were sitting next to them, not talking 'at' them. Faces, he believes, are a distraction from the content. The advantages of recorded videos for learning include the ability to stop, rewind, replay, take notes, listen again (especially useful if English is a learner's second language), practice and revise.

Mastery learning was Khan's adopted teaching method, and he acknowledges that Benjamin Bloom's work was an important precursor. Self-paced learning was the means to deliver this mastery, competence-based learning. Khan is critical of poor testing, claiming that the partial success of traditional assessment and marking can be a problem, which he calls the 'Swiss Cheese' problem. He devised a form of assessment that involves streak tests of '10-in-a-row'. He admits that 10 was an 'intuitive' number, but wanted the tests to be aspirational as well as motivational when the learner got all 10 questions right. In addition to tools for tracking progress and tools for teachers and exercises, there is also an adaptive, online exercise system, that personalizes learning and provides useful analytics.

Khan Academy expanded globally and began to be used in schools. Early work suggested the need to identify who got stuck and where in the learning process, which later became a key mathematical feature in the development of the software. An interesting additional cohort of learners began to emerge – adults and professionals – who wanted to improve or close gaps in their knowledge of maths. The content has now expanded into other fields such as the sciences, finance and medicine, and continues to grow in terms of subjects covered and the number of videos and resources available. The Khan Academy is always available, day or night, freeing both teachers and learners from the tyranny of time and location.

Although there would be no Khan Academy without YouTube, Khan has shown how free learning services on the web can be used by anyone and any organization to good effect. His video resources focus not on talking heads but relentlessly on content.

Adaptive platforms

Adaptive platforms are available that deliver formal learning courses in both education and workplace learning. They provide sophisticated resequencing, with each learner getting a unique learning experience based on their dynamic performance.

Luis von Ahn is a Guatemalan mathematician and computer scientist, who invented CAPTCHA. He then turned his attention to providing free language learning, which eventually became (on a freemium model with subscriptions for a premium service) Duolingo. Duolingo is the 'shooting star' in EdTech. As the world's most downloaded education app, valued at $3 billion and with tens of millions of live users, its use of habitual learning, driven by AI, shows that this is the future of learning, and especially lifelong learning.

Duolingo's success is built on a good business model. The service remains free for most users and there is sound pedagogy at the heart of the learning experience. Based on the premise that most people quickly forget what they learn, it offers repetition, habitual learning, single day streaks, levels and spaced practice. It is mobile-friendly, and the effortful learning has a wide variety of inputs including open input and voice. Recognizing that motivation is a problem in learning, notifications are used to nudge learners forward and keep them going, especially when the app recognizes they are about to falter or stop on their learning journey.

At the heart of the service is an adaptive AI system with a high degree of algorithmic personalization, and it is currently designed to provide basic language learning up to B2 level. The app is indicative of the type of service that is starting to appear on the web – one that uses smart software that is sensitive to the needs of the learner in terms of place, time, motivation and level of achievement. Although online learning remains largely free it is becoming increasingly sophisticated, using more media types and is moving towards adaptivity and personalization. Learners are increasingly using such resources and services, whether in education or workplace training, as they are convenient, easy to use, quick and free.

Self-paced learning courses

Self-paced learning courses which can be taken at any time have become a mainstay of corporate learning. They have recently been dominated by training around compliance, values, diversity, equality and equality. In that sense they have reflected what has been happening politically around ethical problems related to finance, racism and sexism. However, such training has tended to follow the old model of a traditional course, rather than one of process and organizational change, and has led to lots of courses but with little research into their impact.

Such courses are often multimedia (mostly text and graphics but increasingly video) and interspersed with interactions such as multiple-choice, true/false and other similar test items. Scenario-based online learning has become common, and branching simulations are also used. Overall, the design of self-paced learning courses has been remarkably stable over 30 years, using much of the same multimedia plus mechanical question types. They have been criticized as over-engineered, didactic and low on sophistication and generative learning

Text and graphics are often dismissed as inferior media in learning, yet text remains the most important medium in learning. From books to the internet, text is still the primary driver, and is fundamental in a large set of learning experiences.

In self-paced e-learning courses we can read text at about 300 words a minute, faster than we listen, so reading is faster than watching a video. Reading means we, not a narrator, are in control. We can stop, reflect, look something up and take notes in our own time. Text is flexible and searchable, and can be structured alphabetically, by location, chronologically, in menus or by category. Most people have mastered reading and writing, and the tools needed are simple – pen, pencil, keyboard, word processor. Text is also low bandwidth and, if digital, easy to update. Nudges, notifications, checklists, job aids, FAQs, PDFs, blogs, glossaries, chat, discussion threads, infographics, slide decks – there is lots of online text. It is a staple in self-paced online learning, often with accompanying graphics, and is essential for most test items and feedback.

Audio leaves the imagination free from imagery to reflect, while intonation, emphasis and encouragement can provide an emotional connection. Listening is a universal skill, and it leaves hands and eyes free for note taking. Audio is used to offer expert views and of course, podcasts and audiobooks, and is essential in teaching interpersonal skills and language learning. It is also used on smartphones and personal voice assistants in the home.

Video has grown in prominence, with genres such as drama, lectures, documentary style, explanations and procedural videos all providing forms of learning. The way video content is consumed is also changing rapidly. One analysis of US students showed that 85 per cent of students said they 'speed-watched' lecture videos (Murphy et al, 2021). Another study showed learning is as effective at x1.5 and x2 speed (Lang et al, 2020), while another showed that learning at x1.5 speed was better than normal speed and there was no significant difference between x1.5 and x2 (Nagahama and Morita, 2017). In other words, students retain information when watching lectures at up to twice their actual speed.

Simulators were discussed in Chapter 7, when we looked at teaching machines and high-end simulators used in flight training, as well as at simulators at a lower level, such as business simulations, mini-simulation and scenario-based learning. These are an exciting development in learning content that will benefit from further developments in AI and data.

Learning content is also being consumed as games or as gamified content. The pros of this approach are increased motivation, allowing repeated failures and reinforcement, as well as multiplayer and simulation opportunities. The downside is that they are difficult to design/produce and can put off more serious learners. Indeed, poorly designed games can distract from the learning and disappoint users, especially when they are naively behaviourist or seen as inappropriate for the subject. They can also require additional cognitive bandwidth, along with additional learner time and costs.

So the content question is complex, with a wide range of uses, contexts, goals, content types and methods of delivery. Generally, there has been a recognition that online learning needs to deliver a much more varied diet that is more responsive to a wider range of learning needs, both informal and formal, in the workflow rather than just in courses. This variation on content types has been outlined as different types of 'learning experiences' (Clark, 2021). These online experiences vary by media type(s), forms of interaction and goals. It is a very wide spectrum, and getting wider. One of the reasons for this widening of the landscape beyond courses is the rapid maturing of more sophisticated learning technology, using a wider range of devices including smartphones and voice devices. AI and data are also delivering personalized interfaces, more sophisticated pedagogy and more precise solutions to learning needs.

Neither should we forget the learning that goes on across social channels in organizations, where learners have access to others in their community of practice. Huge amounts of content are communicated between professionals, from experts to novices, across established enterprise, communication and social networks, for instance via email and messenger services like Slack and Teams.

Many types of virtual reality (VR) and augmented reality (AR) learning experience have been defined (Clark, 2021). VR has been used for general laboratory training, but also in many cases that free learners from the restrictions of time and place. It works well where training is risky, dangerous and/or uses expensive equipment, and can take the learner to places that are impossible in real life, such as the molecular level or space. AR, despite an initial rush of interest around the phenomenon that was Pokemon GO in 2016, remains a niche application in learning. The technology remains elusive; whether glasses, Hololens or retina projection, it has failed to get consumer traction. Their use is now starting to move from niche training methods such as simulations and soft-skills training to the proposed foundation of the Metaverse.

It is also easy to forget that practice and assessment is driven by a specific type of testing content that gives learners the opportunity to learn, test themselves and be tested by others. Deliberate difficulties, retrieval practice, interleaving and spaced practice are fast becoming, not just types of formative and summative assessment, but powerful ways of effortful learning (Brown, Roediger and McDaniel, 2014).

How is formal content delivered?

Another perspective on the *use* of content is its method of delivery. Context can also be defined by what *technology* or primary platform is used for delivery. We saw in the last chapter how different platforms shape the nature of the content that is delivered, for example:

- An LMS will often deliver self-paced e-learning courses, custom built courses and/or catalogues of generic courses.
- An LXP delivers resources in response to needs through search and pushes notifications and nudges.
- Webinar software is very much presentation led, with additional features for active learning.
- A MOOC platform will tend to deliver a linear set of resources over a period of many weeks, with lots of videos and other resources.

Rooted in creating long-form courses for an LMS, the older and restricted view of content is now breaking free from its legacy status towards the new data-driven, LXP and performance support approach. A wider set of media and pedagogies has also emerged, with audio, video, simulations, VR and AR and social. Content is shifting towards seeing learning as a *process* not an event, with behavioural economics driving micro-learning, notifications, nudges, curation, workflow campaigns, support at moments of need, moments of truth and so on. This drives new forms of content delivery, more sensitive to context, via blended learning, LXP and performance support.

Blended learning

Content as a form of learning technology does not exist in a vacuum, it always has a context. These contexts have been defined by a number of wider frameworks in education, including workflow, blended learning and flipped classroom. We must also recognize that online learning has offline teaching components such as classroom teaching, lectures, seminars, workplace activities and other real-world learning experiences. This is sometimes expressed as a mixture of asynchronous (real-time) and synchronous (non-real-time) delivery.

Blended learning began to emerge in the late 1990s and was seen as classroom learning with technology components as separate activities, when in practice they needed to be integrated. It was developed in response to the impact of increasing online learning, and the impact this was having on traditional learning. It was an adaptive response to changes in attitudes, learner expectations, demographics and above all massive and rapid change in technology. Blended learning, as a concept, allowed the traditional learning system to absorb all of this at a sensible pace, as it was a useful bridge between the new and the old. However, seeing blended learning as just a compromise can lead not to fresh thinking but a defence of old ways, with just a few new adjuncts.

ISSUES WITH BLENDED LEARNING

As a concept, blended learning has suffered from being poorly defined and muddled by metaphor, in particular food metaphors, with learning described variously as recipes, buffet learning, tapas learning, smorgasbord and fast food versus gourmet. The definitions of blended learning have also been described as simple delivery dualisms, either a blend of 'classroom and e-learning' or 'face-to-face and e-learning'. This 'Velcro™' approach to blended learning simply took the old classroom paradigm and added an online dimension. The problem with a definition that fixes a delivery mechanism in advance of the blended design, for example classroom or face to face, is that you have already given up on rational design. We see this in the Zoom+ model rapidly adopted during the Covid-19 pandemic.

More recently, HyFlex (meaning hybrid and flexible), hybrid and fusion learning have all been mooted as blended learning solutions after the Covid-19 pandemic. HyFlex seems to be the worst of both worlds, hanging on to the old while disliking the new. Hybrid merely suggests some fix between two modalities, like a hybrid car – sometimes electric, sometimes petrol. Who is to say that one metaphor is any better than another? Blended learning is not a metaphor.

Blended learning has also suffered from being implemented as something else – blended *teaching*. In practice this has meant teachers/lecturers/trainers have simply sliced and diced existing teaching practices and added a few online extras. Attempts at defining, describing and prescribing blended learning have been crude, involving the usual suspects (lectures/classroom plus e-learning), so merely regurgitating existing teaching methods. Blended learning is not blended teaching.

A better but still flawed approach is to broadly define the world of learning into two exclusive categories: a blend of online and offline or a blend of synchronous and asynchronous. The problem with these definitions is that they are looser but still contain components that may not be needed in an optimal blend. However, the real issue with all of these definitions is that they are really definitions of blended teaching or instruction, not blended learning. We need to look at the concept from a broader learning perspective with definitions that rise above 'instruction' to concepts that encompass context.

The flipped classroom is another species of blended learning. In this model, learners use online learning, usually for knowledge and basic exposition, then live teaching for more sophisticated application of that knowledge. Once again, the focus is on blended 'teaching' not 'learning', making it another fixed, dualistic formula.

Blended learning has certainly taken root, but it has no defined shape, theory, methodology or best practice, making it possible to call almost any kind of offering a blended solution. Blended learning abandoned careful thought and analysis, consideration of methods of learning delivery, sensitivity to context and culture and a match to resources and budget.

IMPROVING BLENDING LEARNING
Truly blended learning is not a back of an envelope exercise. It needs a careful analytic process, where the learners, type of learning, organizational culture and available resources are matched with the methods of delivery. It also needs to include scalability and updatability. Until blended learning is seen as a sophisticated analytic process for determining optimal blends, we will be stuck in this vague, qualitative world, where the phrase is just an excuse for old practices. A blend may have no lecture or no classroom components, or it may have no online components. But an optimal blend will be one where good teaching and learning theory is applied, alongside analysis of what needs to be taught, who is being taught and the resources available for delivery.

In practice, to deliver a quality blended learning experience means considering the learning experience or journey as a whole. This involves imagining your course/workshop/learning experience has no pre-set components and then doing a detailed analysis on what type of outcome you want from this in terms of the learning. Only then, having rid yourself of personal precon-ceptions and institutional forms of delivery, can you really start to rebuild the course/learning experience. So you start with an analysis of the learning and learners, then take into consideration your resources envelope, with a full cost analysis. Also include long-term sustainability issues such as updat-ability and maintenance. To construct a blended learning experience you must deconstruct your natural bias to do what you or your institution have always done, and reconstruct the learning experience from scratch.

Conspiracy of convenience

Charles Jennings sees organizational learning as being stuck in a *conspiracy of convenience* (Rayson, 2006). It is a critique of the 'course as content' model, his description of the tendency to simply order-take on courses demanded by business or driven by HR itself. He is critical of a system that keeps business managers happy because they get a deliverable, learning and development (L&D) happy as they get budgets to deliver courses, and learn-ers happy because they feel they have completed something. BUT there is no evaluated organizational or business improvement. This treadmill of course content production leads to a cycle of wasted effort, money and time. It places learning into a tactical, delivery role, with no real strategic edge.

Jennings uses the 70:20:10 rule, not a set of absolute numbers but a useful reference framework or tool – a reason and call to action to avoid a 'conspiracy of convenience'. The rule allows one to shift from the learning paradigm to the performance paradigm:

- 70 per cent learning from challenging work
- 20 per cent learning from others
- 10 per cent formal learning and reading

Jennings does not get hung up on the exact numbers and ratios. He holds to the general proposition that research shows variations in different cultures, geographies and between employees and executives, but one can still conclude that most learning occurs in the workplace, through work or via other people.

The problem is that L&D mostly does schooling and not training, with too much focus on knowledge and skills and not enough diagnosis of the original problem, along with too narrow a set of solutions. Jennings therefore encourages L&D to move away from this mindset towards a wider perspective on performance, with a deeper take on how people actually learn in practice, with organizational, team and individual performance as its goal.

Jennings sees 70:20:10 as a way of solving problems that are not always due to a lack of knowledge and skills, but problems to do with systems and processes. Human performance improvement (HPI) means developing new roles focused on tasks, not competences. He recommends that we start with organizational results, then look at critical tasks and ask how we can support those tasks, then link back to outcomes.

Jennings has certainly contributed to a shift in mindset in L&D towards at least a recognition that learning is a much wider phenomenon and that frequently the balance is wrong. Although there are many variations on the theme of the 70:20:10 rule using different numbers (and even redefinitions of the types of learning activities associated with these numbers), the shift is palpable. Technologies have also emerged that allow Jennings' vision to take place. It would seem that a convergence of theory and technology is, finally, on the horizon.

Generic content

Large, global vendors sell huge libraries of generic content, and this is the largest portion of the online learning market, covering standard topics such as compliance, soft-skills, sales training, IT training, technical training, leadership and so on. This is useful for large organizations that want to provide 'business as usual' training. The problem has become the imbalance between these huge libraries and great heaps of commissioned content. Sometimes global vendors have a role, but L&D departments must get out of the habit of carpet-bombing organizations with courses, whether from catalogues or bespoke. The people on the ground don't appreciate it as much as organizations assume they do.

Utilizing free content

Rather than always commissioning courses, the trick is not to see content as just what is stored in a library or bespoke content on your LMS, but to first consider options such as free internet content (from trusted sites), videos from YouTube and other online content. If free online resources do the job then it results in massive time and cost reductions. Only then, if the learning needs require, should you consider support resources such as checklists, step guides and job aids. Only after this has been exhausted should you consider generic libraries of content, and if that doesn't meet your specific organizational goal, custom content. The aim is not to calculate a return on investment (ROI) but to finesse the ROI, optimizing the solution to get the right content to the right person at the right time in a way that matches organizational goals.

Smart content

Content is undergoing a fundamental change. Organizations need no longer just purchase content or create online courses, they can analyse its potential benefits, deliver it in smarter ways that are flexible and personalized and then measure impact. This is smart content – resources available in many different forms that can be used intelligently, and which are sensitive to learners, the type of learning needed and real-world contexts.

Rather than holding libraries of content or bespoke content on an LMS, organizations need to employ smart decision-making behind the procurement, design and use of content. Smart software (AI) can take content from various sources and platforms and analyse it for use in a smart content strategy. Such tools deliver an optimal blend, based on inputs such as organizational needs, data about learners, data about learning and data on available resources. Analytic tools provide a model on optimization, transfer and return on investment. The model then outputs an optimal blend. Other systems attempt to do this on the basis of skills maps and gaps, but this has proved to be a difficult task, given the complex and dynamic nature of the problem.

In this way, AI helps find smart content externally and internally through smart content selection solutions, massively increasing the ROI and minimizing the waste and excesses involved in procurement, production and delivery.

Learning experiences and learning resources

The word 'content' has recently been replaced by 'experiences', with the view that attention and engagement matters; but some experiences are better than others. While engagement matters, it is no guarantee of learning, and in some cases may inhibit learning. People can be engaged but not learn or they can be engaged but learning stuff they already know. When the discourse is still simply about making content more appealing, we are stuck in the old paradigm of assuming that event-based content is always desirable. In organizational learning relevance matters, and how the content relates to an individual's job. Learning experiences must be redefined in terms of learning as a process, and that process may mean in the workflow or as performance support.

This is why content must also be seen as resources as well as courses, delivered in a much more targeted way in terms of time, place and need, using smarter forms of learning technology (Clark, 2020). The rise of the LXP and electronic performance support systems has put a new focus on learning resources. Learning in the workflow does not mean interrupting work to deliver a bout of learning content, it means delivering what is needed as part of that workflow. It might be in the form of a PDF, checklist, job aid, set of steps, diagram or FAQ, but it should be the minimum amount of support needed to get that person past the problem, whether it be learning for first time, wanting to learn more, understanding an application, solving a problem or reacting to a change.

This newer dynamic perspective on content was discussed in 'Learning in the workflow' in Chapter 9. Marsick and Watkins (2002) define informal learning in the workplace, and often elsewhere, as not taking place in the classroom through structured courses but in the hands of the learner. They built upon work by Coombs and Ahmed (1974) on non-formal learning and distinctions made by Mocker and Spear (1982) on lifelong learning as well as Reischmann's learning '*en passant*' (1986). Incidental learning is unintentional, rarely planned – the result of something else, a by-product of a task, project, problem solving, social encounters or perceived need. Importantly, people are rarely conscious of it happening as learning. Carnevale (1984) found that 83 per cent of workplace learning was informal and incidental and only 17 per cent formal.

Mihalyi Csikszentmihalyi (1997) researched 'flow' in detail, which he describes as 'being completely involved in an activity for its own sake. The ego falls away. Time flies. Every action, movement, and thought follows inevitably from the previous one, like playing jazz. Your whole being is involved, and you're using your skills to the utmost.' He believes that being in the flow gets rid of fear as it situates learning in the flow of doing and makes it relevant to workflow learning. Conrad Gottfredson and Bob Mosher (2011) gave this movement some solid recommendations with their 5 Moments of Need (see Chapter 9).

This shift away from LMS storage of courses and monolithic libraries of content towards a more dynamic landscape, where content is used not just in courses but in the workflow, has been theorized for 30 years but it finally started to mature when technology arrived that was capable of delivering smart, dynamic content.

Smart content redefines content in terms of context and use. Content is not only to be delivered in courses or stored in repositories of documents, videos and slides for reference, it is something to be used dynamically, both pushed and pulled. Personalized delivery of content will become ever more important, as will the use of data and AI in the delivery of that content, not only in courses but as resources in moments of need.

Resources not courses

Technology has finally caught up with the theory, and learners now want a mix of content ranging from simple resources through to a wide spectrum of content from the web, LXPs in the workflow and performance support systems. Content can therefore also be *resources*.

In an LXP this can be sparked by pull techniques, such as search on the web or search through internally held content. LXPs deliver pushed and pulled content in the workflow, so tend to deliver helpful resources that meet a need at a particular point, rather than courses. They use push techniques such as notifications and curated playlists, and pull content such as checklists, job aids, FAQs, PDFs and short videos to serve a specific moment of need. These needs are quite different, but have been researched and defined.

Where the answer to a current need or concern is required, content needs to follow Occam's Razor – the minimum number of entities needed to reach a goal. In this form of content use, less is more. It may be all that is needed is a concise answer to a query, a short piece of video to show a process or an image of a described object. We see this in the way search now delivers content with a ranked page. Search also often includes a set of other similar but closely related questions, a development from the FAQ (frequently asked questions) concept. This may need to be escalated to a set of steps in a process, a checklist if there are necessary conditions for success. The dynamic, real time use of content has become the new norm, meeting moments of need. This is a good example of how content has been redefined as smart content that suits the context of its use. Performance support is a type of advanced and dynamic content. As we saw in Chapter 9, digital adoption platforms (DAP) provide accurate support when new technology is being rolled out. Other performance support systems are even more targeted towards moments of need in the workflow, at what Bob Mosher calls the moment of truth.

People also use technologies separate from and sometimes unknown to (or forbidden by) their organization – for conversations and revision, for example. In practice we all use much wider sources of content than we realize, from Google to the vast array of content on the web, to social media. Nor does online content exist separately from the real world. For example, Amazon is an online resource for buying even the most obscure of physical books. Content can be blended with real-world activities and learning, reused, customized and even flipped.

Content has also been escaping from the tyranny of time. This is partly addressed with learning technology that gives access to content for anyone, anywhere, at any time. Bloom (1976) laid this out decades ago when he said that learners could master knowledge and skills given enough time. It is not that learners are good or bad, but fast and slow. The artificial constraint of time, in timed periods of learning, timetables and fixed point in time final exams, can be a destructive filter. The solution is to loosen up on time, to democratize learning to suit the many not the few.

Content can also be delivered as retrieval practice, deliberate practice and spaced practice. It is not the learning technology that matters but the things generated, created and applied after learning. Note taking is user-generated content that acts as a bridge between teacher and learner, used after the learning event. A common mistake in learning design ignores the fact that learning is a *process* not an event. Focusing on only designing learning 'experiences' as events is a fundamental error.

How is content created?

Content can also be defined, to a degree, by how it is *created*. For centuries teachers have been designing their own lessons and have been left alone to deliver the content. This is obviously inefficient, so copying manuscripts, then printing and finally digital replication all led to the multiplication of content that could be put into the hands of lots of teachers and, more importantly, learners.

As content is multi-faceted, so is content creation. With the arrival of digital technologies like computers and the internet, teachers and learners were suddenly able to do this for themselves (Figure 10.2). User-generated content is created from a multitude of tools, including the basic word processor, slide creation tools, audio and video editing and capture tools. Learners also use these tools, along with popular flashcard and note-taking tools for learning and revision. AI is now beginning to play a role, too.

Online learning content was not, as some may imagine, created by an army of teachers, lecturers and trainers. That was an early promise when people thought the authoring tools available would make this a possibility. In reality, those tools often needed someone with reasonable design skills and a knowledge of learning to create content in formats that were actually usable online. Just as Microsoft Word doesn't make you a novelist, an authoring tool doesn't make you a learning designer! In online learning, media capture and sharing are useful for some of this effort, but for the creation of good quality content, good authoring tools and specific learning and media design skills are needed to create good content. Authoring tools that can do everything from simple video and screen capture through to high-end 3D games and simulation tools have emerged that make this task easier and faster.

FIGURE 10.2 Content creation

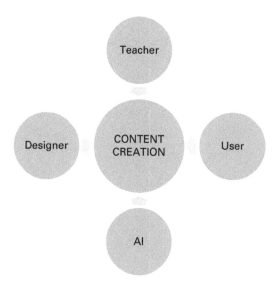

Most self-paced or e-learning courses, either custom built or available in catalogues, have been created using 'authoring' languages, which allow more specialist instructional designers to build courses using different media types and interactions. They usually use templates to save time in the creation of learning experiences and largely port classroom-like courses to the screen.

Early content authoring

In the 1980s, bespoke content authoring was restricted to text and graphics. Many of these authoring languages were 'command based', meaning the designer wrote high-level code straight into the prompt from the operating system. These early authoring languages used character-based graphics rather than bitmaps, and colours were limited to as few as three. Internal memory and external storage were very limited. Nevertheless, these limitations forced designers to be imaginative within these tight constraints. Work produced on the BBC Micro, early Apple computers and PCs had a similar variety to today's online learning, with scenarios, branching, multiple-choice, true/false, matching and other question types. Games and gamification were also common. What was absent were media such as audio, animation and video that had higher processing and storage needs. Storage was via large hard-drives, floppy discs, Laserdiscs, CDi and various CD-ROM formats. These allowed the designer to include audio and video, which led to more sophisticated scenario and simulation work, from point-of-view interviews for jobs to branched drama. Video became, for a while, an important medium in such courses.

However, there are some intrinsic weaknesses with the bespoke content approach. It is labour intensive and therefore expensive. Customer expectations can be high, leading to lots of iterations and scope creep, making content difficult to manage. This approach to content also tends to lead to fossilization, with designers using the same sort of tools to produce the same sort of content (often pages of text with an accompanying graphic, lots of media types with limited interaction around clicking to see more and multiple-choice questions).

However, productivity has now improved due to the use of tools to speed up production, for example, template engines that can reproduce games, quizzes, scenario structures and simulations, quick-to-produce media, like video and audio, agile production and professional project and client management. Automation is also starting to be possible in this area as AI and data-driven technology is now being applied to learning.

Content authoring today

The current model for content production in large organizations includes both generic and custom content, the latter commissioned externally or from an internal team. The dynamic is one where L&D receive a request for a course, and they then deliver that back to the business. Bought libraries of external content are useful for general knowledge and skills but can seem remote, as they lack any real reference to the purchasing organization or hooks that make it relevant to real learners, although they have the advantage of being cheaper than custom content. Custom content has the advantage of being designed specifically for the commissioning organization. The downside is its expense and the complexities of getting an outside company to understand an organization's internal dynamics. However, custom courses are often commissioned before any detailed analysis is done on actual needs and so development companies tend to use similar tools and predictable course designs. Internal content production groups can also get stuck in the steady cadence of producing courses on-demand, to the same templates and tools, resulting in order taking, rather than a focus on business or organizational needs.

AUTHORING TOOLS

Tools often determine output. Simulations and designs that didn't fit into the simple, flat, linear content that the learning management system/virtual learning environment could deliver were rare. This led to a one-size-fits-all approach that was unable to cope with systems that delivered smart, personalized learning pathways. More sophisticated higher-level learning experiences were locked out by the limited ability of the LMS to cope with complexity and innovation. The LMS became a sausage machine through which limited forms of content must be squeezed out. These were fit for purpose in the formal courses that most organizations need to some degree, but unsuited to informal learning (often with a social dimension), performance support (rarely done well from a LMS) and 'learn by doing', or experiential learning, that most LMSs are unable to cope with.

Along with the LMS came a standard known as SCORM (shareable content object reference model). This pushed everyone towards 'course completion', but completion rarely suffices as a measure of success or evaluation. Some argued that learning via a LMS had become a chore, with learners slogging through course after course until they were complete. The concept of personal learning journeys took a back seat, and instead SCORM was used to march learners in lockstep towards completion. The LMS gave the illusion that valuable data was being gathered when in fact, it was merely who did what course, when, and whether they completed it. As the world became more data hungry, the LMS started to become the very thing that stopped valuable data from being gathered, managed and used.

Contemporary authoring tools are template driven with more variety in terms of themes, the variety of interactions and test items. They also support branching and scenario-based learning, while specialist authoring tools for simulations, games and gamification are also available. VR tends to use two main tools, Unity and Unreal, although new Metaverse creation tools are beginning to emerge.

Rapid, agile production also means quicker and shorter courses, which some are calling microlearning. Guerrilla learning has also emerged, which means literally taking a microphone or video camera to grab subject matter expertise quickly, editing the same day, for use within the LMS or LXP. Video and audio (podcasts) are particularly easy to produce. With the rise of more sophisticated definitions of content, the LMS becomes a limitation.

Although the creation of content has never been easier, access to authoring tools does not make you a learning designer. Learning designers tend to assume that all online learning experiences require images. This is not true. Hundreds of millions read books, articles, blogs and text posts. They also listen to radio and podcasts without images. Indeed, the absence of images can be a cognitive virtue. Knowledge of how people learn, matching the type of learning to the right delivery from a range of possible types of learning experiences, along with skills in interface, media and assessment is essential.

There is a vast constellation of content types involving many methods of content production from many types of organizations, groups and individuals. The sophistication of smartphones has also led to a tsunami of user-generated learning resources and content, especially on social media, such as YouTube and TikTok. Organizations themselves often hold rich sources of content, so good search tools can find specific resources such as documents, pieces of text, specific slides and pieces of video within video, which can then be delivered via an LXP.

Artificial intelligence (AI)

AI technology is now being used to create content and questions as well as automate the creation of content and summarize it. Search uses AI, and there are other ways that AI and the data revolution can solve learning problems, as described below.

Content curation

Often using AI tools, content curation focuses on creating fresh content from a range of existing sources. These take external and internal content and produce courses or support that can be made permanent or delivered as playlists.

Content summarization

This is now commonplace and is a great advantage in education and training, where knowledge and skills described by subject matter experts are often too long, poorly expressed or unsuitable for learning. Being able to summarize a document, PowerPoint or video transcript allows the creation of manageable pieces of content, which learners can search or obtain via an LXP. This can be 'extractive', i.e. keeping original sentences intact, or 'abstractive', i.e. producing a precis through rewriting.

AI-created content

AI-created content can use entity analysis to identify key concepts and learning points from existing materials, allowing software to create online content by creating interactive items and supplementary links to external content. AI has also been used to semantically interpret answers from learners who type in open sentence input.

Fresh content creation

Transformers are powerful AI tools trained on enormous amounts of data that work by simply predicting what word comes next, enabling AI to now create fresh content. This is a deceptively simple description, however, as transformers have proved powerful in creating readable, meaningful and consistent text. What has surprised everyone is the cogency of their output.

Full poems, articles, essays and other forms of learning text are possible, so that fresh learning content can be created. This is bound to change the primitive nature of assessment in education, as users can create freshly minted essay and assignment papers, at the click of a button.

Graphics

Graphics have been created from text using AI. DALL-E, a machine learning tool, creates highly sophisticated, high quality and imaginative graphics from simple natural language descriptions. These images place fully rendered images at the correct size in the correct perspective. They can be straight and sober or as wild as your imagination allows. Video, in time, will follow.

Conclusion

Ultimately content is not an end in itself, it is a means to an end – that being to support or change the cognitive state of the learner. Content is the captured and transmitted driver of history and progress. Once we understand that learning technology is foundational we do not see it as a threat but a friend, and learning content, whether on paper, print, platforms, podcasts or internet protocols, accelerates learning.

Content, as a learning technology in itself, is the bridge between teaching and learning. What we are now witnessing is content as something that can be seen in different forms across the learning process, from initial engagement, learning experiences, delivered in the workflow or as performance support. It is a chameleon concept covering all sorts of types and uses, from papyrus, manuscripts and books to Wikipedia, YouTube and online learning. Produced from a multitude of sources and accessed from a range of resources and courses, it receives meaning and purpose from the way in which it is used. It will, of course, continue to surprise and manifest itself in new forms. It is now time now to look ahead and see what the future holds for intelligent, smart content in terms of artificial intelligence and data.

References

Bloom, B S (1976) *Human Characteristics and School Learning*, McGraw Hill Higher Education, New York

Brown, P C, Roediger III, H L and McDaniel, M A (2014). *Make It Stick: The science of successful learning*, Harvard University Press, Cambridge MA

Carnevale, A (1984) *Jobs for the Nation: Challenges for a Society Based on Work*, American Society for Training and Development, Alexandria, VA

Clark, D (2020) *Artificial Intelligence for Learning: How to use AI to support employee development*, Kogan Page Publishers, London

Clark, D (2021) *Learning Experience Design: How to create effective learning that works*, Kogan Page Publishers, London

Coombs, P and Ahmed, M (1974) *Attacking Rural Poverty: How nonformal education can help*, Johns Hopkins University Press, Baltimore, MD

Creative Commons https://creativecommons.org/ (archived at https://perma.cc/ZJ6X-ZWAU)

Cross, J (2006) *Informal Learning: Rediscovering the natural pathways that inspire innovation and performance*, John Wiley & Sons, Hoboken, NJ

Csikszentmihalyi, M (1997) Flow and education, *NAMTA Journal*, 22(2), 2–35

Giles, J (2005) Internet encyclopedias go head to head, *Nature*, 438(15), 900–1

Gottfredson, C and Mosher, B (2011) *Innovative Performance Support: Strategies and practices for learning in the workflow*, McGraw Hill Professional, New York

Hilton III, J et al (2010) The four 'R's of Openness and ALMS analysis: Frameworks for open educational resources. *Open Learning: The Journal of Open, Distance and e-Learning*, 25(1), 37–44

Khan Academy www.khanacademy.org (archived at https://perma.cc/U5DK-RUMT)

Khan, S (2012) *The One World School House: Education Reimagined*, Twelve, New York

Lang, D et al (2020). *Is faster better?: A study of video playback speed*, LAK'20, Proceedings of the 10th International Conference on Learning Analytics and Knowledge, March 2020, ACM

Marsick, V J and Watkins, K E (2002) Informal and incidental learning, *New Directions for Adult and Continuing Education*, 2001(89), 25–34

Mocker, D W and Spear, G E (1982) *Lifelong Learning: Formal, non-formal, informal and self-directed*, ERIC Clearinghouse on Adult, Career and Vocational Education, Columbus, O H

Murphy, D H et al (2021) Learning in double time: The effect of lecture speed on immediate and delayed comprehension, *Applied Cognitive Psychology*, 36(1) https://onlinelibrary.wiley.com/doi/abs/10.1002/acp.3899

Nagahama, T and Morita, Y (2017) Effect analysis of playback speed for lecture video including instructor images, *International Journal for Educational Media and Technology*, 11(1), 50–58

Pearson (2018) Beyond Millennials: The Next Generation of Learners, August 2018, *Global Research & Insights* www.pearson.com/content/dam/one-dot-com/one-dot-com/global/Files/news/news-annoucements/2018/The-Next-Generation-of-Learners_final.pdf (archived at https://perma.cc/JB3E-J878)

Rayson, S (2006) 'Conspiracy of convenience in training must end' says Charles Jennings of Reuters, 20 September 2022, *PRWeb* www.prweb.com/releases/2006/02/prweb343291.htm (archived at https://perma.cc/R7A5-CASS)

Reischmann, J *Learning 'en passant': The Forgotten Dimension*, Paper presented at the Conference of the American Association of Adult and Continuing Education Conference, 23 October 1986

Tkacz, N (2014) *Wikipedia and the Politics of Openness*, University of Chicago Press, Chicago

11

Artificial intelligence

Artificial intelligence (AI) is not just a learning technology, it is a technology that learns. AI is transforming the way we live and work, and, as it continues to evolve, its impact on learning is only going to become more profound.

AI is the new user interface (UI) and one of the most significant ways it is impacting learning is through the development of personalized learning experiences. AI-powered learning platforms are able to analyse a learner's behaviour and preferences and adjust the content and delivery of the learning experience accordingly. This type of adaptive learning is highly effective and allows learners to move through material at their own pace and in a way that suits their individual needs.

Another area where AI is having a big impact on learning is in the development of virtual reality (VR) and augmented reality (AR) experiences. These immersive technologies are being used in a variety of ways to enhance the learning process. For example, VR can be used to provide learners with realistic simulations of real-world scenarios. This is especially valuable for learners who need to develop skills for dangerous or difficult environments. AR, on the other hand, can be used to overlay digital information on the real world, providing learners with layers of useful knowledge, insights or tasks that augment the real world. VR and AR can be mixed.

In *Artificial Intelligence for Learning* (2020), I put forward the idea that almost all online learning will eventually be influenced by AI. Smart tech is needed to produce smart people, and as almost all informal online learning will use data and AI, this seems inevitable. When we search Google, Google Scholar, Wikipedia or YouTube videos, get knowledge from our social media networks or buy books on Amazon, all of this is mediated by data and AI. Formal online learning is also being driven by data and AI. Online content is even being created by AI, with AI used to engage, support, deliver and assess learning in schools, universities and the workplace.

AI has also benefited from the tsunami of data that is produced on the world wide web, with data being the lifeblood of AI for both training of models and implementation. We now see the application of AI to many everyday functions on almost all computing devices in our workplaces, cars, homes and pockets. Our smartphones are powerful, personal pocket devices that pack more punch than the computers that took man to the Moon and back. Engineering has given us the chips that puts AI into our pocket devices, with AI capability resident in the smartphone itself too. AI is being built into almost everything that is online, as well as a good deal of technology that is offline.

AI as a learning technology

AI technology changes everything – how we work, shop, travel, entertain ourselves, socialize, deal with finance and healthcare – all are now subject to mediation by AI. When we browse online, AI intercedes to some degree in almost everything we do. Given its ubiquity, it would be irrational to imagine that AI will have no role to play in online learning.

AI is now embedded in many of the tools real learners use for both formal and informal online learning. For example, Duolingo, one of the largest single global learning services for language learning, is fundamentally driven by AI. Continuous professional development (CPD) mediated by AI is now common on social media. We fail to notice its almost universal presence, as it is largely invisible. Yet its effect is profound for one major reason: as it changes the nature of work, it will undoubtedly change the nature of learning. More generally, AI will change *why*, *what*, *when* and *how* we learn.

AI technology can be used for both teaching and learning. For teachers it can reduce workload and complement their teaching, helping to make it more effective. For learners it can accelerate learning right across the learning journey from search, learning engagement, support, feedback, creation of content, curation, adaption, personalization and assessment. It is becoming a key component in contemporary learning systems, such as learning experience platforms (LXPs), learning record stores (LRSs) and adaptive learning systems.

AI could be said to be the pinnacle of our technological achievements, performing astounding roles in almost every area of human endeavour. In healthcare, finance, entertainment, manufacturing, energy and research, AI is playing an increasingly important role in providing increases in efficacy, productivity and safety. It is playing a similar role in education.

So how did we get here? Well, AI didn't spring from nowhere. It has a long pedigree and has taken millennia of mathematics to get to this moment.

Mathematics and AI

To understand why AI has real potential in learning, we need to understand its history, in particular its 2,500-year gestation period involving mathematics, logic, probability, statistics, algorithmic progress and improvements in data science. AI has been moulded out of these different disciplines and, like most modern technology, it is a mixture of different technologies and approaches.

It is sometimes assumed that AI started in 1956, at the famous Dartmouth Summer Research Project on Artificial Intelligence organized by John McCarthy. This is not true. Although McCarthy did kick-start the 'modern' era of AI by naming it as such, it started well over 2,000 years ago with Euclid of Alexandria, who was the first to formally write down an algorithm in his book *Elements*, around 300 BC. From Euclid onwards, maths and algorithms were laying the foundations for what we now call 'artificial intelligence'. The Euclidean algorithm is a method for quickly finding the greatest common denominator of two integers. There were many other areas of Greek progress in mathematics, from Eudoxus on irrationals, Pythagoras on geometry, Archimedes on volumes (with proofs) and approximating polygons, Apollonius of Perga on conic sections and so on. It is no accident that Plato, in his academy, had above the door 'Let no man ignorant of geometry enter'.

The Greeks, especially Aristotle, also progressed the field with syllogistic logic, the sure foundations of mathematics, which had a renaissance in the 19th and 20th centuries through Frege, Cantor, Hilbert, Gödel and many others. The eponymous Boolean logic is of primary importance in computing and AI. Let us also not forget that the word 'algorithm' comes from the Latinized name of a Persian mathematician, Muhammad ibn Musa al-Khwarizmi, who was born around 780 AD.

Probability theory and statistics

AI also depends on centuries of work in probability theory and statistics that first emerged during the Renaissance through reflections by 16th-century mathematicians Pacioli, Cardano and Tartaglia on games of chance, which then flowered into a full-blown area of mathematics through Pascal, Fermat, Bernoulli and Quetelet's bell curve. Statistical methods underlie many contemporary AI techniques, as do advances in dealing with data in data science.

In 1763, an essay by the Reverend Thomas Bayes was published posthumously. It was to have a profound influence on mathematics and AI. Reworked by Pierre-Simon Laplace, it presented a single theorem that updated a probability. This theorem allows probabilities to be continuously updated in the light of new evidence, new predictors and so on, to create a single, new probability. In learning, such an algorithmic system can continue to update predictions and recommendations for students and content configuration over time, as the learner progresses through a learning journey. In addition to this Bayesian data analysis, one can also use a Bayesian network, a model with known and unknown probabilities, from say, student data, behaviour and performance. As the network has nodes with variables (known and unknown) and algorithms that can make decisions and even learn within these networks, the application of this approach can solve complex problems such as optimal paths for personalized learning.

Andrey Markov, a Russian mathematician, was another significant figure. He introduced the Markov network and Markov models, that can be used to determine what the learner receives next in a learning experience, based on previous behaviours. Most of us are unaware, for example, that these techniques are already used to present us with different web pages.

These statistical theories all advanced the progress of AI by providing the architectures and processing power to perform those huge efforts that now have to be made to train and execute AI. We can see that AI itself is a product of several strands of engineering and mathematics, as well as early mechanical learning machines, calculating machines, electronics computers and finally solid-state AI chips. Much AI has come from academic research including backpropagation and reinforcement learning, but it has also received serious contributions from outside of academia, with advances in machine learning from Bell Labs, IBM, Google DeepMind and OpenAI. The early 21st century is truly the Age of Algorithms.

AI learning systems

We see contemporary online learning design and increasing awareness of AI in user experience and the design of learning experiences (Clark, 2021).

Learning designers now need to be aware of AI and understand its role in delivery (Clark, 2020). This is particularly true of the role of data in smart learning systems. We must now be aware of what data is being gathered, used and in what fashion within a learning ecosystem, as it is data that often drives the functionality of AI, enabling it to execute searchability, recommendations and automation.

It is also the case that in many ways, AI learning systems are themselves learners. For example, data is used to train AI to become ever more powerful. DeepMind's systems will play years of games to train the models before playing the best human in the world at games such as GO... and the learning system will win. There are also several forms of learning in AI, such as machine learning and reinforcement learning, that also learn as they go, improving with scalability and use.

Along with retrieval, spaced practice aids the retention, transfer and ultimate performance of the learner. It is based on the spacing effect discovered in the late 19th century by Ebbinghaus (1885), along with the lag effect which suggests that increased spacing is optimal (Melton, 1970). Research confirms that the process of forgetting, together with the breakdown and subsequent retrieval of learning, helps improve learning (Carey, 2015).

CASE STUDY

Duolingo

Duolingo is a good example of an AI learning system, with one of the largest number of users ever seen for a specifically designed learning platform. Motivation is the primary problem in language learning and most learners give up early on their learning journey, demotivated by a lack of progress and feedback. Using AI, Duolingo delivers bite-size learning with a highly visual sense of progress and completion of levels to drive learners forward. The AI is all about momentum and making learning habitual.

It is easy to underestimate the value of personalization and adaptivity, but Duolingo knows what the learner has learnt, if they have been absent and, importantly, what they have forgotten. Algorithmic personalization has as much to do with rectifying forgetting as learning and Duolingo's approach is novel.

Duolingo employs spaced practice and began with the Leitner sort method algorithm (adaptive), then moved to the Half-life Hybrid (adaptive spacing) algorithm, then to Half-life Regression (advanced). Other more complex AI models are also being researched in this process of continuous learning, improvement and innovation. This requires the gathering of real data from real learners, where data sets not only train the models, they also give insights that lead to continuous improvement (Settles and Meeder 2016).

Duolingo's AI comes into its own in the delivery of 'notifications'. Its sophisticated delivery involves AI deciding algorithmically what to say and when to say it, based on the learner's progress. This automation of the learning process is designed to keep the learner going, as they deliver notifications regularly (but not too regularly). The most powerful notification is the 'final warning', where, if the learner shows signs of dropping off, a timely message encouraging them to keep going can often work wonders. This constant search for ways to increase habitual learning is Duolingo's hallmark.

With open input for full phrases and sentences, it also allows people to type what they hear as well as speak and be understood. Duolingo provides measured remediation when the learner fails and audio when they get things right.

Duolingo is exemplary, showing how learning can be engineered to include good pedagogy and deliver to hundreds of millions on a global scale, massively reducing the cost of learning, while increasing access. This is one pointer towards the democratization of learning at a global scale.

AI for learning

What is AI?

AI is 'the' technology of the age. As it lies behind much of what we see online, it literally supports the global world wide web, driving use through new approaches to UI and personalization. Surprisingly, AI does this as an 'idiot savant', profoundly stupid compared to humans, with nowhere near the capabilities of a real teacher, but profoundly smart on specific tasks. Curiously, it can provide wonderfully effective techniques such as adaptive feedback on a scale impossible by humans, but it doesn't 'know' anything. It is 'competence without comprehension', but competence gets us a long way. The mistake is to anthropomorphize this technology and attribute human attributes when they don't exist.

It is also a mistake to see AI as one thing. It is many different things, from pure symbolic AI that uses logic alone, through to advanced 'transformers'. This form of natural language processing (NLP) trains models on huge corpora of text and are astonishing the world with their power to create text, code and even images. It is a dynamic and developing field that is advancing faster than many thought possible.

AI is the new UI

AI underlies most online interfaces by mediating what we see on the screen. More recently, it has provided voice interfaces, both text-to-speech and speech-to-text. This is important in learning, as most teaching is, in practice, delivered by voice. Then there is the world of chatbots, the return of the Socratic method (see Chapter 6), with real success in engagement, support and learning. There are lots of real examples of how these new interfaces and, in particular, dialogue will expand online learning.

One interface that has emerged in learning is the Netflix interface, a tiled interface that scrolls vertically and horizontally, which is the dominant interface in all streamed services and is now a globally known standard. This interface is being used in LXP to deliver learning to the right people at the right time in the workplace, using AI and data-driven techniques to personalize not only the interface but also what is pushed or pulled to the learner. This has enabled learning in the workflow, a concept that has been around for over 30 years but is only now being realized, as the technology to deliver this 'just-in-time' learning has finally reached the threshold at which it works efficiently.

The invisible hand of AI also allows technology, especially interfaces, to become increasingly easy to use and invisible, for example, voice-based personal assistants such as Siri, Google Assistant and Alexa. Access to the extended mind that is the web is now possible in the workplace, home, cars and on our smartphones, wherever we may be.

AI and searchability

The bedrock of learning is curiosity. Incidental and informal learning takes place when we use AI to access the web to find answers to questions that would have taken much longer in the past. Even at the level of research, the time saved through online access is immense. Search is also becoming much more powerful as AI allows us to search inside documents, while learning systems can now find a relevant video clip for instruction and identify the start and finish timecodes for playback in a learning context, on demand.

Search provides instant access to the knowledge base that is the web but also 'how to' videos and learning services, including Open Education Resources that did not exist before the advent of search engines.

Search is now being used to curate content relevant to an individual's learning needs. By predicting those needs and personalizing delivery, it can continuously recommend useful learning experiences and aids at any point on their learning journey.

AI and teachers

If we look at AI from the teacher or trainer's perspective, we see that it is not a replacement but a valuable aid to teaching, augmenting intelligence. The dialectic between AI and teaching shows that there will be a synthesis and increased efficacy in teaching when its benefits are realized. AI is a powerful teaching and learning tool that saves teachers' time – it does not, as yet, replace them.

One great example of how AI can transform teaching is from the Curra network of schools in South Africa, whose teaching staff gave glowing testimonials about the power of adaptive learning and using AI to personalize learning for students. The teachers presented their results at their annual Conference in 2022, where I gave a keynote address on AI for Learning. Described as a 'game changer' by teachers who used the system, its clear targeting enabled efficient and relevant interventions to be made for individual students. The teachers had clear goals on what the technology had to achieve. They were keen to utilize this technology, implemented it well and cleverly used teacher feedback to spread the word internally. Their big goal, and win, was saving time on marking and correction, which was automated, instantaneous and even provided alternative questions. Diagnostic questions were particularly useful in identifying individual learners' strengths and weaknesses, so that teachers didn't have to wait for an assessment before making interventions. The schools were keen to involve parents in the process and the technology enabled them to access their children's progress, reducing the need for teachers to respond to parent requests.

AI as learning support

When Georgia Tech was faced with a large class of AI students who needed a lot of learning support on their many assignments, they naturally turned to AI (GTPE Communications, 2016). From a total of nine teaching assistants, they swapped one out for an AI assistant without telling the students. The AI teaching assistant was so fast and performed so well in answering student queries that they had to slow it down to mimic the speed at which a teacher would type an answer. The students even put it forward for a teaching award! The following year, Georgia Tech did the same thing, this time with two new AI assistants. Some students thought the real teachers were AI entities, while others thought the AI assistants were human. This shows that by training AI with data sets, namely all the queries and answers given to date, the process of learning support can be automated, taking the pressure off faculty staff and massively improving the student learning experience.

Adaptive learning

Adaptive learning systems work by adapting to the needs of the learner, before or during their learning journey. By arranging the content that is to be learnt into a network of learning objects, each individual learner vectors through that network, taking a different route. Some will move through the content quickly, as they may have higher levels of prior knowledge and cope with difficulties quicker; others will take slower routes as the system recognizes when and why they have problems and provides resequencing and feedback to make sure they do not move too fast, thereby suffering catastrophic failure. This is not unusual in subjects such as mathematics, when students often hit points where they do not master the material and all else from that point onwards is lost to them. An adaptive system will only allow the student to proceed when they have mastered a particular point on which future learning depends. It works by having AI software that gets the user literally back 'on course' if they take a wrong turn or get lost, much like the satnav in a car.

Courses that use adaptive learning systems are now offered in a range of subjects, including maths, physics, biology and history. An example of such a system is that offered by CogBooks, which began in 2005 and received investment from Arizona State University before being purchased by Cambridge University Press and Assessment (formerly CUP and Cambridge Assessment).

AI creates content

A surprising development has been the use of AI to create online content. Tools can create online content in minutes rather than months, with high retention learning using AI to semantically interpret answers and move away from more traditional multiple-choice questions. AI can also enhance video (which suffers from being a transitory medium in terms of memory, rather like a shooting star leaving a trail of forgetting behind it) towards powerful, high retention learning experiences. New adaptive learning platforms are proving to be powerful, personalizing learning on scale, delivering entire degrees. AI pushes organizations towards serious learning by producing and using data to improve performance, not only of the AI systems themselves but also teachers and learners.

In natural language processing, transformers are producing content that is sometimes indistinguishable, when tested, from human output. With a transformer such as DALL-E, even graphics can be created from text descriptions. We can expect to see transformers play a role in learning content in the years ahead.

AI and sentiment analysis

Learning has an affective or emotional component. This has been well researched but tends to be sidelined by the focus on cognitive skills. AI uses sentiment analysis to interpret from text data the feelings and subjective aspects of a learner as they progress through their learning journey. This information can be used to interpret when a learner may be starting to falter or fail. It also provides insights into the design of a course. Motivation matters, and this side of AI analysis is now being used on real LXPs. In the future we can expect more developments in sentiment analysis as the affective side of learning starts to receive the attention it deserves.

AI and learning analytics

AI and data-driven approaches to learning have been around for a long time – the invisible hand of AI has been behind almost every online service you have been using for years. Its invisibility is part of its success. It just works, and in learning this really matters. Interfaces need to be invisible, leaving cognitive bandwidth for learning. Learning is about changing memory, attitudes and behaviours. We don't want to see dashboards and happy sheet data that gives us the illusion that training has worked; instead we want to know if it *has* worked. This is where the combination of business and learning data comes to the fore. By abandoning traditional evaluation techniques, we focus on what matters – organizational outcomes. If you know how to handle data, use learning data and analytics and business data (that is part of an overall dataset), you can look for correlations and causality. Learning then becomes an organizational activity. Only then do you know whether you have a learning organization and that this approach led to real organizational outcomes.

So, accept the fact that L&D will have to become data-driven, as other areas in the business already are or will be. Accept the fact that this is not about LMS descriptive dashboards but about analysis, insights and predictions. Above all, accept the fact that this is about decisions by humans and increasingly software, that deliver real-time recommendations, nudges and support. Data fuels decisions by man and machine, and fuels learning and performance.

Data describes, analyzes, predicts and can prescribe or automate processes. At the simplest level, descriptive data simply harvests what the learner does, and this can be used to track activity. At the next level, analysis can be applied to look for useful statistical insights as to why some learners may be failing. At yet another level, data may be used by AI to predict and recommend courses of action. Beyond this, AI can also prescribe or automate processes.

Data types, the need for cleaning data to make it usable, the practical issues around its use in learning and its use in learning analytics, along with personalized and adaptive learning, shows how AI can educate and train everyone uniquely. Data-driven approaches can also deliver push techniques, such as nudge learning and spaced practice, embodying potent pedagogic practice. New ecosystems of learning, such as LXPs and LRSs, move us towards more dynamic forms of teaching and learning.

AI in assessment

AI enhances assessment and makes it easier. From student identification to the delivery of assessments and types of assessment, AI promises to free assessment from the costs and restraints of the traditional exam hall. Proctoring is now common as AI-driven face recognition, retinal images and fingerprints can confirm identity.

Plagiarism checking is also handled by AI, and plagiarism checkers are now allowing students to write rough drafts and receive feedback on the style, structure and accuracy of their written content. AI can interpret open-text answers using tools such as WildFire. This moves assessment on from traditional multiple-choice tests, where the answer is always on the screen and the cognitive act is one of selection rather than recall and deep thought.

Invisible interfaces are already present on your computer and smartphone in the form of filters (e.g. spam, porn, hate speech), faster delivery, optimized battery life, improvements in quality and editing of photographs and video, subtitling, accessibility features, translations, awareness in 3D space, geolocation and recommendations – and there is more to come. The promise is that AI will now bring this smartness to learning.

Administration and process can be aided by AI, leaving teachers and workers to focus on higher skilled teaching tasks and seeing intelligent agents as colleagues. Standard 101 courses will be increasingly delivered online with personalized learning.

Of course, culture often trumps technology and progress will often be thwarted, to a degree, by those whose interest is in keeping things as they are. As many found during the Covid-19 pandemic, lecturing is easy, teaching is hard. It took an external cause to push online learning to new heights. John Kotter (Kotter, 1995), the change management expert, places 'create a sense of urgency' as the first step in his famous eight-step change management process. During the pandemic, necessity became the mother of innovation and educators had to think, adapt and change.

CASE STUDY

Eric Mazur's redesigned physics course

Eric Mazur, a world-class physicist and teacher at Harvard, has applied his experimental and data-driven approach in physics to teaching and learning (McMurtrie, 2021). This has resulted in a series of practical teaching methods that have been widely applied in higher education and other contexts. For many years, Mazur recommended changing the culture of lecturing to a more learner-active model involving peer learning. During the Covid-19 pandemic, he went one step further, teaching all of his physics classes online and concluded, 'I have never been able to offer a course of the quality that I'm offering now. I am convinced that there is no way I could do anything close to what I'm doing in person. Online teaching is better than in person.'

When synchronous events were minimized and there was increased focus on well-supported asynchronous learning, attainment rose, and students felt better supported than face-to-face students. Mazur concluded that it would be 'almost unethical' to return to classroom teaching and lectures. Mazur used lots of regular, but small assignments, making it acceptable for students to fail and redo work. Students also relied on peer pressure for engagement and completion. The course was still highly structured but with a lot of peer activity, collaborative effort and assignments. Freeing students from the tyranny of the clock freed them up to learn at their own pace. 'When you teach online, every single student is sitting in the front row,' says Mazur.

Another advantage of teaching online using contemporary software like AI is the step-change in digital literacy and skills, now required by learners and teachers alike. AI is undoubtedly the technology of the age and will remain dominant in the 21st century, so it makes increasing sense to create autonomous learners who possess the digital skills necessary for CPD throughout their careers. In the workplace, when experts qualify and become professionals, they already have access to knowledge management systems and knowledge bases that help them do their jobs more effectively. Workplace learning also now recognizes the need to provide learning in the workflow.

As AI progresses in specific domains, with leaps that continue to surprise, it becomes a strategic, organic part of large, global, online learning platforms and delivery. Data is taking on a more significant role in the delivery of learning, as analysis, prediction and automation take hold.

Neurotechnology

What next? One emerging technology that uses AI may accelerate learning through non-immersive and immersive brain-based technology (referred to as neurotechnology) – it is literally mind-blowing.

Neuralink

Elon Musk has many strings to his bow, but one that is of particular interest to learning is Neuralink, which started in 2016. This is the development of extremely thin fibres that can be inserted into the brain so that data can be read, analyzed and turned into actions via what is called a brain computer interface (BCI) system. Research into the possibilities of brain-based technology have been going on since the 1920s. More recently, brain implants have had great success in improving hearing through cleverly engineered cochlear implants, as well as technologies in the brain to help with physical disabilities. This has opened up debate around invasive (and non-invasive) technology for learning, while the idea of plugging the brain into learning experiences is one small step closer to this.

Neuralink implanted a chip in a nine-year-old primate's brain, and in a video the primate, called Pager, is shown playing a computer game (YouTube, 2021). At first Pager plays the game with a joystick and is rewarded by a banana milkshake through a tube. He learns the game and plays well. The joystick is then unplugged and Pager plays the game via 2,000 fibres (each about one-twentieth the width of a human hair) inserted in the region of his brain known to control hand and arm movements. Pager continues to play the game with his mind, ignoring the joystick. The intentional data from the fibres is interpreted by AI and Pager continues to play the game well. The efficacy of the array was obvious.

The learning technology used by Neuralink is a chipset and set of fibres, and it has required a team of high-end electrical engineers, material scientists and neuroscientists to produce the hardware. The software is AI-driven, enabling users to control computers, prosthetic limbs and play games. The goals expand enormously, once intention is turned into code. Note that although experiments where animals controlled actions using implants were first performed in 2002, their genesis goes back more than 50 years. What is different now is the combination of many technologies into one solution and its integration with AI.

Applications of neurotechnology

Neurotechnology's initial use is targeted at people who have paraplegia or quadriplegia, people who have experienced a stroke and those with locked-in syndrome. The technology will enable them to control their own movements and interact with the world. Neurotechnology to control wheelchairs and exoskeletons are obvious applications. Other areas currently being researched include the use of neurotechnology in the management of neurological diseases such as Parkinson's and epilepsy by monitoring to prevent seizures. Other applications are aimed at people who are blind or deaf, as well as psychological applications for those with attention-deficit hyperactivity disorder (ADHD), addictions and depression.

BRAIN TO TEXT

Beyond this, a general application is to control computers at the speed of thought. A wireless interface short circuits the clumsy use of fingers and thumbs and instead links the brain directly with all online resources.

Even if this becomes possible, it is still some way off, but once the brain is linked to the internet, all learning resources become available via a frictionless interface. This is obviously useful for those with disabilities, but it also reduces the cognitive load of traditional interfaces for everyone. This in itself should make learning quicker.

In addition to providing access to the internet, if a feedback loop becomes possible, then personalized learning could be made available with immediate formative assessment and feedback through adaptive learning systems. AI not only reads what a learner does and knows, it provides support and opportunities to learn how to overcome any problems they have in learning. The development of such systems is now underway.

Of course, some researchers believe this approach has limitations and that all discussion of understanding a person's intentions beyond using their motor skills is misleading, never mind interpreting semantic thoughts through language. The underlying neuroscience does not seem to support the bolder claims of thought to text, as sophisticated thought is much more diffuse and interrelated across the brain than simple motor intentions.

RISKS

There is also the issue that such invasive technology is too risky, certainly for mass adoption, and that it is preferable to rely on electroencephalography (EEG) or reflected laser light to read neural activity. The problem with these non-invasive methods, however, is that the data produced is limited and messy. It is also unclear whether they can be used for other purposes or can even develop with the patient's progress. Finally, there is the speed of reaction problem. Such devices may be fine for deliberate action but too slow for fast reactions and decisions. Machine learning may help such devices adapt to patients, and this work is already having some success.

Neuralink has set the pace in this field with proven progress. There are other invasive techniques, such as stents in major blood vessels and others such as Kernel that uses non-invasive techniques to send light into the brain and read the signals received. This is a fast-moving area that holds promise as human-machine brain interfaces develop (Clark, 2020).

Musk has also launched thousands of low-level satellites called Starlink (a division of SpaceX) to provide low-cost 5G internet at any spot on the planet. The ambitious engineering plan is to launch 4,200 satellites by 2027. The possibility of delivering quality online learning to anyone, anytime, anyplace may be realized by this initiative.

Conclusion

AI opens exciting new possibilities in learning and its smart creation, curation and delivery are already being used to make us smarter. AI is the most important technology of our age and its use is irreversible. It is therefore inevitable that AI will play a major role in learning. New technology is always on the horizon, just ahead of us, and one piece of technology that is receiving massive investment by all the major technology companies is the Metaverse.

References

Carey, B (2015) *How We Learn: Throw out the rule book and unlock your brain's potential*, Pan Macmillan, London

Clark, D (2020) *Artificial Intelligence for Learning: How to use AI to support employee development*, Kogan Page Publishers, London

Clark, D (2021) *Learning Experience Design: How to create effective learning that works*, Kogan Page Publishers, London

Clark, D (2022) Exemplar of successful implementation of tech in schools, 14 January 2022, *Donald Clark Plan B*, https://donaldclarkplanb.blogspot. com/2022/01/exemplar-of-successful-implementation.html (archived at https:// perma.cc/LV25-QJQ3)

CNET (2021) Elon Musk's Neuralink monkey brain demo explained, 9 April 2021, www.youtube.com/watch?v=3Ya-bAYri84 (archived at https://perma.cc/ PS5Z-5G4E)

CogBooks www.cogbooks.com (archived at https://perma.cc/9LKV-CLDM)

DeepMind www.deepmind.com (archived at https://perma.cc/6M2Q-RBSG)

Duolingo www.duolingo.com/ (archived at https://perma.cc/5SD8-8VWP)

Ebbinghaus, H (1885) Über das Gedächtnis: Untersuchungen zur experimentellen Psychologie, Duncker & Humblot, Leipzig

GTPE Communications (2016) Meet Jill Watson: Georgia Tech's first AI teaching assistant, 10 November, *Georgia Tech Professional Education*, https://pe.gatech. edu/blog/meet-jill-watson-georgia-techs-first-ai-teaching-assistant (archived at https://perma.cc/54V6-3JE4)

Kernel www.kernel.com (archived at https://perma.cc/DF45-5GNP)

Kotter, J P (1995) Leading Change: Why transformation efforts fail, *Harvard Business Review*, 2(1), 1–10

McMurtrie, B (2021) Teaching: Why an Active-Learning Evangelist is Sold on Online *Teaching*, 27 May, *The Chronicle of Higher Education*, www.chronicle.com/newsletter/teaching/2021-05-27 (archived at https://perma.cc/E968-SG4F)

Melton, A W (1970) The situation with respect to the spacing of repetitions and memory, *Journal of Verbal Learning and Verbal Behavior*, 9(5), 596–606.

Settles, B and Meeder, B (2016) A trainable spaced repetition model for language learning. In: *Proceedings of the 54th Annual Meeting of the Association for Computational Linguistics*, August 2016, 1, 1848–58, Berlin

Starlink www.starlink.com (archived at https://perma.cc/8ESU-9AVH)

12

Metaverse

From the first stories told by our ancestors, it has been our constant endeavour, over thousands of years, to create ever more elaborate and wonderful new places. Our drive to seek out new places, even new worlds, has been a central feature of our culture for at least 50,000 years. We began by representing our enclosed world through instructional images in cave art. Aspirational, alternative worlds have been imagined in religious thought for millennia, as heavenly realms, free from the pain and suffering of earthly existence and were represented, in print and art, as places of peace, pleasure and harmony. The fascination and pull of the idea of a Metaverse is similar to these religious, transcendental ideas. The Metaverse is a heaven on earth.

Until the Metaverse – the first truly new medium – the internet was the last great convergence of technologies and experiences. Older commentators whose cultural references are mostly novels and movies quote *Snow Crash* and *Ready Player One* and virtual worlds like *Second Life*; young adults quote Web 3.0, NFTs, cryptocurrencies and blockchain, while the younger still are already building and inhabiting their Metaverses, such as *Minecraft*, *Fortnite* and *Roblox*. VR and AR have also opened up possibilities in VRChat, AltspaceVR, Rec Rooms and many other virtual worlds, for new ways of experiencing new worlds. Flight simulators and Google Maps also point to possibilities.

We Met in Virtual Reality (2022) is a documentary that follows several real users as they explore, find friendships and love in the multiuser world of VRChat. It shows just how deep these social encounters can be, especially for people who experience isolation and loneliness in the real world. A sign language teacher finds it a place where the deaf and hearing impaired can find companionship, others take real-world activities, such as dance, and make a life for themselves as teachers. What the documentary reveals is a rich world where people find things they could not find in the real world.

Their experiences are surprisingly rich and full of accidental encounters, fun, humour and disappointment, essentially all the good and bad stuff that comes with social interaction.

Metaverse and learning

We have seen how novels, movies, early virtual worlds and games have provided experiments for the Metaverse, but are there any that envision what *learning* could look like in the Metaverse? It does not yet exist, so dismissing it outright is to dismiss the yet unknown, and we would do well to recall Douglas Adams' (1999) sage advice, that 'Anything that's invented between when you're fifteen and thirty-five is new and exciting and revolutionary and you can probably get a career in it. Anything invented after you're thirty-five is against the natural order of things.' We must also be careful in dismissing something just because some early prototypes failed, as it is not yet clear what it is or what it will end up being in learning.

Defining the Metaverse

The Metaverse is still an open book, and definitions tend to use present technology such as virtual reality, the internet and games' worlds as comparators. In truth, it is likely to be very different with yet unimagined features. The digital world does not have the constraints of the physical world, such as physics, biology and even social norms. We see glimpses of it in the various types of existing immersion, but it is an open world, with unimagined opportunities. Think for a moment of the existing worlds that you currently interact with, probably online, such as work, entertainment, government, finance, health and learning. Each has its own requirements or needs in terms of authentication and data, in order to for you to be in that particular digital layer. What seems likely is the model that emerged with the internet, where the internet provides the substratum for the identity of people, communications, presentation and learning to develop at several different levels. The substratum may be 'Meta' but there are many layers and types of 'verses'.

If, as seems possible, the Metaverse will be realized as a major technology, we can also start to imagine how we could teach and learn within it. This vision and a simple learning manifesto reflect our experience of the current

FIGURE 12.1 Metaverse layers and components

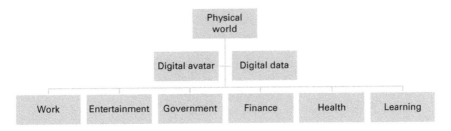

TABLE 12.1 Rules for learning in the Metaverse

Rules for Metaverse	Rules for learning in the Metaverse
There is only one Metaverse.	There is only one learning world.
Metaverse is for everyone.	Metaverse learning is for everyone.
Nobody controls the Metaverse.	Nobody controls Metaverse learning.
Metaverse is open.	Metaverse learning is open.
Metaverse is hardware independent.	Metaverse learning is hardware independent.
Metaverse is a network.	Metaverse learning is networked.
Metaverse is the internet.	Metaverse is a learning world.

internet, both its successes and failures. It sees the Metaverse as a new form of internet, completely open, with full interoperability. Tony Parisi (2021), who created the first 3D web programming language, VRML, has come up with a useful manifesto for what the Metaverse should be. The promise is that learning could mirror Parisi's democratic vision. Let's imagine open access to learning in anything, by anyone, anywhere at any time.

Similar to the internet, where we first had informal and formal learning through search and knowledge bases like Wikipedia, YouTube and free learning services like Khan Academy and Duolingo, we could see a similar explosion of informal and formal learning opportunities in the Metaverse. There are as yet unknown approaches that institutions and other bodies could make full use of with this new medium.

Advantages in Metaverse learning

The science of learning suggests the Metaverse will be a powerful context for learning, as it may deliver several strong conditions for good learning:

- attention – holds learners' complete visual and total cognitive attention
- emotion – achieved through powerful immersion
- experiential – learners will learn by doing
- context – provides useful virtual environments
- collaboration – provides virtual/real multiplayer tasks that are easy to implement
- recall – increase in recall due to all of the above
- transfer – increase in transfer from learning to performance

There is ample research and evidence for these principles in simulated environments, although the research has also uncovered some downsides. However, media rich does not always mean mind rich. Cognitive overload can hinder learning, and a lack of deliberate learning design can lead to learning experiences that have lots of novelty but lack efficacy.

What has emerged with VR, and points towards opportunities in the Metaverse, is the possibility of using our natural affinity with 3D perception to put the Metaverse to good use in learning. We know that virtual 3D worlds hold attention, indeed it is hard to escape being wholly attentive, and this is a necessary condition for learning. VR also provides emotional stimulus and this affective dimension in learning is at its most powerful in these evocative worlds. As an experiential learning tool, one can also learn by doing a 3D activity, something that education and training struggles to deliver. This makes the Metaverse a potential experiential learning tool.

Context is also provided, as the world in which the learning takes place, the Metaverse, is a designed context, whether it is place, things or other people. There is also a strong argument for the Metaverse being a place where there is a high probability of retention and transfer. Transfer to the real world is easier if you have learnt and practised in a similar, congruent virtual world. We know this with certainty from flight simulators. All pilots train extensively on simulators, so we know this form of learning works. Learning in the Metaverse is likely to involve more 3D simulation learning and, in particular, training. Extended realities, whether wholly immersive, mixed or augmented, will also play a role in learning, and it is only a matter of the degree to which they will be adopted.

Metaverse VR and AR

VR is a medium, not a gadget. Learning must match its uses and benefits and there are some very strong cases for this, based on costs, safety and efficacy, which enable the learner to:

- move in or through a 3D place
- use or manipulate 3D objects
- learn in inaccessible and dangerous places
- remember step-by-step processes and procedures
- learn in a team or group.

Note that many learning tasks are assumed to need 3D representation, but in fact they may not. Take for example laboratory work: learning using 2D representations of procedures and/or actually learning in a real lab may be just as effective. What really matters is psychological, not physical or even 3D fidelity.

VR may (or may not) be the window into the collective consciousness of the Metaverse. It is certainly a front runner, but a problem with a purely VR-based Metaverse is that it limits learning to that world and ignores the simple fact that much learning, especially work-based learning, is about application and performance in the real world. It is one thing appealing to virtual workers in a virtual world, but in the real world we will still need plumbers, refuse collectors and pizza delivery people. There is a need for the Metaverse to seamlessly interact with the real, physical world.

What to learn in the Metaverse?

As already mentioned, there is little doubt that some forms of learning could be delivered in the Metaverse, and our instinctive thoughts on what VR may be especially good for are sound. VR is not necessarily the ideal medium for teaching factual knowledge. It is less useful for 'knowing that', more useful for 'knowing how' and this, indeed, is what most of the successful learning projects show.

Projects using VR in learning have been underway for many years (Clark, 2021). There is some promising research on VR learning in sectors including health, the military, oil and gas industries and other practical domains. It is clear that learning in the context of a 3D environment, with its ability to manipulate objects and be with other learners (or people) in simulations, does work. In virtual reality, a learner can manipulate objects in the same way as in real life, for example to load trucks, conduct medical procedures and so on – the opportunities for training are endless. More specific training in using handheld tools and equipment will also be possible. The haptic effect, feeling the object as it would feel in the real world, is starting to be realized through clever controller and glove technology. From using a scalpel to wielding sports equipment, learners will be able to do things with things. Procedural training will also be possible, safely and without risk, in areas such as health and safety, healthcare, retail and manufacturing tasks. Avatars can provide an endless supply of patients in medicine where all sorts of procedures will be possible.

Soft skills

In the difficult area of soft skills, learners can be given context and opportunities to learn and practise using other Metaverse trainees, tutors and AI-driven avatars, including managing others, listening skills and interviewing. Customer avatars, patients, students and employees are all possible and can cover a wide range of situations. The technology is repeatable and scalable. AI will no doubt play a role in analyzing behaviour, empathy, speech and actions, and those who are neurodiverse may also benefit from social training available in the safe environment of the Metaverse.

Physical and psychological healthcare issues may be dealt with in this new environment. VR has already helped with physical disabilities such as paraplegia, stroke and amputations. It can also be used for disorders such as post-traumatic stress disorder, phobias and depression to deliver therapy such as CBT, and may be helpful for those with dementia, too. Body swapping will allow a person to become someone else through an avatar swap and enable them to gain a better insight and understanding of issues such as sexual harassment, racism and how it feels to live with a disability.

Collaborative and blended learning

Team learning in planning, communications and execution of projects can be practised safely, which is useful in the workplace and especially in dangerous or critical environments such as the emergency services and military.

New forms of blended learning may also be useful in the Metaverse, where the learner is in a 3D world but can also interact in the real world.

Teachers, lecturers and trainers can operate within the Metaverse or stay outside of it, setting tasks and challenges for learners and then giving guidance, instruction and feedback. Sequences can be recorded for reflection and further feedback. Assessment for practical tasks, jobs, certification and relicensing can also be executed.

Beyond learning, prototyping of objects, processes and procedures will be possible, from simple products to entire city planning. This will lead to creative ventures within the Metaverse, where new unimagined phenomena will be realized and where it will be possible to walk around or step inside created worlds and share that experience with others.

How can we learn in the Metaverse?

Good training mirrors real life, and as the Metaverse mirrors real life, it can be a good place to learn. Yet the reality of learning this way, by donning a headset and entering either real or imagined worlds, has been around only recently. We might assume that learning in an immersive environment is the same or similar to the real world, but there are considerations with VR media, including immersion, presence, what is experienced visually and agency. Headsets shut out the external world. They have the advantage of greatly increasing the user's field of view and, being stereoscopic, present a powerful 3D effect. While inside these worlds, the learner can move around and participate in the learning experience, but this can be controlled by deciding how much freedom is allowed or designed into the learning experience, what is possible within the limits of the technology in terms of physical movement and the inclusion of other functionality, such as sensors and haptic devices. At present, the Metaverse is far from being a wholly functional second world.

The advantages of the Metaverse for learning will become evident when learners are able to manipulate 3D objects, move in or through 3D space or use real 3D equipment in difficult, expensive, even inaccessible or dangerous places. It can replace learning that, in real world set-ups, would be impractical or expensive. Initial projects are likely, therefore, to involve 'experiential' learning of physical processes and procedures, self-awareness or team or group learning, where decision-making can be simulated.

Presence in the Metaverse

'Presence' is a word heard often in VR, but it is not a simple concept. It refers to the user experiencing presence again, in the same way they did as child, by learning to deal with the world, other people and objects all over again. It varies from the visual feeling of just being in that second world, through to fuller senses of moving around and interacting with other people and things in that world. Presence is the fundamental sense of self in VR – what it is just to be there, move slightly, look around, be aware of your own self – that makes it so different. Also that sense of strangeness, awkwardness, even fear and angst, followed by curiosity about the possibilities being revealed. This feeling of presence depends on all sorts of factors including the field of view, fidelity of the images and smoothness of the experience.

In multiuser worlds, it is possible to see and interact with other software generated avatars and people outside of that world, for example, an external tutor giving voice instructions. Social behaviour and interaction in virtual worlds may not be quite the same as in the real world. This social dimension can, to some extent, be impoverished by the lack of social signals, but also enriched and varied in ways not possible in the real world. The social side can also extend over time, as seen in VRChat and *We Met in Virtual Reality* (2022), the documentary referred to earlier.

Presence can also involve interaction with other things in that world. This depends on how they are presented, what it feels like to touch them and what it is possible to do with them. Again, this can generate a sense of wonder, even awe, but can also be either an impoverished or rich experience, depending on how it is designed. Finally, there is the presence of 'flow', being in the flow of the VR experience to such an extent that the user forgets they are in VR and that the 'people' they meet are just avatars. This is a deeper form of presence and immersion across time.

How best to learn in the Metaverse?

Research into learning in VR is maturing with some well-established results and recommendations.

Does 3D VR immersion result in more learning than 2D immersion on a flat screen?

We can tentatively conclude that there is a difference between 2D desktop VR and 3D headset VR, especially when there are specific pedagogical approaches in the design of the learning experiences that play to the immersion and interactivity of the medium. When 2D was compared with 3D VR, children were found to have greater improvement in 3D VR (Passig, Tzuriel and Eshel-Kedmi, 2016), a result also found in a study of 89 biochemistry students, where the 3D VR group outperformed the 2D VR group when asked to teach other students (Klingenberg et al, 2020). Makransky and Lilleholt (2018), Olmos-Raya et al (2018) and Villena Taranilla et al (2019) think our higher sense of presence in VR raises interest, attention, enjoyment and intrinsic motivation.

Does 3D VR lead to better learning?

Makransky and Petersen (2019) claim that desktop VR leads to more and better learning. First there is the emotional or affective path through the VR features of presence, intrinsic motivation and self-efficacy; second, a cognitive path through VR features of usability, cognitive benefits and self-efficacy. They concluded that desktop VR simulations offer real benefits when strong VR features, along with good usability, are used to positive effect. But this only works if the VR training is well designed. Interaction and agency certainly have positive effects and self-efficacy is a particular strength, especially through immediate feedback on actions (Johnson-Glenberg, 2019).

There are also studies reporting a lack of efficacy in learning. This is partly to do with the poor design of learning experiences and the focus on creating worlds rather than carefully considered learning experiences. Makransky, Terkildsen and Mayer (2019) confirmed motivation and presence but less learning, showing the danger of the novelty and allure of VR creating the illusion of learning. Importantly, they showed that immersive VR needs to be deliberately designed as a training experience, not just general VR immersion experiences.

It is clear, therefore, that learning experiences must be designed specifically for VR. Too many projects assume that immersion will be enough, but these may simply encourage and exacerbate cognitive overload and distraction. Deliberate design with simplification to reduce cognitive overload, along with strong signaling, chunking and generative activities, make all the difference. There is also the issue of cost. The return on investment for using VR for learning can result in significant savings to alternatives that are expensive in the real world.

Vanity projects, where the goal is to simply appear innovative or contemporary, are often a feature of the early stages of a new technology. There is a need for less of these mosquito projects, which usually have no long-term implementation and quickly die, as opposed to turtle projects, which may be a lot duller, but where long-term impact is the goal.

GENERATIVE LEARNING

Generative learning is the ability of learners to create and apply their learning. VR allows for the deliberate design of reflective and generative activities, and they appear to have a positive effect. For example, Makransky et al (2020) took 165 learners and compared a 2D video of a simulation with a full 3D VR experience. The VR resulted in better learning compared with 2D video learning because adding generative activity to the VR experience allowed immersion and interactions, or presence and agency, which led to reflection and integration into prior knowledge.

COGNITIVE OVERLOAD

More detailed lessons have also been learnt as a result of VR learning research conducted so far. As stated above, VR learning can lead to cognitive overload (Sweller, 2011) and can actually inhibit learning (Schrader and Bastiaens, 2012) and (Makransky, Terkildsen and Mayer, 2019). Overstimulation can be a problem. Users may be overwhelmed and develop a kind of stage fright or wonderment in fully immersive environments, as they are flooded with sensory information. They can also become obsessed with detail. There is also the allure of the new and novel that can distract from learning. In addition, increased interactivity and agency may lead to more cognitive load and reduced efficacy of learning. All of this can hinder, rather than help, with other tasks and efficient learning.

How much information should you use in immersive environments?

Lokka and Çöltekin (2017) found evidence that too much information can increase cognitive load and reduce performance. Various levels of visual realism and fidelity can provide useful context for many learning tasks, especially with the use of judicious highlighting and landmarking, but one should not get obsessed with visual realism unless it is necessary for the learning task. Interestingly, learner perceptions, especially preferences for high fidelity, are often at odds with what actually works in improving learning.

Another often touted advantage of VR is that it is fun, but this may actually result in less or more superficial learning (Makransky et al, 2020). We should not see the Metaverse as a proxy for delivering 'fun' or 'novelty' in learning, although there will, undoubtedly, be plenty of such projects in the early phase. It is important, however, not to mistake fidelity, novelty, fun and excitement for learning. The allure of the new should not blind us to what we actually know about how people learn.

The implementation of learning will need to focus on the actual 'learning', not just the creation of VR/Metaverse projects. Real decisions have to be made about the appropriate level of user autonomy; for example, should the tutor be real or an avatar within the world, or should tutor guidance come from outside the world as audio, or even be automated. Designers will need to consider haptic needs and focus on audio, not video and text, as well as build in practice so that skills transfer to the real world. New skills will be required from learning experience designers (Clark, 2021).

Evolution of learning technology

The Metaverse is likely to be more like a Multiverse, in other words, multiple worlds that differ in purpose, scale and appearance. We can learn a lot from games here, which have been creating such worlds for decades. These contain full, hi-fidelity graphic worlds, low simple block and polygon worlds and everything in between.

Decentralization has been a promise of Web 3.0 and it is to be hoped that Ivan Illich's famous dream of a more open 'web' of learning services (1971) will emerge in the Metaverse. But the virtual 'reality' is likely to be a compromise between what Niall Ferguson (2017) calls *The Square and the Tower*, where every open space or agora has a regulatory or hierarchical tower. It is unlikely to be a single vendor, centralized world. Instead, it may well turn out to include thousands of little Metaverses, like small theme parks, all competing for our attention. Multiple sizes will emerge, some very large, expansive and open, some of moderate size and others specific, precise and small. Multiple build strategies will also emerge, some created centrally, some by professional designers and some by users.

We will get the usual educational brands and traditional forms of learning delivery, but it may also provide a new and unique environment in which learning technologies and techniques, some known, some yet unknown, will flourish. This may turn into a new gold rush, creating a wonderful new educational market. What makes this different from previous proto-Metaverses, such as *Second Life*, is that the underlying technologies and standards and a ubiquitous, high-bandwidth, cloud-based internet can make it a much more sophisticated world. As we spend more time in such places, we may well be willing to spend money on learning in the places we inhabit. This is the economy of experiences which may also be valuable learning experiences.

Flat 2D learning

Flat 2D learning came relatively recently in our evolution, around 5,000 years ago, with the invention of writing, manuscripts, books and eventually 2D screens for film, TV and computers. All of these media involve perspectival shifts:

- In the theatre, the viewing distance is a fixed perspective with scene changes.
- In cinema, the close-up, medium, long, pan, cuts and other techniques give more freedom with multiple perspectives, as the camera can be anywhere relative to the action, yet you, as the viewer, have no choice in where to watch or go as you are depending on the view shown by the camera.
- Computer games were the next advance, with their created worlds, freeing the viewer to roam and do things within these worlds.
- Multiplayer VR literally swaps out the real world to present worlds that are virtual but social, with many of the possible dimensions of real life. It is possible to be a single viewer in a VR movie as an observer or with limited participation or with different degrees of participation, all relative to others in the VR world.

One interesting question is whether VR will change the cinema experience or create an alternative form of cinema and storytelling. This requires massive bandwidth for fully rendered, seamless branching. Such storytelling will have a different set of creative rules. This is an interesting possible shift to a much more sophisticated Metaverse. Artificial intelligence will also have a huge role to play in this, for example, by imbuing avatars with human behaviours. AI may even help create and build these worlds and the stories told and watched within these worlds. Beyond this are technologies that truly augment and enhance cognition and consciousness, such as neural implants.

In all of this there has been a steady freeing of the user from time, place and fixed perspectives, which is why the Metaverse fits into the general evolution of learning technology.

Arrival of the Metaverse

There is no clear consensus over the arrival of the Metaverse, although a sudden arrival is the wrong way to look at this. There will be no 'BC to AD', 'before and after' or 'Big Bang'. Forecasts vary from 'it is already here', 'in the next five to ten years', 'in the coming decades' or just 'in the future'. In short, no one knows.

There are currently lots of parallel initiatives with no real coalescence. However, efforts are focused on open standards in a world that looks towards learning experiences being taken with a persistent identity and an ability to move across different worlds as one learns. There was a thriving learning community in *Second Life,* and there are several examples of learning taking place within proto-Metaverses including Minecraft Education and Facebook's $150 million investment in 10 US Metaversities (Whitford, 2022).

Bellini et al (2016) predicts that VR will reach 15 million learners by 2025 and the economic forecasts for the Metaverse have been consistently in the trillions of dollars. Jensen Huang of Nvidia, has even claimed that the GDP of the Metaverse will be greater, at some point, than that of the real world (Kindig, 2021)! It is clear that this will be a huge market, including those involved in education. Some are already gearing up for that market, but these are immersive learning companies, not those with technology deeper in the technology stack. The world of education must therefore take the Metaverse seriously. There is a thirst to know what it is and how it can help in learning, specifically in learning by doing, something that is often neglected in education and training. VR has already become a common method of this form of training and the Metaverse is a natural expansion of this, both on 2D screens and 3D virtual worlds, as well as through AR. No one in learning can ignore VR and the Metaverse.

Metaverse standards

The Metaverse Standards Forum was set up in June 2022. It is a major milestone, but is just the start of a long journey relating to standards and governance. Note that the forum will not be defining or policing standards, only bringing the major players together to discuss standards. These standards on interoperability will take years to develop and these are necessary before any form of learning standards will emerge.

Matthew Ball (2022) has examined the full stack options, along with their challenges, having researched the considerable technical and cultural challenges posed, and has concluded that interoperability is possible and that standards will emerge. The evidence from existing massive online virtual environments, along with current levels of investment by almost all of the major tech companies, standards work and technical progress, all point towards some sort of 3D virtual layer, as part of the internet. The need for users to move through these different environments with a persistent identity and presence is clear.

Conclusion

Think for a moment about the following:

- Spending time inside worlds, both physical and psychological, spun from our imagination, with or without technology.
- Being so engrossed in a book that we emerge changed and surprised that mere words could so envelop the mind.
- Entering a building so stupendously beautiful that all thought of the outside world disappears.
- Watching a movie and coming back out into the dark night seeing the real world in a different light.
- Researching something of deep interest on the web and losing all track of time.
- Pouring over Google maps, exploring a place to visit.
- Entering into virtual reality and literally swapping the world for another.

The Metaverse is the continuation of all of these processes of the imagination. We have always created new worlds and we always will. Learning, above all, will benefit all of those who have the imagination to see that its purpose is to change minds. We change minds by taking them somewhere else. That somewhere could be the Metaverse.

Throughout this book we have seen mainstream technologies as learning technologies, as that turned out to be their most potent use. Although we cannot say with certainty that the Metaverse will happen, there is enough momentum among the standard organizations on interoperability, the major tech companies and the sheer scale of a generation brought up in virtual worlds to make it seem likely.

Learning technology is unique in that it lies at the root of and propels the process by which we create new culture, knowledge and technology itself. Time will tell if the Metaverse will revolutionize learning, but it is clear that learning technology will continue to play the role it has always played, as something fundamental to our species and civilization.

References

Adams, D (1999) How to Stop Worrying and Learn to Love the Internet, Douglas Adams.com, https://douglasadams.com/dna/19990901-00-a.html (archived at https://perma.cc/RB2R-HEMJ)

Ball, M (2022) *The Metaverse: And how it will revolutionize everything*, Liveright, New York

Bellini, H et al (2016) Virtual & Augmented Reality: Understanding the race for the next computing platform, 13 January, *The Goldman Sachs Group, Inc*, www.goldmansachs.com/insights/pages/technology-driving-innovation-folder/virtual-and-augmented-reality/report.pdf (archived at https://perma.cc/S3BQ-GK76)

Clark, D (2021) Learning Experience Design: How to create effective learning that works, Kogan Page Publishers, London

Ferguson, N (2017) *The Square and the Tower: Networks, hierarchies and the struggle for global power*, Penguin, London

Illich, I (1971) *Deschooling Society*, Harper & Row, New York

Johnson-Glenberg, M C (2019) The *Necessary Nine*: Design principles for embodied VR and active stem education, *Learning in a Digital World*, 83–112

Kindig, B (2021) The Key To Unlocking The Metaverse Is Nvidia's Omniverse, 2 September, *Forbes*, www.forbes.com/sites/bethkindig/2021/09/02/the-key-to-unlocking-the-metaverse-is-nvidias-omniverse/ (archived at https://perma.cc/7B94-C83L)

Klingenberg, S et al (2020) Investigating the effect of teaching as a generative learning strategy when learning through desktop and immersive VR: A media and methods experiment, *British Journal of Educational Technology*, 51(6), 2115–38

Lokka, I E and Çöltekin, A (2017) Toward optimizing the design of virtual environments for route learning: empirically assessing the effects of changing levels of realism on memory, *International Journal of Digital Earth*, 12(2), 137–55

Makransky, G and Lilleholt, L (2018) A structural equation modeling investigation of the emotional value of immersive virtual reality in education, *Educational Technology Research and Development*, 66, 1141–64

Makransky, G and Petersen, G B (2019) Investigating the process of learning with desktop virtual reality: A structural equation modeling approach, *Computers & Education*, 134, 15–30

Makransky, G, Terkildsen, T S and Mayer, R E (2019) Adding immersive virtual reality to a science lab simulation causes more presence but less learning, *Learning and Instruction*, 60, 225–36

Makransky, G et al (2020) Immersive virtual reality increases liking but not learning with a science simulation and generative learning strategies promote learning in immersive virtual reality, *Journal of Educational Psychology*, 113(4), 719–35

Olmos-Raya, E et al (2018) Mobile virtual reality as an educational platform: A pilot study on the impact of immersion and positive emotion induction in the learning process, *Eurasia Journal of Mathematics, Science and Technology Education*, 14(6), 2045–57

Parisi, T (2021) The Seven Rules of the Metaverse, 22 October, *Medium*, https://medium.com/meta-verses/the-seven-rules-of-the-metaverse-7d4e06fa864c (archived at https://perma.cc/W66R-KK8H)

Passig, D, Tzuriel, D and Eshel-Kedmi, G (2016) Improving children's cognitive modifiability by dynamic assessment in 3D immersive virtual reality environments, *Computers & Education*, 95, 296–308

Schrader, C and Bastiaens, T J (2012) The influence of virtual presence: Effects on experienced cognitive load and learning outcomes in educational computer games, *Computers in Human Behavior*, 28(2), 648–58

Sweller, J, Ayres, P and Kalyuga, S (2011) *Cognitive Load Theory: Explorations in the Learning Sciences, Instructional Systems and Performance Technologies*, Springer, Berlin

Villena Taranilla, R et al (2019) Strolling through a city of the Roman Empire: an analysis of the potential of virtual reality to teach history in Primary Education, *Interactive Learning Environments*, 30(4), 608–18

We Met in Virtual Reality (2022), HBO, www.hbo.com/movies/we-met-in-virtual-reality (archived at https://perma.cc/JB4R-S7YK)

Whitford, E (2022) After two years of Zoom classes, colleges are warming to the idea of holding classes in the metaverse. With $150 million invested, Mark Zuckerberg's Meta is leading the charge, 3 September, *Forbes*, www.forbes.com/sites/emmawhitford/2022/09/03/metaversity-is-in-session-as-meta-and-iowas-victoryxr-open-10-virtual-campuses/ (archived at https://perma.cc/4QHE-F8QF)

INDEX

Note: Page numbers in *italics* refer to tables or figures

Lightning Source UK Ltd.
Milton Keynes UK
UKHW021107060123
414889UK00002B/18